WHEN TOMORROW COMES

Eileen D. Frost

authorHOUSE™

1663 LIBERTY DRIVE, SUITE 200
BLOOMINGTON, INDIANA 47403
(800) 839-8640
WWW.AUTHORHOUSE.COM

First published by AuthorHouse 01/23/06

ISBN: 1-4259-0028-3 (sc)

Printed in the United States of America
Bloomington, Indiana

This book is printed on acid-free paper.

To my late father and mother,

on whose lives this story is loosely based,

to my husband William

and to our children,

Ann, Rosemarie, Geoff and Graham

PART ONE

The Fragile Peace

1932-1939

PROLOGUE

It might as well have been the middle of winter for all the difference the sunshine of an April day made to the grey, bug-ridden houses crumbling away on either side of Wimple Street, and the labyrinth of dark alleys and footpaths surrounding it. The Shambles, a nickname given to the district by its long-suffering residents, was a grim place in which to live. Tiny homes, splitting at the seams by the ever increasing size of the families that existed in them, shared lavatories, sewers that overflowed into the streets, rats, some the size of small dogs, and the constant emission of soot from the nearby railway station, covering everything in a grey blanket of grime, had earned the place its reputation. In the decaying streets, children, many in rags and with bare feet, played games in the gutters, sang their skipping songs and, knowing nothing better, cheerfully accepted their lot. Disease among them was rife, and the sight of a little white coffin being borne away to the Cemetery so commonplace it scarcely raised an eyebrow.

As he stood on the corner and surveyed the festering squalor of the place he'd brought his wife to some five years' earlier, the man, whose immaculate appearance bore no resemblance to his surroundings, wondered how she could have put up with it for so long without one word of complaint. He also wondered if the letter he knew would have arrived today, - the letter he was half-afraid to open, - would mean a better life for his family, and be the means of their escape from the misery of living in such a hellhole of a place.

He entered his house, took the brown envelope from the kitchen dresser, tore it open and read the contents.

CHAPTER ONE

At two o'clock on the afternoon of 12th September 1932, Harry Cartarett, having finished his milk round for the day, arrived home at number twelve Kestrel Road to find the Midwife's bicycle propped against the wall of the house. As he stepped inside the front door, the familiar smell of antiseptic and strong carbolic meant that either his wife Esther had given birth or it was imminent. He hung his coat and cap on a peg in the hallway, went through to the back of the house and sat down in his armchair, past experience telling him to keep well out of the way of the ministrations going on upstairs.

One of the advantages of starting work at four o'clock in the morning was that he finished early in the afternoon and could spend what was left of it dozing in his armchair, and catching up on his early morning start. There would be no such pleasure for him today. The thumping back and fore of two pairs of feet across the room above sounded like a regiment of soldiers on the parade ground, the first belonging to the Midwife and the second to his sister Frances. Frances would, as usual, be holding Esther's hand and mopping the perspiration from her face while urging her to push the child she had carried for the past nine months out into the world. He sat with his head in his hands until, some half an hour later, he heard Esther cry out, then the first wail of a newly born baby. It was all over, and he had another mouth to feed.

He glanced around the room of their smart new Corporation house, his thoughts drifting away to the place from where he and his family had just moved. Wimple Street. He recalled the day the letter from the Corporation had arrived, telling him he could have one of their new houses at Eastbrook, and the look on Esther's face when he'd told her they would be moving there in time for the birth of their child. Within days, the news had taken years off her age, and they had both looked upon number twelve Kestrel Road as a new start for them, and a far better place in which to bring up their four, soon to be five, children.

'It's a boy.' He jumped back to the present with a start as Frances, her face beaming, stuck her head around the door and announced that Daniel Albert had arrived safely. 'Ten pounds the little beggar was, and poor Esther is exhausted.' She gave him one of her meaningful looks. 'I just hope this is the last, Harry.'

'Can I go up?' he asked, ignoring her last remark. It was all very well for Frances. She and her husband Albert didn't have any children due to reasons known only to themselves. They could make love morning, noon and night, although he doubted if they did, and still nothing would come of it whereas he, Harry, had only to look at Esther for her to end up with a baby in her arms.

'Yes,' Frances said. 'But don't stay long. Esther's worn out.'

He took the stairs two at a time and found his wife sitting up in bed, her dark eyes heavily shadowed, nursing their latest arrival whilst midwife Mary Williams stood at the window, staring down into the street below. 'Good job you've moved to this new house' the nurse said, turning an accusing stare on him. 'Wimple Street was no place in which to keep bringing children into the world. I've always said that.'

Harry nodded. He didn't need to be told something he already knew. They had moved to Kestrel Road at Eastbrook just over two weeks' ago. Set back off the road, with a garden back and front, the house was at the end of a terrace and had a sideway to the back door, leading into two spacious rooms, a kitchen and bathroom, and upstairs, three good sized bedrooms. After Wimple Street, Esther thought it was Paradise. Harry planned to grow his own vegetables, and if the Corporation would allow him, perhaps keep a few chickens.

They were also now living just around the corner from Frances whose help with the children Esther found invaluable.

He parted the blanket in which the nurse had wrapped Daniel, dropped a kiss on the baby's head and turned his attention to his wife. Her tired face made him feel guilty. 'Beautiful, as usual,' he said, 'and so are you.'

Esther smiled, too exhausted to talk.

'Right,' Mary Williams snapped, 'time for mother to rest and father to find something useful to do.' She took Daniel from Esther's arms, placed him in his crib and dismissed Harry with a look and a nod towards the door.

In the kitchen, Frances had prepared a tray of tea for everyone. She handed a cup to Harry. 'I'll just take these upstairs,' she said, 'then you and I will have a little talk before David and Alex come in from work.' She went into the hallway.

'What about Catherine and Edwin,' Harry called after her. 'Shall I go and get them from across the road?'

'Not yet,' Frances shouted as she went upstairs. 'They'll be all right with your neighbour for now. I'll go and fetch them later.' And to herself she muttered, 'You don't get out of it that easily Harry Cartarett. With Catherine under everyone's feet wanting all the attention as she does, and Edwin demanding his tea, there'll be no chance for me to try and talk some sense into that thick skull of yours.'

Mary Williams, who had never married, and whose opinion of men couldn't get much lower if she tried, eventually took her leave. 'Your wife is sleeping now,' she said to Harry. 'And what she needs after that little lot is a good rest, but what she *doesn't* need is to have any more babies,' and with a sniff, she mounted her bicycle, promising to call back later that evening to check that everything was all right.

Harry wondered why everyone seemed to be giving him dark looks as if it was all *his* fault. After all, it took two to make a baby. He finished his tea, and Frances sat down in Esther's chair opposite.

'Esther had a lousy time of it,' she said. 'I know it's not your fault she gives birth to these big babies but she oughtn't to have any more.'

'I know, I know. I've just had man-hater Mary Williams on at me about the same thing. And you and I went through all of this the last time, didn't we?'

'Yes, we did,' Frances agreed, 'and Catherine is just a year old and here you are with another mouth to feed.' She pulled a piece of paper from the pocket of her apron. 'Here,' she said, handing it over to him, 'have a look at this.'

'What is it?'

'Just read it.'

It was an address for a clinic where women could get advice on "Matters of a Delicate and Personal nature", including how to practice birth control. 'It's run by the National Birth Control Council with the backing of a lady called Marie Stopes who started opening these clinics all over the country some years' ago,' Frances said, 'and it's free.'

Harry turned the paper over in his hands. He shouldn't be discussing these things with his sister but she was a difficult woman to deal with, and so he read on. 'Where did you get this?' he said. 'I can't see Esther wanting to discuss our private business with strangers.'

'Never mind where it came from,' Frances said, pointing a finger to the room above. 'I think you'll find that Esther'll do anything if it means not going through that lot again, especially if I offer to go with her. Think about it Harry.' She left her chair and started clearing away the cups. 'I'd best go and fetch Catherine and Edwin now, before the others come home.'

Left to himself for a few minutes, Harry wandered out into the back garden, which was still full of builders' rubbish, and lit up a Woodbine. Too often these days, he was allowing his mind to drift back to when he and Esther had first met. Maybe it had something to do with the fact that he'd turned thirty-eight, or perhaps subconsciously, he longed for the days when he'd had no responsibilities and plenty of money in his pocket. He couldn't understand it. He loved Esther and their children and was happy enough but there were times when he felt so bowed down with responsibility that he didn't know which way to turn. He wanted what was best for them all but it wasn't easy trying to bring up a large family on what he earned, and he lived in hope that a better job might come his way one of these days. And at least he'd been able to move them away from the odious Wimple Street.

His thoughts wandered off to a warm Sunday afternoon in 1914 when he and Jimmy Styles, both out on a short leave pass from the Army Barracks where they were stationed, went for an afternoon stroll in Southampton Park. A crowd had gathered around the bandstand, and were enjoying a rendition of Franz Lehar's Merry Widow, when Harry spotted two girls heading in their direction.

'They're a bit of all right,' he said. 'I like the look of that one on the right with the gorgeous black hair.'

Jimmy pulled a face. 'Not much use me looking. I'm already engaged to be married in case you've forgotten.'

'Doesn't mean you can't have any fun,' Harry replied as the girls drew level and stopped. The one he had his eye on gave him a wide smile.

'Going somewhere soldier?' she asked, her lovely dark blue eyes looking straight into his. And that was the moment Harry Cartarett fell hopelessly in love with Esther Elizabeth Wilding.

They started going out together after that but Esther was only sixteen, and her parents disapproved of her walking out with a soldier who was nearly five years' older. They tried everything to put a stop to it but their daughter was a wilful girl and she refused to give Harry up. When she told them she was expecting a baby they were beside themselves with rage and told her she would have to marry the child's father, get out of their home and have her child somewhere else. Harry rushed the wedding through and they were married on 6th June 1915, just two days' before he went to France with his regiment.

They set up home in rooms in his mother's house where Esther gave birth to a son, but Harry never saw the child, as the boy, named Harold after himself, was sickly from the start and lived for only six weeks. If he had known how much Esther would suffer at the hands of his mother, he would never have left her to live there without his support, but he'd had no time to find a place of their own. Once the war was over, he and Esther remained in his mother's house until David was born and they were able to find a room in a house in Copnor. A year later, Alex arrived. Then Esther had two stillbirths followed

9

by the arrival of Robert who, at six months, caught Diphtheria from which he never recovered. By this time, they were jammed together like sardines and when a house in Wimple Street came empty, despite its reputation, Harry took it, thinking it would be just a temporary move until they could find somewhere better. But Edwin came along next, and when he was three, Catherine was born. With four children, there was nowhere else to go, the years rolled by, and it wasn't until the Corporation built a small estate of houses at Eastbrook that they were able to escape. Now there was *another* mouth to feed, and Harry made up his mind that, come what may, he'd make sure there were no more babies.

Alex came in from work, and Frances took him, Catherine and Edwin upstairs to see their new baby brother before getting tea ready. Then, knowing how strict Esther was about early bedtimes, she stayed long enough to get the two youngest washed and ready for bed by six o'clock.

'I'd best be off now,' she said to Harry. 'There's a pie each in the oven for you, Alex and David.' She slipped into her coat. 'I'll be back first thing in the morning.' She raised her eyebrows. 'And give some thought to what we've just talked about.'

'I will. And thanks for all you've done, Frances.'

Harry didn't know how they'd manage without his sister's help. She was a bit on the bossy side but a good sort and he often thought what a pity it was that she and Albert had never been able to have children of their own. Albert drove trams for a living and some years' before had come into a small inheritance, which he had wisely used to buy his own house. Sometimes, Harry felt guilty when he had envious thoughts about what they had, and how comfortably off they were.

'Mind how you go now,' he said, giving Frances a swift kiss on the cheek, 'and my regards to Albert.'

He watched as she set off down the street, and saw her stop for a quick word with David, who had just turned the corner on his way home from Joe Rigby's Shoe Repair shop, where he'd been working for the past year.

'So it's another boy,' David said, hanging his coat on a peg in the hallway. 'Auntie Frances just told me.'

Harry nodded. 'Yes. Daniel Albert we've called him.'

'Is Mum all right?' David was the eldest son and worried a lot about his mother. She kept having these babies and worked too hard looking after them, and the rest of the family.

'She's very tired of course,' Harry replied. He didn't know how much David knew about babies and how they were born, or, for that matter, how they were made in the first place. 'He weighed over ten pounds,' he said. 'Some heavyweight, eh?' They went into the kitchen where he took the pies from the oven and set them on three plates.

'Dad,' David said presently, as he finished his last mouthful and Alex had gone upstairs to get ready to go out.

'Yes son?'

'Could I talk to you?'

'Of course you can,' Harry said. He couldn't remember the last time any of his children wanted to talk to him. They usually went to Esther for anything they wanted. 'But you should go upstairs and see your mother first, and meet your new brother.'

David left the table. 'Yes, I suppose I'd better,' he said, going through to the hall leaving his father puzzled. David was a strange boy and Harry hoped he wasn't in any sort of trouble.

The bedroom door was half-open and David crept in. He didn't want to disturb his mother if she was sleeping but she was sitting up in bed with the baby in her arms and he thought how pale and tired she looked, the dark smudges under her eyes showing up the pallor of her face.

He leaned over and kissed her. 'How are you Mum?' he said, stealing a glance at Daniel who was sleeping soundly.

'I'm very well, son,' Esther lied, with a smile. She felt far from well after going through such a long, tough labour but David was too young to understand the facts of childbirth, and all that it entailed, and she didn't want to bother him with all the details.

'He's big, isn't he,' David said.

Esther held the baby out for him to hold. 'Here, take him. Give him a cuddle.'

David did as she had asked but Daniel wasn't having any of it, and when he woke up and started to cry, was quickly handed back to his mother.

'He doesn't like me,' David said, pulling a face.

'Nonsense.' Esther started to bare her breast. 'He's hungry, that's all.'

David averted his eyes. 'I'd better go,' he said, not wanting to see her feed the baby. 'I want to have a talk with Dad.'

'Is anything the matter?' Esther asked.

'No Mum, nothing at all,' he reassured her. He could hear the baby making horrible sucking noises and was desperate to leave the room. 'I'll come up and see you later,' he promised and fled out onto the landing, unable to make out why the sound of his mother feeding the baby had made him feel sick. It was only natural, and he'd been fed like that once, but why couldn't she have waited until he'd left? He went downstairs to find his father.

Harry sat hunched over the fire, looking as if he had all the cares of the world on his shoulders. He pointed to Esther's chair. 'Sit down, son,' he said and David dropped into the seat, not sure how to begin but deciding to come straight to the point.

'I know Joe Rigby gave me a job when I left school,' he said, 'but I don't want to go on mending shoes for a living Dad.'

Harry poked at the fire. He'd had an idea for some time that his eldest son wasn't happy with his job. 'I see,' he said. 'So what is it you'd like to be doing to earn your living?'

David told him. 'I'd like to learn carpentry. You know, make nice things from wood, like furniture and stuff.'

There was nothing worse than being stuck in a job you hated, and Harry knew it. 'Well, son,' he said when David had finished, 'having ambitions is fine as far as it goes but learning a proper trade like woodwork costs money, which is something I don't have a lot of.'

'I know that Dad, but I'd be willing to stay on with Joe Rigby if I could go to night school and learn carpentry. I'd work hard, honestly I would.'

'I know you would,' Harry replied, 'but there are other things to think about. For a start, I don't know if there are any night schools around here.' He shook his head. 'And your brother Alex is working now in that Jam factory, and there's no future in that. Suppose *he* wants to learn some sort of trade. How am I supposed to find the money for the two of you? Tell me that. And another thing, have you asked Mr. Rigby for his opinion on this? Don't forget he took you on when work was scarce, and he pays you well.'

David rested his head in his hands. 'No Dad, I haven't spoken to him yet but I will tomorrow. And Alex isn't interested in learning any trade. He told me ages ago.'

'He might change his mind if he gets fed up with that factory,' Harry said, 'but I'll think about it, though I'm not making any promises.' He moved towards the door. 'Now I'd better go an' see if your mother is all right before Mad Mary comes back on her broomstick. I don't want to listen to any more of her lectures, thanks all the same.'

David laughed at his father's description of the nurse, and started to clear away their dirty plates. His Dad had promised to think about it, which was a start, and maybe Joe Rigby might understand if he, David had a word with him. He swilled the plates under the tap, dried them off in a tea towel then answered a knock on the front door and let Mary Williams into the house. She does look a bit like a witch, he thought, with her long black hair, thin face and hooked nose.

He smiled to himself as he went through to the kitchen to make his sandwiches for the next day.

CHAPTER TWO

Joe Rigby's Boot and Shoe Repair shop had stood on the corner of Ash Terrace and Potters Row in The Shambles, for as long as anyone could remember. It had a sad, neglected air about it, with peeling paintwork, and unwashed windows full of faded, flyblown advertisements. The sign over the window had long since ceased to mean anything, its gold copper-plate lettering now unreadable behind several layers of grime from the nearby factories and railway station. Inside, yellowing cards of boot and shoelaces, metal studs and brads covered the walls, and tins of Cherry Blossom boot polish, Dubbin, dusters and cleaning brushes filled the dusty shelves. At one end of the woodworm-eaten counter, old newspapers, their edges curled and yellow with age, sat in an untidy pile, and on the other, cardboard boxes of assorted pieces of leather were on sale for anyone who wanted to do their own repairs. Everywhere, the odour of rows of sweaty boots and shoes awaiting their turn on the last overshadowed the sweet smell of polish and new leather.

Behind the counter, David sat at a wooden bench trimming the edges of the leather sole he'd just nailed to a pair of ladies' shoes. He glanced at the clock on the wall. It was 4.30 and another hour-and-a-half to go before he could escape from the job he hated so much. His thoughts drifted to home and the new baby. He might be only fifteen but he knew a bit about the procreation of children and wished his father would do something to stop adding to his mother's already overloaded burden.

A door leading from the living quarters at the back of the shop opened and Joe Rigby appeared. A small man with a stoop, acquired from spending most of his life bending over a last, he also had quite a noticeable limp due to an injury to his leg when, as a young man, he'd been trampled in the road by a runaway horse. He leaned against David's workbench to catch his breath. 'How're you doin' son?' he said in his gravelly voice. 'I can't get me breath at all this afternoon. It must be the dry weather or summat.'

And the sixty fags you smoke every day, David thought to himself, but saying nothing. He held up the shoe he was working on. 'I've finished Mr. Garbutt's boots Mr. Rigby,' he said, 'and I'm just starting on Mrs Smith's shoes.'

Joe studied the young boy closely. He was a good lad was David Cartarett; well spoken and from a decent family and he'd had no hesitation in taking him on to teach him the trade. He knew, however, that the boy's heart wasn't in it. Not that he didn't make a good job of repairing boots and shoes; he did that all right. But it wasn't what the lad wanted and somehow Joe, who had a feeling for these things, had sensed that some time ago.

'This aint what you really want to do, is it lad?' he said, as David picked up a shoe and fitted it onto the last. 'And put that bliddy thing down for a minute while we talk.'

David pushed the last away from him. 'I'm really sorry Mr. Rigby,' he said. 'I've tried, I have, but I just can't get on with it.'

Joe gave a toothless grin. 'For someone who can't get on with it, you've done very well son,' he said. 'I've not had one complaint about your work in the year you've been with me.'

'Thanks Mr. Rigby.'

'Tell me,' Joe went on. 'What is it you really want to do for a livin'?'

'Carpentry,' David replied. 'I want to make things from wood. That's what I'd really like to do.'

Joe stroked his beard thoughtfully. 'Um', he said, 'you realise of course that you'd have to go to College, and Colleges cost money.

Or mebbe find an apprenticeship, which aint easy and wouldn't pay much. An' could your father afford to let you do that?'

David knew the answer to that. 'I could go to night school though,' he said. 'Couldn't I?'

'Mebbe.'

'P'raps I could work here during the day and go to school at night. What do you think Mr. Rigby?'

Joe didn't want to say what he thought. There was no point in raising any hopes in the boy. Even going to night school would cost money, and the cost of things like books and such would have to come from somewhere. Harry Cartarett wouldn't be earning much at the dairy, and he had a large family to support, plus the extra rent he now had to find for his new house at Eastbrook. 'Have you talked to your Dad about this?' he said. 'Have you told him how you feel?'

'Yes Mr. Rigby,' David said. 'But Mum had just had the baby when I got home from work yesterday and everything was upside down.'

'What did he have to say about it son?'

'He said he'd think about it.'

'Well, that's a start innit. An' if you like, I'll try and get to have a word with him an' see what he thinks. Mind you, it wouldn't be easy workin' all day, and then goin' to school at night. But then a sensible lad like you would know that.' The old man limped towards the door. 'An' now I'm just off to get meself some fags. You get on with Mrs Smith's shoes and we'll see.'

David had always felt sorry for Joe Rigby. The old man lived alone at the back of the shop, his wife having died some fourteen years' earlier from the Spanish Flu, not long after their only son was killed in France during the Great War. As far as anyone knew, Joe had no other relatives and was a lonely man. David didn't like the idea of letting him down as he was a good boss, and a generous one too. Not only was David learning a proper trade, but he also earned more than most of the boys he'd left school with. The trouble was, mending shoes for the rest of his working life wasn't what he wanted to do.

Joe was back within five minutes, puffing away at a Woodbine. David had never been able to understand what people saw in smoking.

He'd tried it once, behind the bicycle sheds at school but it had made him feel so sick and dizzy that he'd vowed never to do it again. And he never had.

'I'm off for me tea now,' Joe said through a cloud of grey smoke. 'Give me a shout before you go home an' I'll lock up behind you. See you in the mornin.''

'Goodnight, Mr Rigby.'

'Goodnight then son.'

At ten past six, David called through to the back that he was off, and let himself out into the street where, just ahead of him, two of his old school mates were larking about in the road. He caught up with them and stopped for a chat.

'What you up to these days?' he said to Alfie Blatt, well known around the local streets as a bit of a ruffian. 'Working for a living are you?'

'Nah,' Alfie replied, kicking an old tin can into the gutter. 'Got the sack I did an' I aint found nothin' else yet.'

'What about you, Tom?' Tom Trippet had always stuck to Alfie like glue, and it came as no surprise to anyone that the two of them had found jobs working together when they left school. Tom shook his head. 'I got booted out, same as Alfie,' he said, sounding proud of the fact. 'Me an' Alf was workin' t'gether over at the scrap yard but ole man Stallard didn't like us, did he Alf?'

'Nope,' Alfie said, 'he didn't an' that's a fact. An' stop calling me Alf.' Steering the conversation away from work, he asked David how he liked the new house.

'It's nice,' David said. 'Bit far to come for work but I'm hoping to get an old bike to do up soon, then I won't have to walk.'

'Blimey!' Alfie said. 'You have t'walk there an' back?'

'Yes,' David replied, 'but I don't mind. It's better than living round here.'

'Yeh, I suppose *anythin's* better than livin' round 'ere,' Alfie agreed. 'You gonna be doin' anythin' on Saturday night?'

David didn't usually do anything on a Saturday night, or any other night for that matter. There wasn't a lot you could do if you had to hand over your wages and didn't get much back in the way of pocket money, he told Alfie.

'Want to come over to the Mission Hall to a Social?' Alfie asked. 'It's only thruppence to get in.'

David hesitated. He'd like to go out somewhere just for a change. Trouble was, he didn't have anything decent to wear. Still, it didn't matter too much if you were only going to the Mission Hall. No one dressed up for that.

'I might,' he said.

'Belle Summerford will be there,' Tom put in. 'You always liked her didn't you David.'

David gave that some thought. Tom was right, he'd always liked Belle and they'd been good friends when they were at school, although he didn't really want to start going out with girls just yet. He couldn't afford it. Still, it would be a nice change to go somewhere and the thought of seeing her again not an unattractive one. 'All right then, I'll come,' he said.

'See you there.' Alfie said. 'It starts at eight.'

They parted company and David whistled as he continued his journey home, his head full of whether or not Belle Summerford already had a feller and if not, would she be interested in him. He hadn't seen her since they had both left school but he'd heard she'd been seen walking out a few times with Russell Porter and if that was the case, David didn't fancy the competition. Russell Porter stood over six feet tall in his socks, and was a heavyweight, with a reputation for enjoying a good scrap with anyone who upset him. He'd make mincemeat out of someone only five feet six and skinny like David and no girl was worth that he decided as he walked on. It took him a good half an hour to walk to Eastbrook and as he neared the corner into Kestrel Road, he spotted his Auntie Frances crossing the road on her way home.

'Everything all right Auntie?' he called out.

'Everything's fine David,' she replied. 'Your Mum's looking better today. I had to dash off as your Uncle Albert will be waiting for his tea.'

After David had left the shop, Joe Rigby locked and bolted the door then wandered over to the workbench and picked up the shoes the boy had just finished working on for Mrs Smith. A neat job if ever he saw one. He pottered about for a minute or two then turned out the light, went back into his living quarters and sat down by the fire to think. The shop was on a lease; Joe didn't own it, but over the years, he'd been careful with his money and had a nice, tidy little sum tucked away in the Building Society. What would happen if he offered to help David go to night school to learn carpentry? Or even better, Joe's old friend Jim Dangerfield was known to be looking for a lad to help out in his cabinet-making firm. It might be worth asking if he'd consider taking David on. But would David's father be offended? Joe knew that Harry Cartarett was a proud man who might take any offer of outside help as a suggestion that he couldn't properly support his own family. Still, it might be worth a try. Young David would make a good carpenter, and Joe had no one else to spend his money on so there was nothing to lose by talking to the lad's father. Sound him out and see what he thought.

He poked at the fire, sending a shower of sparks up the chimney, sat back in his old armchair, went through his usual evening ritual of thinking fondly about his late wife Adeline and the son they'd lost, then closed his eyes and drifted off to sleep.

David stood in front of the mirror that hung by a piece of string in the hallway, studied his reflection and wasn't pleased with what he saw. The face that stared back at him was pale and thin, accentuating the prominent nose he'd inherited from his father. In one respect, he was lucky for there wasn't a spot or blemish to be seen on his skin, unlike some other boys of around his own age whose faces were a mass of angry-looking pustules, made worse by being picked or squeezed with dirty fingers. Leaning forward, he peered closely at his hair, or what was left of it after he'd had orders from his mother last week to get a short back and sides at the barbers in Dundee Street. 'You look like a tramp,' she'd said. It was a nondescript, brown colour but a spot of his father's Brilliantine would make it appear darker and give it a shine. His eyes were his best feature. Dark blue, just like his mother's, they were large and expressive and fringed with thick, silky lashes, the envy of all the girls who had been in his class at school. Up until now, much to his annoyance, he'd not started shaving. At odd times, he'd spotted a bit of fluff growing on his chin but that was all it was, a bit of fluff, and nothing that required the assistance of a cut-throat razor.

He went through to the kitchen to have a wash then upstairs to the bedroom he shared with his younger brother Alex where, on the bed, he laid out his only pair of grey flannels, a blue shirt and a sleeveless Fairisle pullover, knitted by Auntie Frances for his last birthday. Then, wanting the use of his father's Brilliantine, he crept along the landing and tapped lightly on his parent's bedroom door where Esther was still in bed after giving birth to Daniel five days' before. She called out for him to come in.

'Ah,' she said, 'a visit from my eldest son.'

David felt guilty that, since the night of Daniel's birth, apart from putting his head around the door before leaving for work each morning, he had kept well out of the way. He couldn't face seeing her feed the baby again although he still didn't know why he felt the way he did about it. He could remember some women living in Wimple Street who'd sat on stools outside their homes to feed theirs. It happened all the time. He'd seen them. So what was so bad about his mother doing it indoors in front of him?

'Sorry Mum,' he said. 'Could I use some of Dad's Brilliantine?'

She nodded. 'You're going to the Mission Hall tonight, aren't you?'

'Yes.'

'Who are you going with?'

David hesitated. He thought he'd better tell the truth even though he knew she didn't like Alfie Blatt. 'I'm going with Alfie,' he said, adding quickly, 'but I'm not going *with* him. Just meeting him there, that's all.'

'He's a bad influence is that one,' Esther said. 'And I don't want you getting into any trouble.'

'I won't,' David promised, 'and I'll be in by eleven.'

'You'll be in by ten, young man.'

'Aw, Mum, it doesn't finish 'til half past ten.'

'Ten o'clock or you don't go at all,' she insisted.

David knew better than to argue any further. All the same, he resented her treating him like a child when he was out earning a living *and* handing over his wage packet unopened at the end of each week too. He took his father's tin of Brilliantine from the dressing table, gave his mother a peck on the cheek and went back to his room to get ready. She could say what she liked, he wasn't going to look a cissy in front of everyone and he'd get home at whatever time he pleased.

He smeared some of the grease onto his hair and combed it back. It didn't look too bad and he made a mental note to save up and buy some of his own. As he climbed into his trousers, he found himself shaking. Standing up for himself was something new, but this time he was going to do what *he* wanted, and take no notice of his mother's orders.

The Mission Hall was in Lucan Street, about twenty-five minutes' walk from Eastbrook and as he approached it he could hear the sound of music drifting through the open door. He wasn't over fond of modern music and couldn't dance a step but it didn't matter. He'd come to see Belle Summerford. Ever since they'd parted at the school gates for the last time, over a year ago, he'd wondered what had become of her. He knew she lived in a posh street at North End and had found work in one of the swanky shops at Southsea where all the Big Nobs bought their stuff, so it was unlikely that she'd be interested in him. Still, there was no harm in trying.

Alfie and Tom were already there and David wandered over to join them. On a small, raised area, a man was playing records on a wind-up gramophone, although there was no one up on the floor dancing, all the action centred on a table at the opposite end of the hall where refreshments were being served. David scanned the room but he couldn't see anyone who looked anything like Belle Summerford. Then Alfie nudged him. 'That's 'er, with the blonde hair and long legs,' he said, pointing to two girls who were standing by the refreshment table. He laughed and gave David a shove. 'Go on, go over an' talk to 'er.'

David sauntered across the room, trying his best to look casual. At first, he thought Alfie had made a mistake, for the girl who turned round when he called her name was nothing like the Belle Summerford he remembered. This one was just about everything he hated to see in a girl. Thick makeup and pencilled-in eyebrows that made her look like a clown he'd once seen in a picture book, and a low-cut blouse showing too much bare flesh. She looked cheap and common.

'Well, if it isn't Davey Cartarett,' she said, moving closer and fluttering her eyelashes at him.

The smell of her cheap perfume was overpowering, and made him want to sneeze. He took a step back. 'How are you Belle?' he asked, trying hard to be polite and keep his distance at the same time.

She smiled at him archly. 'All the better for seeing you,' she replied. 'It's been a long time, hasn't it?'

'Yes, it's been over a year.'

'Do you dance, Davey?' She wriggled her hips suggestively and he wished she would stop calling him Davey.

'Sorry,' he said, relieved that he wouldn't have to get that close to her, 'I don't.'

'Don't worry,' she cooed, 'I'll show you how,' and before he could do anything to stop her, she had her arm around his waist and was guiding him onto the floor. He stumbled along to the music, treading all over her feet and feeling such a fool with everyone watching them until in the end she gave up and drew him across the hall. 'Never mind,' she said, 'we'll sit here and you can tell me all about yourself and what you've been up to since we left school.'

David had no wish to sit and talk to this awful girl. In fact, all he wanted now was to go home. The music was getting on his nerves, the air was full of cigarette smoke and he had a headache. 'I'm going outside for some fresh air,' he said and immediately wished he'd kept his mouth shut.

She jumped up, linking her arm in his and, in her eagerness to get him outside, almost shoved him through the doorway. 'I'll come with you,' she said.

It was a lovely night. The sky was awash with stars, and there was a full moon. They walked for a few yards to the end of the street before she stopped and leaned provocatively against the wall of a house. 'Aren't you going to kiss me?' she whispered, putting her arms around him and lifting her face to his.

David had never kissed a girl before and he didn't want to kiss Belle Summerford with her painted lips either, but suddenly her mouth was on his, all warm and soft and moist. He felt funny, as if he should do be doing something, but wasn't sure what, and he'd no idea what to do with his hands. She was pushing herself up against him, her hands everywhere, the overpowering smell of her perfume making his nostrils smart. Suddenly, she unbuttoned her blouse, grabbed his hand and shoved it inside. 'Go on,' she whispered, 'touch them. I don't mind a bit.'

He could feel the firmness of her breasts but, as a picture of his mother feeding Daniel passed briefly before his eyes, he wanted to be sick and snatched his hand away. Belle laughed and by the light of the gas lamp, he could see the lipstick on her teeth and the lines on her once pretty face where her make-up had gone all blotchy. She looked disgusting. 'What d'you think you're doing?' he shouted, frantically trying to extricate himself from her clutches.

'Don't you *know?*' She yelled back at him, and then burst out laughing. 'My God, you *don't*, do you?'

He felt such an idiot. How could someone who was fifteen years' old not know what a girl wanted when she was inviting a boy to go further than a kiss? 'Get off and leave me alone,' he muttered. 'Go on. Go back and find someone else to do whatever it is you want.'

She stared at him in disbelief and, with a toss of her long hair, buttoned up her blouse and turned to walk away. 'At least anyone else would act like a man,' she called over her shoulder, 'which is more than can be said of you. What are you anyway, some kind of Nancy Boy?'

He waited until she had disappeared back into the Mission Hall before setting off for home and as he walked through the darkened streets, he tried to make some sense from his odd behaviour. He thought he knew how babies were made, but his knowledge of what to do with girls was limited to that gleaned from other boys at school during dinner breaks. Some of them had seemed very knowledgeable about petting and stuff but he, himself, had left school none the wiser. In any case, you should be married if you wanted to do things like that. He wished there was someone he could talk to about it. His own father would be uncomfortable with the subject, and he certainly couldn't ask his mother. Uncle Albert might be willing although David doubted it, and that left Auntie Frances. No, he couldn't ask a woman. Had he worked in one of the factories with other men, he would probably have learned all he needed to know by now but he spent his days alone in the shop with no one to talk to except Joe Rigby. And he certainly couldn't ask him. He'd just have to find out some other way. Eventually, he reached Kestrel Road and, thankful to be home, opened the back door and went in.

Harry, who was sitting at the living room table sorting out the milk money he had collected that day, looked up in surprise on seeing his son back so early. 'Didn't expect to see you 'til later,' he said. 'What happened?'

David took a chair by the fire. He'd already rehearsed his excuses. 'I couldn't stand the noise and the cigarette smoke,' he said, 'and I was getting a headache.' He rubbed his hand across his forehead. 'I suppose I shouldn't have gone. I don't really like dances and things like that.'

Harry set aside his money counting for a minute and moved over to his fireside chair. 'Well,' he said, 'I had a visitor this evening while you were out. You've only just missed him in fact.'

'Oh, who was that then?'

'Joe Rigby.'

David's ears pricked up. 'Joe Rigby?'

'That's what I said.'

'What did he want?' David asked. 'And how did he manage to find this place?'

Harry took hold of the poker and riddled the fire. 'Well, it seems he knows Eastbrook quite well,' he said, 'and as he had our address, he hopped on a bus to the top of Barnwell Road and asked for directions from a man out walking his dog.'

'Are you going to tell me what he wanted then?' David said, anxious to know whether it was something to do with what he and Joe Rigby had discussed the other day.

'He wants to be your benefactor,' Harry said.

David laughed. 'Blimey Dad, that's a big word. What does it mean?'

'Not sure me'self,' his father replied, 'but it sounds good, and as I understand it, means he wants to help you. He has a friend called Jim Dangerfield who owns a furniture-making business and is looking for a lad to help in the workshop. Mr. Rigby has asked him if he'd take you on and he's agreed. That's if you want to of course.' He shook his head. 'I must admit I wasn't very happy about it at first and told him so, but when he said he'd lost his only son in the war and didn't have anyone else to spend his money on, I said I'd talk to you about it, and think it over.'

'It's what I want to do, Dad,' David said, 'and I'll work hard, honestly I will.'

Harry reached across and laid a hand on the arm of this sensitive son of his. 'I know you will,' he said, 'else I wouldn't have agreed to it.' He left his chair and went back to the table. 'And now I've to finish counting me takings,' he said, gathering up a pile of the silver disks the Co-op customers used as cash for their milk, 'and you'd best be off to bed. We'll sort this out tomorrow. Goodnight son.'

'Goodnight Dad. And thanks.'

Harry looked up. 'It's Joe Rigby you've to thank,' he said, 'so make sure you do, first thing on Monday morning.'

'Yes Dad.' David went upstairs to bed, pausing on the way to say goodnight to his mother. She didn't ask why he was back so early from the social and he was glad. He wanted to forget all about this evening and concentrate on his future. He climbed into the bed he shared with Alex, who was fast asleep, and lay staring into the darkness until long after he heard his father come up the stairs to bed. The baby started to cry, and he was aware of his mother moving about trying to quieten the child. Alex, who could sleep through anything, stirred and turned over without waking.

For some time, David lay there listening to the movements in the next room. He tried to, but couldn't, make some sense from his reactions to Belle Summerford, until at last everything went quiet and he fell into a deep sleep, not waking until Alex shook him and said that if he wanted any breakfast, he'd better get out of bed.

CHAPTER THREE

'You'll never guess who's moving in across the road,' Harry said to Esther one Sunday morning as she sat by the fire feeding Daniel.

'Who would that be,' she said, 'anyone we know?'

'Yes. It's Jack and Phyllis Martindale and their three boys, who live on the corner of Wimpole Street and Pegasus Place. Jack works at the dairy with me.'

'Oh I know them,' Esther said. 'Mrs Martindale always passed the time of day but never stopped for a chat. She kept her head down and didn't seem to want to talk to anyone.'

'Well, maybe you'll get to know one another now,' Harry said. 'Jack says she's been going through a bad time, and he's at the end of his tether with the boys. He can't control them and Phyllis doesn't want to be bothered. I think he's hoping that she will be better once they've moved away from The Shambles.'

'*Anyone* would be better moving away from that place,' Esther said, handing Daniel over to him. 'Could you hold him a minute while I find a clean nappy.' She made the baby comfortable then put him down to sleep. 'When are they moving in?' she said.

'Tomorrow.'

'All right,' Esther said, 'I'll give them a couple of days to settle and then I'll call and see this Phyllis if you like. I could do with a bit of female company myself.'

It didn't take long for the two women to become firm friends, and the change in Phyllis was, Jack told Harry, a miracle. Her depression seemed to disappear overnight and once she began to take an interest in everything again, even the behaviour of their boys improved. 'I can't believe it's the same woman,' he said.

Harry sympathised. 'That Hell-hole we've just moved from was enough to get anyone down,' he said.

Once Esther was able to go out after the birth of Daniel, she and Phyllis started going for walks together of an afternoon. More often than not, they went along the seafront but sometimes, it was Highland Road and gazing into shop windows at all the things they'd love to buy but couldn't afford. It was on one of these afternoon walks that Phyllis confided in Esther about her marriage. 'I think Jack is seeing another woman,' she said, one fine October afternoon, as the two of them, with the children, strolled along the seafront savouring the late autumn sunshine.

'Don't be silly,' Esther said, parking the pram next to a bench. 'You've taken the wind out of my sails saying a thing like that. Let's sit down a minute.' Jack Martindale was seeing another woman? Esther didn't know him that well, but he didn't seem the type. The idea was ridiculous. 'Anyway,' she went on, 'what makes you think he is?'

Phyllis was silent for a minute. Then, 'I haven't … well … *you know* … let him do anything for ages,' she said.

Esther stared at her friend in disbelief. Was she saying that they didn't make love any more? 'That's awful Phyllis,' she said. 'But, if you don't mind my asking, why?'

'It's all my fault,' Phyllis confessed. 'I can't bear him anywhere near me since Robert was born. At the time, I hadn't wanted any more children when I found I was expecting him, and although I wouldn't be with out him now, I suppose I'm afraid of having another baby.'

'I knew women in Wimple Street like that,' Esther said, 'who didn't want any more babies, but they still gave their men what they wanted or ran the risk of losing them to someone who would.' She rushed to defend Jack. 'Anyway, I'm sure you're wrong,' she said. 'Your Jack would never do a thing like that.'

'Well,' Phyllis said, 'could you blame him if he did? He's only forty and still has needs, *and* rights the same as any man.'

'Men *don't* have "rights", as you put it Phyllis, but all the same, if what you say is true, it's not very fair on him.' She placed an arm around her friend's shoulder. 'I'm sure you're wrong, but why don't you ask him?'

'If I did, he'd only deny it.'

Esther thought for a minute. 'Do you remember that clinic I went to?' she said. 'They have women doctors there and you can talk to them about anything to do with that side of things. They're really very helpful.' She rummaged in her bag and found the piece of paper Frances had given her. 'Here, all you have to do is make an appointment.'

'Oh, I couldn't talk to a stranger about anything like that,' Phyllis said, her face turning scarlet at the thought, 'it's too embarrassing.'

Esther lost her patience. 'For goodness sake,' she snapped, 'do you want to lose your husband altogether? You can't let things go on like this and if you don't do something about it, he *will* look elsewhere, and then what will you do?' She took her friend's hand. 'Go on,' she urged, 'give it a try. I'll come with you if you like.'

Phyllis felt a great sense of relief that at last she had been able to confide in someone about a matter that had been worrying her for years, especially lately. She loved Jack very much and knew that her behaviour was just not fair on him. It was true that these days he didn't seem to mind much about her refusal to make love, and that made her suspect that he might be getting what he wanted with someone else. Also, for the past few months, he had given up trying to persuade her and now just gave her a peck on the cheek when they went to bed, before turning his back on her. She'd like to take Esther's advice and do something about it but what if it the clinic *could* help and then Jack didn't want to be bothered with her after all this time. And did she really want to turn the clock back?

'All right,' she said. 'I'll think about it. Only not a word to anyone mind.'

'Of course not,' Esther said, as Daniel woke up and began to cry. 'We'd best be going back now. He's due for his feed.'

As the two women strolled along the seafront towards home, Esther tried to reason with herself about Jack and the likelihood of him having another woman. She couldn't imagine him cheating on his wife and yet, she supposed, any man might be driven to it if he wasn't getting his needs met back home. But Jack? She found it hard to believe.

Ambrose Street was at the other end of the town and in the kitchen of number twenty-seven, Jack Martindale was finishing his cup of tea. He put his empty cup down on the table and smacked his lips together. 'That was good,' he said to the woman sitting opposite.

Maisie Gilliman smiled. 'Not the only thing that was good,' she said, reaching across and slipping her hand into his. 'Will you be calling in tomorrow?'

Jack shook his head. 'Sorry,' he said, 'I've promised to stand in for one of the other Milkies who wants a day off. I won't be finished the rounds until late in the afternoon so there won't be time.'

'Oh.' Maisie sounded disappointed. 'Well never mind; perhaps the day after?'

'I'll see what I can do,' Jack said, careful not to promise anything. He was very fond of Maisie but it was really Phyllis he'd rather be tucked up in bed with, and his conscience had begun bothering him lately over his behaviour. He wished with all his heart that he could do something to help his wife but until she was able to show him some love and affection, nobody could blame him for seeking his pleasures elsewhere. Maisie was undemanding. She knew how things were and wanted nothing more than to have him to visit her as often as he could. Her own husband had died in an accident at sea some five years' ago and she didn't want to marry again. This rather surprised Jack because she wasn't an unattractive woman but, she'd told him, giving pleasure to an unhappy man like him was enough for her at the moment. He often worried about how long she would be willing to go on like that without asking for more because he would never leave Phyllis and the children and had made that plain. Sometimes it occurred to him that Phyllis might suspect what he was up to but she had never asked questions, so telling lies to cover up his activities had so far not been necessary, for which he was thankful.

He left the house and walked to the end of the street where he had left his empty milk cart, away from the prying eyes of Maisie's neighbours. His thoughts, as he pushed it back to the dairy, were on what Harry would say if he knew about his unfaithfulness to Phyllis. Despite having put Esther in the family way before they were married, Harry was a man of very high principles and would most likely be shocked if he found out that his friend and neighbour was, for whatever reason, cheating on his wife. Maybe once Phyllis had settled in the new house she loved so much, things would change and they would be able to live like any normal married couple. Just like Harry and Esther for instance. He hoped so because the strain of keeping his liaison with Maisie a secret was beginning to tell.

The yard was empty when he arrived back, Harry having finished work and gone home. Jack washed the cart down, put it away and went into the office to sign off. When he arrived home, Phyllis was in the kitchen preparing dinner. She looked happy, and he was therefore surprised when she asked if he had someone else. He went over and put his arms around her, giving her a hug and for the first time since his carrying on with Maisie had to tell his beloved Phyllis a lie for there was no way he wanted to hurt her by telling the truth. 'Don't be silly,' he said. 'Of course there isn't. What do you take me for?'

For once, she didn't push him away, but rested her auburn curls on his chest and gave him a hug. 'I wouldn't blame you Jack,' she said. 'You've had to put up with a lot from me over the past few years, what with me being depressed and that.'

Surprised at this unusual display of affection, and a little worried that her behaviour might mean that she suspected something, he held her away from him and noticed a bit of a sparkle in her eyes. She'd also done something to her hair, and put some powder and rouge on her face. She had always been a pretty woman, with her auburn curls, delicate features and slightly freckled skin but lately, she'd not bothered too much with her appearance. Today, she looked beautiful.

'What have you been up to?' he said. 'You look really *different.*'

She couldn't tell him that she'd talked about their private life to Esther; he wouldn't like that. But the relief of bringing it out into the open and telling someone of her fears had been enough to bring home to her the danger her marriage was in. And she'd already made up her mind to visit the clinic Esther had told her about. She smiled up at him. 'Now that would be telling, wouldn't it,' she said, 'but I do love you Jack, I really do. And I don't want to lose you to someone else.'

Jack had to look away, afraid the guilty look on his face might give him away. 'Want to prove it?' he said, expecting her to freeze and turn away from him as she had done so often these past few years. But this time she didn't. Instead, she looked up at him and smiled, and he could hardly believe what he was hearing when she said that yes, she would ... but later, once the boys were all in bed.

Chapter Four

From the front room window of her top floor apartment overlooking the sea front at Southsea, Lydia Cartarett had an uninterrupted view of the Solent and, beyond that, the rolling hills of the Isle of Wight. She never tired of sitting in the window, surrounded by her five Persian cats, watching the activities on the strip of water that separated the Island from the mainland. Or waiting for her son Harry to turn the corner with his milk cart on his way to visit her, which he did twice a week after he'd finished his milk round for the day. On this particular November afternoon, it was twelve-thirty when he appeared and as soon as she spotted his familiar figure, she left the window seat and went into the kitchen to put the kettle on.

Harry parked his cart in the road fronting the block of flats. He knew it was his duty to call in on his mother now and then but he was getting tired of these regular visits, which she had come to expect even though she was perfectly able to call on him and Esther had she wanted. Her total dislike of Esther was the reason she didn't and she had never been to Kestrel Road, nor had she seen Daniel, and it was this indifference towards his children that made him so angry. Still, it was her loss and if she felt like that, she would just have to get on with it.

He tapped on her door and let himself in with a key she had given him. He wished she didn't have so many cats. She kept them shut in the apartment for twenty-four hours' a day and the place stank of them, and the fish diet on which she fed them. He wasn't fond of animals himself, except for horses, and not only that, Esther could always tell when he'd been visiting his mother by the smell on his clothes. It was the one thing guaranteed to cause a row between them.

'Do you have to go there so often?' she would say, with bitter resentment in her voice, 'after the way she's treated me all these years.' He couldn't blame her for the way she felt but his mother was his mother and there wasn't anything he could do to change that.

'You look tired,' Lydia said, breaking into his thoughts as she handed him a cup of tea, served in a bone china cup and saucer when he would much rather have had an enamel mug like the one he used at home.

'That's probably because I've been up since four o'clock,' he replied.

'That job is too much for you,' she said, sipping her tea. 'Isn't it time you found something better?'

'You know I can't, as you put it "find something better", mother,' he replied irritably. 'We have this conversation every time I come here.'

'Too many mouths to feed,' she said, 'that's your trouble.'

Harry felt his anger rising to the surface. Why did she always have to say things like that about his family? 'Did I tell you,' he said, in an effort to control his temper, 'that David might be starting an apprenticeship to learn woodworking?'

She shifted around in her seat to make room on her lap for one of the cats. 'No,' she said, 'you didn't. Why is he doing that when you can barely afford a decent pair of shoes to walk the streets in?'

'He wants to be a carpenter. And why shouldn't he?' Harry's voice had an edge to it. 'He'll still be working and paying his way if that is what's bothering you. And Alex has just started in his first job. He's managed to find work at the local Jam factory until he can make up his mind what he wants to do, so that's two of them earning.' He finished his tea. 'And I haven't yet got to the stage where I have to do my milk round in bare feet.'

'And what is that wife of yours doing these days?'

Harry finally lost his temper and slammed his cup and saucer down on the table beside him. 'My wife has a name,' he said, 'and I'll thank you to use it.'

Lydia stared at him, her dark eyes glinting. 'I do have a name for her but you wouldn't like it.'

He shot out of his seat. 'I've had just about enough, and I'll not stay and listen to any more of this, Mother,' he said. 'And in future if you want to see me you can come to my house for I'll be buggered if I'm going to put myself out to come and see you again.'

Lydia knocked the unfortunate cat to the floor and stood up. 'Don't you dare use that kind of language to me,' she said as he snatched up his cap and made for the door. 'Save it for that woman you're married to. I'm sure it won't offend *her*.'

He stopped in his tracks and turned round to face her. 'I don't know what it is that makes you hate Esther so,' he said with surprising control, 'but from the day I brought her home to meet you, you've had it in for her. And I would remind you that I've been married to her for seventeen years now and she's been a damned good wife to me and a good mother to our children. She put up with living in Wimple Street for all those years without a single word of complaint, when most other women would have given their man hell over it. And apart from all that, I love her.' He shrugged his shoulders. 'Esther would have made a friend of you if you hadn't treated her so badly when I was in France and she had to live in your house.'

Lydia's face registered surprise.

'Oh yes,' Harry went on, 'I know all about the business of when our first child died and how you told her that it was God's punishment on her for being a sinner.'

'So she was,' Lydia said. 'And as for putting up with living in Wimple Street, if you had done as I asked and trained for one of the professions, you'd have met and married a decent woman from a good family, and had your own house by now. Esther Wilding trapped you into marrying her, only you were too stupid to see it. And where did it get you after you left my house? First, living in one pokey room, then that filthy place in the slums, and now in a Corporation house, with nothing to call your own, and with goodness knows *what* kind of people for neighbours.'

'You are a snob, mother,' Harry replied, 'and I suppose it never occurred to you that I didn't *want* to be an accountant, or a doctor or solicitor or go in for any of the other fancy careers you had lined up for me. And as for my being "trapped" into marrying Esther, I think that *I* had something to do with her getting into trouble.'

'Men like you wouldn't take advantage of fast and loose girls who didn't ask for it,' Lydia replied, determined, but failing to have the last word.

He moved to open the door and turned once more to face his mother. 'The number twenty tram to Eastbrook passes this block of flats every fifteen minutes,' he said his voice quiet and steady, 'and if you want to see me – *us* –, get out of your chair and get on it. You know where we live.' And leaving her speechless, with her mouth hanging open, he let himself out.

As he pushed his cart back to the dairy, he wondered why it was that his mother couldn't, or wouldn't, accept something that had happened such a long time ago. She had always been of the opinion that Esther wasn't good enough for him, her father having been just an ordinary seaman of lower rank, when his own had been a well-respected businessman of some note in the town. Douglas Cartarett had been on the point of becoming a Councillor when, at the age of forty, he'd died suddenly of a heart attack, leaving his wife to raise their three children on her own.

This last thought brought Harry to a halt. Wasn't he being just a bit hard on his mother? After all, even though money had not been a problem, she'd made sacrifices, one being the chance to marry again which she had declined because she knew her children wouldn't want to replace the father they'd loved so much. She had always been, and still was, an attractive woman and had not gone short of offers from men who could have made a big difference to her life. But she'd turned them all down.

Harry had always been a disappointment to her since he'd refused to train for one of the professions. His older brother Charles had become an Accountant, married into a good family, and his only son Walter was doing well in the Police Force whilst Harry had preferred to do any job that would take him out into the fresh air. He couldn't stand the thought of being shut in a factory or office day in and day out and besides, he wasn't academically minded like Charles and would never have been able to apply himself to study for years on end as he had. At sixteen, Harry had started to make plans to emigrate to Canada or America as soon as he was old enough but nothing had come of them because, with the possibility of a world war looming on the horizon, he'd joined the Army instead. He'd met and married Esther, fought in France, gone missing for a while then, when it was all over, returned to her and the problem of his mother, and trying to find somewhere else to live.

'You've been to see her again, haven't you?' Esther said, sniffing the air as Harry walked in through the back door. 'I can smell those cats.'

Harry, tired of being some sort of piggy-in-the-middle between his mother and his wife, lost his temper. 'For God's sake, woman,' he shouted. 'what's the matter with you?' He flung his cap across the kitchen. 'Of course I've been to see my mother and I've just about had enough of the pair of you. You're one as bad as the other.'

Esther slammed a saucepan full of stew down on the cooker. 'How dare you say that,' she flung back at him. '*She's* the one who causes all the trouble. She hates me and isn't even interested in any of her grandchildren.' Her hands trembled as she struck a match and lit the gas under the saucepan. 'Not quite like your brother Charles and his little snot of a son who, she thinks, is God's Gift to the Police Force.' She fought back the tears. 'And I don't see the need for you to visit her twice a week.'

'She *is* my mother.'

Esther raised her eyebrows. 'Yes, and don't I know it. But there's no reason why she couldn't call in and see us now and then. She visits Frances often enough.'

Harry threw his hands up in the air in despair. 'I'm going out into the garden,' he said, 'where I might be able to find a bit of peace and quiet.'

Esther picked up an empty saucepan and threw it at his disappearing back, but it missed and landed with a crash on the path. As he turned and gave her one of his contemptuous looks, she went back with a heavy heart to her pot of stew. Her own parents both long dead, there was nothing she'd like more than to be friends with her mother-in-law, but the old lady, in seventeen years, had never shown any sign of wanting to make amends for the dreadful things she'd said and done. And Esther had never seen any good reason why she should be the one to make an effort to put things right, which meant that the situation between the two stubborn women had reached stalemate.

Harry wandered into the garden, his eyes moving over the piles of builders' rubble that had yet to be cleared by the Council workmen. They said it would take at least a month to clear every garden in the road but he was getting impatient to get started. It was a wide plot and he'd already drawn up plans for how it should be. In his mind's eye, he saw neat rows of vegetables, a small salad bed in the far corner, some soft fruit, raspberries, red and blackcurrants and gooseberries and, close to the house a chicken run with enough hens to keep a good supply of eggs going. He might even be able to find enough space for a few rows of potatoes. There was nothing to beat them, freshly dug from the earth, then scrubbed and boiled in their jackets and served with a generous knob of butter and some boiled bacon. Just like his mother used to do. This last thought brought him back with a jolt to the reason he was out here in the garden making his plans. His mother and Esther; what was he to do about the two of them?

A voice from over the fence broke into his thoughts. 'Settled in yet?'

Harry swung round and came face to face with a tall, fair-haired man dressed in Merchant Navy uniform. 'Chad Garnett,' he said. 'And this is my wife Molly.' The two men shook hands over the wire fence, and Harry nodded to the young, attractive woman who was clinging possessively to her husband's arm.

'Harry Cartarett.'

'Pleased to meet you, Harry.'

'Half a mo,' Harry said, 'I'll give the wife a shout. We might as well all get to know one another, seeing as we're going to be living next door.' He went down the side of the house, opened the back door and the smell of neck of lamb stew set his gastric juices rumbling.

'Are you there Esther?'

'Yes.' Her voice was cold and distant. 'What do you want?'

He ventured inside to where she was spreading a cloth on the table. 'Come outside and meet the people next door,' he said, wanting, but not daring to put his arms around her and tell her that everything was all right.

'I'm *busy.*'

'Well *stop* being busy for a minute and come outside.' It was a command, and the tone of his voice made her remove her apron and follow him out into the garden. It really wasn't his fault, this business with his mother, but the problem had been going on for seventeen years now and it was time he did something to put a stop to it.

Esther liked Molly at once but took an instant dislike to her husband. There's something unpleasant about him, she thought, although she couldn't say what it was that had made her shiver when they were introduced and he squeezed her hand much too tightly over the fence, holding on to it far too long. While the two men talked about the new houses, she and Molly exchanged views on having a large family, Molly and Chad also having had five children.

'Three girls and twin boys,' Molly said. 'The twins are ten, and the girls, eight, seven and two. And that's it as far as I'm concerned, although Chad wouldn't mind another one.'

'That's all very well,' Esther said. 'Men don't have the bother of looking after them. If they did, it would be a different matter.' They chatted for a while before Esther remembered the stew on top of the stove. 'I'll have to go,' she said, 'else we'll all be eating burnt offerings.'

'Perhaps we could walk to the shops together tomorrow,' Molly suggested. 'That's if you don't have anyone else to go with.'

Esther thought of Phyllis. 'Well, there's a friend of mine, lives across the road. I usually go with her but I don't suppose she'll mind if you come along.'

'About ten o'clock then,' Molly said.

Back indoors, Esther served up plates of stew with dumplings for herself, Harry and the two boys who had just arrived home from work. Edwin and Catherine had already had their tea, and Daniel lay sleeping in his pram in the hall. They ate in silence, Harry having always forbidden talking at table. Working class they may be but that didn't mean they shouldn't have good manners. Perversely, he wiped his plate clean with a huge chunk of bread. To him, that was an acceptable way of finishing off a plate of delicious stew, mopping it up with a piece of bread. 'Mmm, that was good,' he said, smacking his lips together appreciatively. 'What did you think of next door then Esther?'

Esther told him of the plan to go shopping with Molly. 'I hope Phyllis won't mind her coming along.'

'Shouldn't think so,' Harry said, thankful that the disagreement over his mother seemed to be over, at least for the time being anyway.

Esther collected the dirty plates together. 'Molly seems very nice,' she said.

'Yes. So does Chad.'

Esther kept her thoughts about that to herself. She filled the kettle and set it on the cooker to boil for the washing up then told the boys to go into the garden.

'I'm sorry Harry,' she said, once they were out of earshot. 'I just can't help getting angry when I know you've been visiting your mother. She could easily come here for a change, but she won't, and the children don't even know they've a Grandmother. It makes my blood boil.'

Harry pulled her down onto his lap and gave her a kiss. 'Well,' he said, 'you'll be pleased to know that I've told her if she wants to see me, then she'll have to hop on a tram and come here because I'm not doing any more visiting.' He ran his fingers through the silky thickness of her mane of hair. 'And I *mean* that.'

CHAPTER FIVE

One Friday afternoon, two weeks' before Christmas, Alex, after collecting his wages from the cashier at Meldrew's Jam factory, opened the brown envelope and took out half-a-crown. Unlike his brother David, he saw no reason why he should take his wage packet home unopened, even though he knew there would be trouble from his mother when she discovered what he'd done. Meldrew's Jams & Preserves paid well and there would still be plenty left for her from the sixteen bob, which was his take-home pay. If he handed over the lot, all he'd get back would be a shilling and that wasn't enough for his plans for Saturday night.

He swaggered back into the factory, a handsome young man who looked older than his fourteen and a half years. Taller and heavier than David, he had an unusual combination of their mother's dark, curly hair and blue eyes, and father's fair complexion and as he walked through the shop floor, he was aware of the admiring glances of the girls who were at work on the lines. Winking at Mary Sadler, he bent down and whispered in her ear. 'See you tomorrow night Mary,' he said, watching the other girls from the corner of his eye and enjoying the attention he was getting. 'Seven o'clock, outside the Regal. And don't be late.'

She smiled up at him. 'I won't.'

Mary had never been able to understand why, from all the girls Alex Cartarett could have gone out with, he'd chosen her. She was very ordinary with not a lot to say for herself. Not a bit like most of the other girls she worked with, some of whom, to use her mother's expression, were "common as muck and with mouths big enough to drive a tram through". It had come as a surprise when Alex Cartarett of all people, had singled her out for attention. She'd only been out with him twice and despite rumours around the factory that he was old beyond his years and had tried his luck with some of the other girls he'd taken out, he treated *her* with respect. So far, she'd had no trouble with wandering hands or requests to do things she knew were wrong.

Esther was angry when Alex presented her with an open wage packet that evening. 'You've no right,' she said, 'to open it yourself. Your brother never has and neither should you.'

'It's me that has to work for it,' Alex protested, 'an' it's *my* money.' He was sick of hearing about his older brother, who was so weak-willed, with no mind of his own, and allowed their mother to run his life for him, even though he was old enough to decide things for himself.

'Well I don't care what dear Saint David does,' Alex said, 'if I want to take some money out my wage packet, I will. So there.'

'How *dare* you speak to me like that.'

'Well stop treating me like a child then.'

'You *are* a child,' she said, 'else you wouldn't behave like this. Now go to your room.'

'No!'

She raised her hand, and the blow across his face when it came, nearly knocked him sideways. He stared at his mother, his eyes filled with hatred. 'I'm leaving home,' he shouted, 'to get away from being bossed about by *you*.' And with that, he bolted through the door and up the stairs.

Esther sank into a chair. Whatever had made her do that to her own son, when she and Harry had never resorted to slapping their children, preferring instead to use persuasion and reasoning to get them to do as they were told? True, Alex was far more headstrong than David, who had always been easy to handle, but she should never have slapped him like that. She glanced at the clock on the mantelpiece. Harry wouldn't be home for at least an hour, and he'd do nothing to help anyway. She pulled herself up from the chair, crept upstairs and pushed open the bedroom door to find Alex lying on his back on the bed, staring up at the ceiling, an angry-looking red wheal across his left cheek. He looked as if he'd been crying.

'I didn't mean to slap you,' Esther said, perching on the edge of the big iron bedstead shared by the two boys. 'But sometimes, you're too mouthy for your own good.'

'I meant it,' Alex said. 'About leavin' home, I mean.'

Esther laughed. 'And where do you think you'd go?'

Alex propped himself up on one elbow. 'Auntie Frances would 'ave me. She likes me. She told me so.'

'Well,' Esther replied, 'she might like you but having you to live with her all the time's a different matter. And I doubt if Uncle Albert would be too pleased to find he'd a lodger in the house.'

'I'll find somewhere else to go then,' Alex said. He didn't really want to leave the comfort of his home, he liked his mother's cooking too much for that, but neither did he want to be told what to do with his hard-earned money. And hard-earned it was. For six days' a week, he worked from seven o'clock in the morning until six o'clock at night, with just a short break for sandwiches in the middle of the day. He unloaded delivery lorries, wheeled heavy crates full of jars of preserves from factory floor to Goods Out, swept and washed floors, cleaned out the huge vats in the mixing room and, in between, ran errands for the snotty management and their even snottier secretaries. He wasn't allowed to stand still for a minute, but the wage packet at the end of each week was generous and made it all worthwhile. Well, it did until he could find something better.

'Is it a girl?' Esther asked presently.

Alex sat bolt upright on the bed. How did his mother know about Mary? 'Yes it is,' he said. 'She's nice and I want to take her to the pictures.'

Esther had never been able to feel close to Alex. Strange that, she thought, for apart from the colour of his hair, he looked very much like his father and for that reason, if no other, she should have been able to love him as intensely as she loved her other children. Yet she didn't. She was fond of him of course, as a mother should be of her son, but there had always been a distance between them and as he was growing up, that distance seemed to be getting wider until she sometimes felt she didn't know him at all.

'Not one of those fast and loose hussies you work with, I hope,' she said.

Alex stared sullenly at his mother. Was she now going to start telling him who he should go out with. 'No. Well, she *does* work at the factory. But Mary's not like all the others and that's why I want to go out with her.' That was true. He was far too young to get involved with girls of the sort his mother was going on about. Besides, with their painted faces and dirty talk, he found them repulsive and there was certainly no truth in the rumours going around that he'd "tried it on" with any of their kind. Why, some of them even smoked cigarettes and there was nothing more disgusting than that in a girl, he thought. All the same, he might have a bit of fun with some of them when he was older.

'Well,' Esther said at last, 'just be careful, that's all. And you can keep the half-a-crown this time but don't let it happen again.' She left the room and, as she closed the door quietly behind her, felt sure she heard Alex mutter something that sounded like 'I won't Mum. Next time, it'll be three-bob.'

Mary was waiting for him at the Regal cinema when he arrived at two minutes' to seven. She was dressed in a long, plum-coloured coat with a big fur collar, her dark brown curls spilling out from beneath a tiny hat pulled over one eye. 'You look nice,' he said. 'Is that a new coat?'

She giggled. 'It's not mine,' she confessed with refreshing honesty. 'My sister lent it me. I could never afford one like this, but she's much older and earns a lot more money.' She pulled a face. 'It's a bit big really but I wanted to look nice for you.'

Alex was flattered, and a little bit embarrassed. 'Where would you like to go then?' he said. 'There's a Fred Astair and Ginger Rogers film on here, or we could go to the Odeon and see Tarzan if you like.'

'Fred Astair,' please.'

It wasn't really Alex's kind of film; he preferred something a bit more exciting, but Mary enjoyed it and all through the performance they held hands which had the effect of taking his mind off what was happening on the screen anyway. As they were walking home, he pulled her round and kissed her, his mouth brushing against hers; her lips soft as velvet. He came over all funny … just as he did sometimes when, in the middle of the night, he woke from a dream and found himself wetting the bed. He always worried about that in case his mother might notice but if she had, she'd never said anything, and it was only when he told one of the lads at the factory about it that he discovered that most boys of his age did the same.

'Wet dreams,' Ronnie Tucker told him. 'We all 'ave 'em an' it's nothin' to worry about.' And a puzzled Alex, none the wiser, had to be satisfied with that.

'We'll do it again sometime,' he said as they reached Mary's doorway and she held her face up for another kiss. In the light of the street lamp outside her house, her face glowed and he knew he wanted to do more than kiss her goodnight. Instead, he gave her a quick peck on the mouth then, to her surprise and amusement, shot off down the street as if all the dogs from hell were after him.

'How many girls have *you* kissed?' he asked David later, when they lay in the double bed, each thinking his own thoughts.

Memories came flooding back to David of the night he'd gone to the Mission Hall and met up with Belle Summerford. Since then, he'd not even bothered to go out of an evening and certainly didn't want to start kissing girls if they were all like her. 'Only one,' he replied. 'And *she* kissed *me*.' He shuddered. 'It was horrible. Like having a wet dog slobbering all over you.'

Alex couldn't understand that. Although he'd been scared of his feelings tonight when he'd kissed Mary, he'd found it very enjoyable. What was wrong with his older brother? Surely, kissing and that, was natural wasn't it? He propped himself up on one elbow. 'Have you ever had a wet dream?' he said.

David turned to look at his brother. 'You ought to have your mouth washed out with carbolic soap,' he said. 'That's dirty talk. And no, I haven't if you must know.'

'You're a liar. I bet you 'ave.'

'I *haven't*,' David insisted. It wasn't quite the truth. Of course he'd had funny dreams but they'd always left him feeling dirty and confused and he wasn't going to admit anything to anyone.

'An that's not all Ronnie Tucker told me either.'

'Who's Ronnie Tucker?'

'Bloke at work. He told me about this other thing boys do, like …'

'Shut your mouth and go to sleep,' David said, clapping his hands over his ears and turning his face to the wall. 'I don't want to hear about things like that. It's just filthy talk and if Mum hears you, she'll clip your ear.'

'You're odd, you are,' Alex said, sliding under the covers, pleased with himself that he'd succeeded in annoying the older brother he'd nicknamed Saint David.

Long after Alex had dropped off into a deep sleep, David lay staring into the darkness. He still couldn't understand his own lack of interest in girls. Maybe it had something to do with seeing his mother feeding Daniel, or his experience with Belle Summerford, or both. All he knew was, at this moment, his thoughts were on more interesting things … the new job he would be starting after Christmas.

Joe Rigby had decided to close the shop and retire but not before he'd fixed David up with a job working for Jim Dangerfield, who was more than pleased to take on someone well known to Joe. 'T'will be better than goin' t'night school,' Joe had told David. 'An' to be honest, I aint as young as I was an' 'tis time I put me feet up.' He would pay all expenses, he said, plus a regular sum to bring David's wages up to what he was earning now. 'An I've made a Will, leavin' whatever's left in me bank, to you. It won't be much but it's yours when you're twenty-one, by which time, it'll 'elp you to start up your own business.'

David was grateful for the old man's generosity and, having visited the workshops of Jim Dangerfield, Makers of Fine, Hand Crafted Furniture for the Discerning Customer, was now looking forward to the new year when he'd be able to start learning the trade for himself. He'd rather get his hands on a nice piece of solid oak than on any girl. And what was wrong with that?

Esther was thankful when Christmas was over. It had been a lean year for money, what with the cost of moving house, and having to find the extra rent. Still, the move to Kestrel Road had been worth it and, even though there was still no lino on any of the floors and only enough curtains for the front room, she was happy. Everything else would come later. With both David and Alex now working, things should soon start to get a bit easier. The children hadn't gone without as Harry had given her some extra cash to buy each of them a small present; a Teddy Bear for Catherine, a Kaleidoscope for Edwin and a rattle for Daniel. David and Alex each had a new pair of socks, and an appreciative, well-off customer had given Harry a Capon, which meant a proper Christmas dinner on the table.

What she was going to do about Alex, she'd no idea. Although, after the last incident, he hadn't opened his wage packet again, he'd grown more and more difficult, spending as much of his spare time as possible out of the house, refusing to say where he was going or what time he'd be home. If she was worried about David's unsociable habits, she was even more concerned about Alex and his strong will. He was going to be a problem to handle, she could tell. A tap on the front door brought her back to the present. It was Phyllis, and Esther invited her in.

'I've something to tell you,' she said, in a whisper, so that Esther could barely hear what she was saying. 'Only I don't want anyone else to know, so not a word, except to Harry if you like.'

Esther put the kettle on to make tea. 'Not a word,' she promised.

Phyllis's face was animated. 'I'm expecting a baby,' she said, patting her stomach gently. 'It's due in July.'

Esther almost dropped the kettle in surprise. 'Oh, Phyllis, that's wonderful,' she said, 'isn't it?'

'Of course it is.'

'And what does Jack think?'

'He's like a puppy with two tails,' Phyllis said, her eyes sparkling, 'and I think he's hoping it's a girl this time.'

'And what would you like?'

'I'd love a little girl too,' she said, 'but as long as it's all right, that's all that matters to me.'

Esther caught hold of Phyllis's hand. 'Bet you're glad you listened to me and went to that clinic, aren't you?'

'Of course I am,' she replied. 'The best thing I've ever done.'

'You must start taking better care of yourself, and make those boys of yours give a hand around the house.'

'Oh, they're thrilled to bits,' Phyllis said. 'Even Luke can't do enough for me.'

Esther looked sceptical. 'Are they behaving themselves these days?' she asked.

Phyllis nodded. 'Better than when we were in Wimple Street,' she said. 'Luke still plays truant sometimes, though not nearly as often as he did, and thank goodness he'll soon be leaving school and getting a job. Terry and Robert like Milton School and have settled down really well. Robert has even taken up reading and always seems to have his nose in a book these days.'

'That's a good sign,' Esther said. 'And by the way, changing the subject, I've been meaning to ask you what you think about Molly. Do you like her?'

'Yes. She seems very nice. A bit on the quiet side but otherwise she's all right. Why do you ask?'

Esther hesitated. 'I don't know,' she said. 'She's very nervous sometimes and I'm not very keen on her husband. There's something odd about him.'

'What does Harry think?'

'Oh, he likes him,' Esther replied. 'And he thinks I'm imagining things but I've seen bruises on Molly's arms, and the other day I heard them having a row, then she was screaming as if she was getting a hiding.'

Phyllis looked surprised. 'Do you think he's knocking her about?'

'I'm not sure,' Esther said. 'But Harry says it's their business what goes on and I'm to keep out of it.'

'He's right,' Phyllis replied. 'There's nothing anyone can do, even if you're right and he *is* hitting her. It happens to lots of women. So I should forget it if I were you.'

'But why should women have to put up with being knocked about like that?' Esther said. 'Why *should* we be treated like serfs and underdogs?'

'That's life,' Phyllis replied.

'Well, it shouldn't be like that. But that's not all. I don't like the way he looks at me sometimes.'

'What do you mean?'

Esther shivered. 'Well, it's the way he eyes me up and down. Makes me feel as if I'm stark naked. Gives me the creeps it does.'

'Well all you can do,' Phyllis advised, 'is to keep out of his way. And for goodness sake don't say anything to Harry about it else there'll be trouble.'

Catherine, who had been playing with her toys in the corner, started to whimper. 'She's getting hungry I expect,' Esther said, scooping the child up in her arms. She looked up at the clock on the mantelpiece, 'and Daniel's due to wake up for his feed at any minute.'

Phyllis stood up. 'I'll be going then,' she said. 'The boys'll be in from school soon and I like to be there when they come home.'

A few minutes' after Phyllis left, Frances arrived with Edwin who had been spending the day with her. 'I've just passed your friend outside,' she said. 'My, doesn't she look well these days.'

Esther smiled to herself. Phyllis had asked her not to tell anyone about the baby and her secret would be safe. Or would it? 'It's living here,' she said quickly. 'Wimple Street was enough to get *anyone* down and this place is so *different.*'

'It certainly seems to suit Phyllis,' Frances said, noting the rising colour in her sister-in-law's cheeks. 'That's unless of course, there's something you're not telling me.'

Esther laughed. There was no keeping anything from Frances, and Phyllis wouldn't mind her knowing. 'She's going to have a baby,' she said. 'But you're not to tell a living soul. She doesn't want the whole wide world to know just yet, in case something goes wrong.'

'I'll not say anything,' Frances said. She pulled a chair from under the table and sat down. 'Now am I going to get a cup of tea or not?'

Esther gave Catherine and Edwin their jam sandwiches, made a pot of tea for herself and Frances then lifted Daniel, by now wide awake, from his pram and put him to the breast.

'I don't know if Harry would be interested,' Frances said presently, 'but the Dockyard's looking for labourers. Our next door neighbour went for an interview last week and he's been offered a place.'

'Harry would be too old, wouldn't he?' Esther said.

'Nonsense. Forty-five and under they're taking on. And the money's good. More than he brings in pushing that old milk cart around in all weathers, I'll bet.'

Esther's face brightened. For ages now, Harry had been feeling more and more fed up with trudging the streets day after day, but as he'd said many times, 'A job's a job, and it's better than no job at all.'

'I'll tell him about it,' she said. 'See what he thinks. And thanks Frances.'

Later that evening when the children were in bed, Alex had gone out and David was at Joe Rigby's shop helping him to clear out, she gave Harry Frances's piece of news.

'Doubt if I'd get in,' he said. 'I'll be thirty-nine soon don't forget.'

'Yes, I know that,' Esther replied, 'but Frances said they were taking men on up to forty-five, so why not see if you can get an interview?'

Harry thought about it for a few minutes. He'd love to find another job but whether or not he would be up to starting something new at his age, he'd no idea. Still, there was nothing to lose, was there.

'All right,' he said. 'I'll nip round to see Frances tomorrow after work and see if she can tell me a bit more about it.' He left his chair and pulled Esther from hers. 'But now,' he said, 'this husband of yours needs his requirements met.'

Esther laughed up at him, her eyes sparkling. It was a two-way thing, this need for love between them and, even though they had their differences now and again, and some of their rows ended in Esther throwing whatever she could lay her hands on at Harry, theirs was a happy marriage. 'It's only just eight o'clock,' she said, willingly following him up the stairs and into the bedroom before closing the door quietly behind them.

'Nothing like an early night,' Harry murmured, pulling the ribbon from her hair and pressing her down onto the bed.

Afterwards, when she lay quietly with his arms around her, she told him about Phyllis and the baby. 'She says she's a different woman since we all moved here,' she said. 'And Jack's thrilled to bits about it.'

Harry smiled to himself. He already knew, Jack having told him about the baby a week or two ago. 'Only don't tell Esther,' he'd said, 'Phyllis would want to do that for herself.'

Esther raised herself up on one elbow. 'Do you think Jack might have had another woman? 'You know ... when things were going badly for him and Phyllis.'

Harry's voice was angry. 'You just watch your tongue, Esther,' he said. 'Jack would never do a thing like that, no matter what. He's always loved Phyllis and he'd never do anything to hurt her.'

'Well, she seems to think he has.'

'Then she's wrong.'

Esther leaned over and planted a kiss on his thinning hair. 'I just wondered, that's all.'

'Well stop wondering, and go downstairs and get my supper for me woman,' he said, giving her a playful slap.

It was late the next afternoon when Jack called to see Maisie to tell her that there would be no more visits. He was sorry if she was upset, he said, but Phyllis was expecting now and it would have to stop.

Maisie's reaction filled him with alarm. 'So I'm to be put out to grass,' she said, 'is that what you're saying?'

Jack took her hand but she snatched it away. 'Of course not Maisie,' he said, his heart sinking into his boots. It hadn't occurred to him that she would put up any objections. After all, she'd known right from the very beginning that one day he would have to finish the affair.

She left her chair and wandered over to the window. 'Just supposing that I don't want it to end. What then?'

'It can't go on any longer,' he said, 'not now.'

'Not now that you're getting what you need at home, you mean.'

'No. It's not like that Maisie.'

'Oh, but it is,' she replied bitterly as she turned to him, the expression on her face wretched. 'And don't think you'll get rid of me that easily.'

He stood up. 'I'm sorry,' he said, 'but you knew all along that it would come to this sooner or later and I've never pretended otherwise.'

'Get out!'

'Maisie ...'

'I said, get out. Go on. Go back to your wife, who's too stupid to see what's been going on under her nose, and see if I care.'

He fished in his trouser pocket. 'Better have this back then,' he said, handing over the house key.

She snatched it from him then marched over to the door and opened it. 'Don't think you've heard the last of me,' she warned as he stepped out into the hallway. 'I won't let you get away with this.'

As he walked along the road to collect his milk cart, he shook his head in bewilderment. The last thing he'd expected of Maisie was that she would cause trouble. They had discussed their affair many times and she'd always insisted that, should he ever want to finish it, then she'd step aside and not stand in the way of his marriage. Whatever had come over her? And what plan did she have to get her own back? It would just about kill Phyllis if she were to find out what he'd been up to behind her back all these months.

From an upstairs window, Maisie watched him walk away and out of her life for good. She hadn't asked to fall in love with him but that's what had happened. There were other men in her life, although Jack didn't know about them, but they were just lonely, usually in sterile marriages, and willing to pay for the kind of comfort she offered. They meant nothing to her and she couldn't see herself living without Jack's visits, baby or no baby. Turning away from the window, she flung herself across the bed and cried until her eyes were red and raw. An hour later, embittered and filled with despair, she had come to a decision about what she would do to make him suffer for what he'd done to her. Something he wouldn't forget in a hurry.

Consoling himself with the thought that Maisie had only made those threats in temper and didn't mean anything by them, Jack made for home where he found Phyllis dozing in her chair by the fire. For the first time in years, she looked peaceful and contented, and he'd kill Maisie Gilliman if she did anything to destroy the newly found happiness he and Phyllis had found.

CHAPTER SIX

David began working at Dangerfield's at the beginning of February 1933. His first month was spent sweeping up, making tea and running errands and towards the end of it, he was beginning to wish he was back in Joe Rigby's shop mending boots and doing something worthwhile. On the Monday morning of his fifth week, he had a message to report to the office of the owner Jim Dangerfield, a tall, fearsome looking man with dark brown eyes that bulged frog-like behind his glasses, iron-grey hair and a magnificent, bushy moustache to match.

'Take the weight off your feet my boy,' he said, indicating a chair facing him across the desk. 'And don't look like a frightened rabbit. I won't bite.'

David, who had no idea why he'd been summoned to the Great Man's office, sat down. Jim Dangerfield rested his elbows on the desk, pressed his fingertips together and fixed him with one of his inscrutable looks, his eyes like two enormous brown marbles. 'Well, Cartarett,' he boomed across the desk, 'you know how to make a good cup of tea, I'll give you that, though your sweepin' up aint that good. Still, you came highly recommended by my old friend Joe Rigby and so I'm going to give you a chance to prove him right.' He leaned across the desk. 'Only one mind you. I never give anyone a second chance, d'you hear?'

'Yes, Sir,' David said.

'Good. From tomorrow, you'll be working alongside Vinnie Totter, who is a real craftsman if ever there was. There's nothing he doesn't know about wood and how to work with it so you pay attention to everything he tells you and you'll learn a lot.'

'Yes Mr. Dangerfield.'

'And make your mind up whether you're going to call me Sir or Mr Dangerfield. One or t'other, I don't mind which.'

'Yes, Sir.'

Jim Dangerfield leaned back in his chair and studied his newest prodigy. The boy was clean and well-mannered but, unlike some of the loud-mouthed little tykes who'd passed through the firm, this one seemed not to have any self-confidence and was far too quiet for a lad of fifteen. He looked a bit "girlish" too. Perhaps a year or two in the workshop with the older men would bring him out of his shell, or more likely drive him further back into it.

'Anything you want to ask, Cartarett?'

'Where can I get some tools Sir?'

The older man went across the office to a cupboard. 'In here,' he said, 'is a set of the finest carpentry tools you'd ever wish to find. Bought for you by your benefactor Mr. Rigby, who must be out of his mind to spend so much money on a scallywag of a boy who probably won't appreciate them.'

'Oh, but I will,' David promised, unable to believe his good fortune. He'd been wondering how he, or his father, would be able to find the money for the tools necessary to learn his trade.

He handed David the toolbox. 'Well just don't you ever forget what you owe Joe Rigby. If it weren't for him, you would still be nailin' bits of leather on to boots, with nothing to look forward to.' He pointed to the door. 'Off you go then,' he said, 'and don't forget what I said. One chance you get. No more.'

Thankful the ordeal was over, David stood up. 'I won't forget Sir,' he said. 'And thank you. I'll always be grateful to Mr. Rigby for what he's done.'

After David had left, Jim Dangerfield sat scratching his head for a minute. What a strange mixture that boy is, he thought. An' I hope that lot in the workshop, especially Totter, won't make his life too much of a misery. I've seen many a stronger lad reduced to tears by them clever Dicks on the benches, and Totter has more tricks up his sleeve for tormenting them than all the rest put together.

At the same time as David was seeing Jim Dangerfield, his father was having an interview at the local Labour Exchange for one of the vacancies in the Dockyard. He'd met Frances's neighbour who'd persuaded him to apply and less than a week later, here he was, sitting before a panel of men who were asking questions as to his suitability. The interview wasn't as bad as the grilling he'd had when he'd applied to the Corporation for one of their houses, but there were still many things they wanted to know, although they were mostly to do with his employment record and not how many children he'd fathered.

The wages would be three pounds for a forty-eight hour week and after a trial period of one month he would have to work some extra time if needed. Harry was more than happy to agree to that. There were still things they needed for the new house, which he couldn't afford on his present wage of two pounds, five shillings, and the extra hours would come in very useful, although he doubted whether Esther would be too pleased. Well, if she wanted lino on the floors and curtains at the windows, she'd have to put up with it. Eventually, after convincing the panel that he was more than up to learning something new, he was offered the job on a month's trial, to start once he'd worked his week's notice at the dairy.

On the way home, he thought of Jack, who had refused to be persuaded to try his luck in the Dockyard, as he didn't want to make any changes now, what with the baby coming and all that. Besides, Don Spiller the dairy Foreman was retiring soon and he, Jack was going apply for his job. 'It's not the right time,' he'd told Harry. 'Maybe if I don't get Don's job, I'll think about it.'

There was something bothering Jack lately but whatever it was, he didn't want to talk about it and Harry thought it best to leave well alone. He was sure his old friend would tell him when he was ready, and not before.

Esther was less than excited at the thought of the long hours Harry might have to work. 'I hardly see anything of you now,' she said, when he told her about the overtime he'd be expected to do. 'And how do you think I'm supposed to deal with Alex if you're not around to make him do as he's told?'

Harry laughed. 'He doesn't take any notice of me anyway,' he said. 'What he needs is a good kick up the backside, but he knows I won't lay a finger on him. Never have on any of our nippers and I'm not about to start now.'

Esther, who was making pastry, slammed the rolling pin down hard on the table. 'Then it's a pity you've got this idea in your head that giving them a slap now and then when they deserve it is wrong.' She squared up to him. 'Do you know, you are the only father I know who doesn't.'

'Well,' Harry replied, 'that makes me different from all the rest, doesn't it. And that's the way I like it.'

Esther turned back to her rolling pin, angry that he was unable to face the truth about Alex, who was out every night of the week now, mostly with some of the boys he worked with at the factory. Now and again, he took Mary out and Esther didn't mind that, although she'd never met the girl and only had Alex's word for it that she was respectable. And Alex couldn't be relied upon to tell the truth about anything. He'd lied, for instance, about the night he was seen by a neighbour in a public house opposite the Royal Marine barracks. 'It wasn't me,' he'd said when Esther had tackled him about it the following day. 'I didn't go anywhere near the place, so there.' He'd also started defying her over the business of opening his wage packet before handing it over. Now, he always gave her five shillings, keeping the rest to himself. She was always arguing with him, and Harry did nothing about it.

'He's feeling his feet,' was all he would say. 'I was the same at his age.'

Knowing Harry's mother as she did, Esther doubted that.

About a week later, the very thing she had been dreading happened. She answered a knock at the front door one evening to find herself staring into the arrogant face of Harry's nephew, Walter Cartarett who now sported three pristine white stripes on the sleeve of his Police tunic. 'Evening Auntie Esther,' he said, 'may I come in?'

Esther's heart sank as she stepped aside to let him in. He was a big man, and she felt intimidated by his presence in her home. She sent David across the road to fetch Harry who had gone to see Jack about something.

'Whatever is the matter?' she said, showing Walter into the living room where he removed his helmet and, without being asked, sat himself down in Harry's armchair.

'Best wait until Uncle Harry's here,' he said, drawing a notebook and pencil from the top pocket of his tunic. 'Don't want to repeat everything twice.'

She asked after his father and mother and he said they were well.

Harry shot through the back door like a whirlwind. 'What's happened?' he said, his eyes darting from his nephew to his wife and back again.

'Your son, Alexander George Cartarett,' Walter began, tapping his notebook with a pencil, 'is in trouble with the law and is, at this very moment, down at the station, along with several other miscreants, waiting to be charged.'

'Charged? What the devil with?' Harry was already putting his coat on, as Esther dropped onto the sofa, her head in her hands.

'Affray,' Walter said importantly. 'Along with a number of other boys of a certain age, he was creating a disturbance of the peace.'

Harry had a sudden urge to wipe the smug look from his nephew's face. 'What exactly do you mean by "causing an affray"? And why are you writing down everything I'm saying?'

Walter ignored that and stood up. 'Shouting and bawling in the street,' he said. 'Disturbing the residents and terrorising a certain Mrs Delaney's tom cat by tying a tin can to its tail before chasing it up the road with a stick and almost into the path of an oncoming tram.'

'Is there anything else?' Harry was finding it difficult not to laugh.

'Drinking,' Walter said, 'in the pub opposite the Marine Barracks, and that, as you well know, is against the law for someone of fourteen. And he was seen smoking too.'

'Well,' Harry replied, 'I was smoking long before I left school, but the drinking is another matter, though I still don't see why my boy has been arrested when a good telling off would have been enough. Boys will be boys, as I'm sure you know. Or didn't you ever get up to mischief when you were a lad?'

Walter puffed his chest out. 'Boys being boys is one thing,' he said, 'but being cruel to dumb animals, and drinking and carrying on outside people's own homes is another. And no, I certainly didn't get up to those kind of tricks. I wouldn't have been allowed to.' He put his helmet on, gave Esther a quick peck on the cheek, and he and Harry left for the Police station.

David, who had made himself scarce while his cousin was there, came back into the sitting room to find his mother crying. He'd never seen her do that before and didn't know what to say.

'What are we going to do about Alex?' she said presently, drying her eyes in her pinafore. 'He's not really a bad boy, is he David.'

'I don't know Mum.' David wasn't sure what she was expecting him to say. 'But perhaps this will frighten him into behaving himself.'

'I do hope so,' she said. 'And how are things with you, David? How's the new job going?'

David averted his eyes. The new job wasn't going as well as he had hoped, mainly due to Totter and the rest of the gang in the workshop. Totter had taken a dislike to David and had made that plain from the start. 'Creepy little Sod,' he'd been heard to say to the others. 'He needs takin' down a peg or two if you ask me.'

His idea of taking David down a peg or two had led to a number of unpleasant incidents that, much to Totter's annoyance, David had chosen to ignore. That was, until the day when someone had thought it funny to sabotage his lunch box and fill it with live maggots, which made him violently sick. He'd always had a delicate stomach and he'd had to throw his sandwiches in the dustbin. That incident had made him wish he were still with Joe Rigby.

'It's all right I suppose,' David lied.

'Just *all right*?' Esther sensed there was something was wrong. 'What's the trouble?'

David shrugged. 'Well, nothing really,' he said. 'It's just the men and their tricks, that's all.'

'Oh, *that.*' Esther knew all about the things older men got up to when they had a young lad at their mercy. Harry had told her. 'I shouldn't worry,' she said. 'They'll soon get tired of it and start on someone else. It's because you're new, that's all.'

David had thought his mother would understand. And there wasn't much chance of anyone new being taken on for some time so he supposed there was nothing else for it but put up with it until the men grew tired of playing stupid games and left him alone. 'One of them called me a Nancy Boy the other day,' he said. 'Why do you think he did that, Mum?'

Esther covered her face in her hands. There was no way she could explain to her son what *that* meant. She only had a vague idea herself, and Harry would have to deal with it. 'I shouldn't worry about it David,' she said. 'I'll have a word with your father and he'll put you right.'

It was ten o'clock before Harry returned home with a shamefaced Alex. David, at a nod from his father, made his escape to bed, and Harry rounded on his other son. 'What d'you think you're playing at?' he said, pushing him down into a chair. 'Bringing that snotty-nosed cousin of yours round here like that.'

'Sorry Dad. I didn't mean any harm. *Honest.*'

'Too late to be sorry,' Harry shouted back. 'And I'll tell you this, my lad. I've never laid a finger on any of you but if there's any more of it, you'll feel my razor strop across your backside. D'you hear me?'

'Yes Dad.'

'Now get off to bed and out of my sight before I lose my temper.'

'Yes Dad.'

After Alex had gone upstairs, Esther asked what had happened down at the Police station.

'They all got off with a good talking to,' Harry told her. 'But so help me, I'd have given anything to wipe the sneer off that high and bloody almighty little bastard's face. Only it would've made things worse so I just had to stand there and let him talk down to me like I was some sort of villain myself.'

'*Harry.*'

'Well, so he is. He thinks he's so bloody important just because he struts around wearing a uniform.'

'Calm down and let me make you a cup of tea,' Esther said. 'Then we'll sit down and talk about what's to be done about our Alex. And there's something I need to ask you about David.'

'Not having trouble with him as well, are we?' Harry said, beginning to wonder what was going wrong with this family.

Esther told him what David had told her. 'So, they called him a Nancy Boy. I've heard worse than that,' he said. 'It's time that boy stood up for himself, then they might leave him alone. He's as wet as a rice pudding.'

'You don't think he is, do you?' Esther said. 'One of those *queer* men, I mean.'

Harry looked at her as if she'd gone mad. 'Don't be so daft, woman,' he said. 'No son of mine's a Nancy so forget it. And if he is, he can pack his bags and get out of my house.'

'He's unhappy,' Esther persisted.

'Then, he should've stayed with Jo Rigby, shouldn't he.'

Esther sighed. 'Would you talk to him about it? I can't discuss that sort of thing with my own son.'

'No Esther, I'm sorry but I've enough to think about as it is,' Harry said, not wanting the unpleasant task of having to go into details about the meaning of homosexuality to his son. 'He'll have to sort it out for himself. The same as I had to.'

Esther couldn't imagine Harry ever having had problems in that direction. She gave up on the issue and asked why he'd gone across the road to see Jack, the business of what to do about Alex temporarily forgotten.

'Oh, just some little problem he was trying to sort out,' he told her. 'He thought I might be able to help.'

'And did you?'

'No. There wasn't anything I could do.'

Esther was puzzled. 'Can't you tell me?' she asked.

'Sorry love, no I can't. It's Jack's personal business.'

Later that night, Harry, unable to sleep, lay tossing and turning in the big double bed, trying to make sense from what Jack had told him. He'd had had an affair with one of his customers, Maisie Gilliman? It just didn't seem possible. And she'd threatened to get her own back on him in some way. That was really something to be worried about.

'I must tell Phyllis,' he'd said to Harry. 'In case she finds out from someone else. I can't keep it to myself any longer.'

'Did Maisie Gilliman threaten to tell her?' Harry asked.

'No.'

'Well then ...' Harry had just been about to advise him against making a confession when the doorbell rang and David arrived to announce that the Police were at their door and could his Dad come quickly.

Before he dropped off into a fitful sleep that night, Harry prayed that he'd be able to talk some sense into Jack to persuade him not to tell Phyllis about his carrying on with this woman. Surely, Maisie Gilliman wouldn't be spiteful enough to tell her, and what was more likely was that she'd only threatened Jack to try to keep the affair going, that was all. A form of blackmail was Harry's last thought as he finally drifted off.

On arriving at the dairy one morning, about two weeks' after Jack had finished the affair with Maisie Gilliman, he was called into Don Spiller's office to be asked if he'd heard the news.

'What news is that?' Jack said. What was he supposed to have heard that would be of any interest to him?

Don cleared his throat. 'It's about one of your customers. Name of Mrs Maisie Gilliman, of twenty-seven Ambrose Street. A neighbour found her dead last night. Gassed herself it seems.'

Jack went cold. 'Oh, my God,' he said, grabbing at a chair as the room swam before his eyes. 'Did she leave a note or anything?'

Don's face registered surprise. 'That's a funny question to be asking,' he said. 'At this stage I shouldn't think that anyone knows except the Police.'

'The Police?'

'Of course the Police had to be called. It looks like suicide and suicide is illegal in case you didn't know. What the devil is the matter Jack?'

Jack buried his head in his hands. What had he done? He'd only driven Maisie Gilliman to kill herself, that's all. He was shaking and wanted to be sick. Supposing she'd left a letter about their affair, the whole wide world would find out, including Phyllis.

'There'll have to be a post-mortem,' Don said, not realising that, by giving Jack that piece of information, he was making things ten times worse than they already were.

'Why d'you think she went and did a thing like that?' Jack said, trying to pull himself together and bring some semblance of normality into the conversation in case Don became suspicious.

Don pulled face. 'Who knows,' he said. 'Maybe one of her gentlemen visitors might have the answer to that one.'

'What gentlemen visitors?'

'Mrs Gilliman "entertained", if you know what I mean. There were quite a number of them apparently. Mostly high-class businessmen by all accounts. I'm surprised you didn't know, seeing as she was one of your customers, and everyone else seemed to.'

Jack shook his head in disbelief. It didn't make any sense at all. Maisie had never asked for a single penny from him and he'd no idea she'd been taking other men into her bed for money although there had been times when he'd wondered how she could afford some of the expensive frills and furbelows she decorated her home with. And if it were true, then she'd been nothing more than a common prostitute and he a stupid idiot.

'Better get on then Jack,' Don said, breaking into his thoughts. 'There's milk to be delivered.' He sniggered. 'Only don't go calling on number twenty-seven Ambrose Street will you. There won't be anyone at home.'

Jack glowered at him. 'I don't find that funny,' he said.

Don leaned back in his chair and, with one eyebrow raised, gazed at Jack quizzically. 'If I didn't know you as well as I do,' he said, 'I'd be wondering why you're more than a bit upset about this business. You weren't one of her clients by any chance, were you?'

It was all Jack could do to keep his temper. 'If I was,' he said, going to the door, 'it wouldn't be any of your bloody business so keep your dirty suggestions to yourself.'

He had deliveries to make in Ambrose Street, and as he approached Maisie's house, he averted his eyes, but all the same, as he drew level with her front gate his head became filled with the sound of her voice. "I said you wouldn't get away with it, didn't I," he heard her say, before the unmistakeable and infectious laugh that had always amused him, echoed along the empty street.

Phyllis gave birth to a daughter on 20th July 1933. Delighted that they now had a daughter, she and Jack decided to call their latest arrival Sarah, after Jack's mother who had died two years' before. Harry had managed to persuade Jack to keep his affair with Maisie a secret, and suggested he should push the unhappy business to the back of his mind. Jack no longer delivered milk, having succeeded Don Spiller as Supervisor at the dairy, and not having to pass Maisie's house every day made it easier to cope with his guilty conscience, although there were still times when he couldn't sleep because of it. It was lucky that the Coroner had returned a verdict of Suicide while the Balance of her Mind was disturbed, with no known reason for Maisie Gilliman to have taken her own life. At least she hadn't left a note implicating Jack. Sometimes though, Phyllis looked at him in such a way that he felt sure she knew something, but she never asked any questions, and they were happier now than they had been for years.

Esther was keeping Phyllis company one evening, while Jack did a spot of overtime at the dairy, when it suddenly came to her that she hadn't seen anything of Molly for nearly a fortnight. 'I would have thought she'd want to see you and the baby,' she said. 'But there's not been a sign of her. I do hope everything's all right.'

'Have the children been about?' Phyllis asked.

Esther thought for a minute. 'To tell the truth,' she said, 'I've not seen anything of them either. It's very odd.'

'Why don't you knock the door and find out?' Phyllis suggested. 'She might be ill or something.'

Esther pulled a face. 'I don't want to see *him*,' she said. 'I told you, he makes me feel uncomfortable and I don't like him.'

'I know that but it's the only way you'll find out, isn't it.'

'Yes, I suppose so.' Esther looked at the clock. 'I'll have to go now,' she said. 'It's time to start thinking about getting supper. Send one of the boys over if you want anything from the shops tomorrow.'

'I will.'

Esther decided to call in on Molly before going home. She tapped lightly on the knocker. At first there was no answer and she was about to try again when the door opened very slowly and she found herself staring into the grinning face of Chad Garnett. 'What a nice surprise,' he said, his eyes moving boldly down to her breasts. He opened the door wider. 'Come in.'

'No, I won't stop thanks.' Esther could feel the colour rushing to her cheeks. 'I've only called to see if Molly is all right, only I haven't seen her for a couple of weeks and I wondered if she was ill or anything.'

The grin widened. 'That's because she isn't here,' he said. 'She's gone to stay with that old witch of a mother of hers.'

'Oh.' Esther took a step back. 'I'm sorry to have troubled you. When is she coming back?'

He leaned towards her and she could smell whisky on his breath. 'Are you sure you won't come in?'

'Yes. No thanks.'

'She won't be coming back at all,' he said eventually. 'Left me she has. Though how she thinks she's going to manage I don't know.'

'What about the children?'

He shrugged. 'Farmed out among the relations I expect,' he said without interest.

Esther couldn't think of anything to say. Molly must have been desperate to walk out on her husband, and as if that wasn't bad enough, having to pass her children around the family must have been terrible. And Chad Garnett didn't seem to give a damn.

'I'm very sorry,' she said.

'I'm not.' He leaned against the doorpost and drew on a cigarette and Esther couldn't help thinking how handsome he was. 'In fact I'm almost glad.' His eyes wandered over her and she felt as if he were stripping her naked. 'There are plenty more fish in the sea, and more attractive ones at that.'

Esther backed away. Her first impression of him had been right. 'You're disgusting,' she called over her shoulder as she went down the path, his laughter ringing in her ears. 'I'm not surprised Molly's left you.'

'There were good reasons,' he said, 'and it wasn't all *my* fault. Not that it's any of your business.'

Esther didn't believe a word of that. 'I'm quite sure he's been knocking her about,' she said later to Harry. She didn't dare tell him about Chad inviting her in or staring at her the way he had. 'She'd never have left unless she had a good reason.'

'I suppose you could be right, but if that was the case, why was she always clinging to him like a limpet?'

Esther smiled. 'Women put up with a lot from their men,' she said, moving closer to him. 'Whatever you did to me wouldn't change that, though don't go getting any ideas.'

They were laughing together when Alex arrived home, unusually early. His brush with the law had frightened him and there had been no more trouble in that direction. He still went out most evenings but was always in by eleven o'clock, although Esther had given in to his insistence on opening his own wage packet.

'Where's David, Mum?' he said.

'He's in bed,' Esther replied. 'Why?'

'I've got something to ask him.' Alex gave her a funny look and Esther thought how much like Harry he was these days.

'Well, you'd better be quick, else he'll be asleep.'

'More likely to be sittin' up in bed with his nose in a carpentry manual,' Alex said, scornfully.

Esther sighed. Whatever was it with Alex that he was forever having a sly dig at his brother? David was doing well in his job, even though the older men were still tormenting him. Still, that would harden him up a bit and perhaps in the end make a man of him. She was still worried about his lack of social life but as Harry had said many times, one of these days he'd be off and out and then she'd be fretting about where he was and what he was up to.

Alex took the stairs two at a time, and when he opened the bedroom door, found David, exactly as his mother had said, pouring over a book. 'You're always bloody reading,' he said.

David closed the book and put it on the floor. 'Do you *have* to swear indoors,' he said. 'I hear enough bad language all day at work without you starting.'

Alex stared at his brother in disbelief. 'What is it with you,' he said. 'All the boys I know swear ... except *you*, of course. You're too bloody good to be true.'

'Anyway,' David said, 'you're in early for a change. What happened? Did the Pub run out of beer?'

'Oh, that's *very* funny. No, Mary wanted to wash her hair or something so I thought I'd come home. And I've something to ask you.'

'What's that?' David was wary. Alex wasn't in the habit of asking him anything.

Alex perched on the side of the bed. 'D'you fancy coming to the pictures with me and Mary ... and Mary's friend?'

David's stomach turned over. 'Why you asking me?' he said. 'What about all those pals of yours. Won't one of them do?'

'No,' Alex said. 'Sally's a quiet girl and wouldn't care for goin' out with some of the riff-raff I work with. An' what's wrong with takin' a girl to the pictures then?' He eyed David suspiciously. 'Not one of *them* are you?'

David leapt out of bed. 'What d'you mean by that,' he said, his face scarlet. 'Just because I don't go chasing girls around doesn't mean there's anything wrong with me so shut your mouth.'

Alex laughed. 'You just aint natural that's all,' he said. 'D'you know what they're sayin' about you where you work? They say you're a Nancy Boy. Sam Totter's Dad, who works at your place, told Sam and he told me.'

'Sam Totter's Dad's a dirty-mouthed sod.'

'Weeee ... you swore.'

'I'll do more than swear in a minute, but this'll do to be going on with,' and before a startled Alex could move out of the way, David's fist caught him full in the mouth. 'Now perhaps you'll keep your filthy mouth shut for a change.'

Alex, wiping the blood from his rapidly swelling lip, stared in amazement at his brother. 'Well, I'll be buggered,' he said. 'Fancy, Saint David standing up for himself. Wonder what Mummy would say if she knew what you'd just done.'

David climbed back into bed, angry with himself for losing his temper. All the same, he was tired of having to put up with being called things for reasons he didn't understand. He'd found out exactly what the expression Nancy Boy meant but his mother hadn't kept her promise to ask his father to talk to him about it, and he still didn't know why the label seemed to be sticking to him like glue.

'Well, are you coming with us or not?'

David didn't really want to go out with a girl but the only time he went anywhere was when he visited Joe Rigby every Thursday evening. It had become a regular thing, and he didn't mind but it might be nice to do something different.

'When?'

'Saturday after next.'

'All right, I'll come, but only this once.'

Alex laughed. 'You wait 'til you meet Sally,' he said. 'She's a real good looker and you'll want to take her out more'n once, I bet. That is unless ...'

David said nothing. He was too busy worrying about what he'd do if this Sally turned out to be another Belle Summerford.

CHAPTER SEVEN

Harry had settled down well in his new job. He enjoyed the company of other men, and there was something gratifying, after a hard day's work, to be one of the surge of workers leaving the Dockyard on bikes at finishing time. Through the Unicorn Gate, like a swarm of bees, with barely six inches between one set of handlebars and the next, it gave him a sense of camaraderie he'd never felt when pushing a milk cart around the town on his own. The Charge of the Light Brigade he called it, although Esther said it sounded mighty dangerous to her.

He'd bought an old bicycle to do up for David, and the two of them spent a whole Sunday taking it to bits, cleaning it and putting it back together. Not once, during the time they were working in the back garden together did Harry mention to David the problem of the name-calling and David decided to say nothing more about it. If his father didn't want to talk about it then there was no more to be said.

Most of the talk in the Dockyard at the moment seemed to be about a Dictator called Adolph Hitler who had recently been responsible for stirring up trouble over on the continent. 'He's evil is that one,' Reggie Davies, who worked alongside Harry, said one lunchtime as they stopped for a break. 'And I can see another war breaking out afore very long.'

Harry didn't agree. 'No-one in their right mind,' he said, 'would start another war ... not after the last lot.'

'That's just it. This Hitler bloke *aint* in his right mind, so I've 'eard. A few months' ago, he ordered all books belonging to the Jews to be burned, an' now he's havin' the poor blighters thrown out of their own homes. He's takin' away their businesses and thousands 'ave been left homeless and destitute. He's a bad man and a dangerous one too.'

Harry bit into a sandwich. He wasn't convinced, but from then on he stopped every day on the way to work to buy a Daily Herald. And when he heard that someone had an old wireless for sale, he bought it. Esther thought he'd lost his reason, but when she discovered that, if she twiddled a couple of knobs, she could listen to dance music on it, she changed her mind.

She was hanging out the washing one Monday morning when the sound of a van drawing up next door caught her attention and she went down the side of the house to the front gate to see what was going on. There was a removal van parked outside Chad and Molly's house and she watched as three men, directed by Chad, loaded the van with furniture and belongings.

As she turned to go back to her washing, Phyllis appeared. 'Do you see what I see?' she said, pointing to next door.

'He must be moving out,' Esther said. 'I wonder what's happened to Molly and the children.'

'I wish we could find out.'

'He wouldn't tell us anything,' Esther said, 'and I don't want to see him again anyway.'

Phyllis nudged her with her elbow. 'Get away. I'll bet you enjoyed him making eyes at you.'

Esther laughed, her face turning pink. She had to admit to herself that it *was* a nice feeling to think that someone, other than Harry, found her attractive. Phyllis went home and Esther finished hanging the washing on the line then went back into the kitchen where she found Daniel up on his feet and toddling towards the open door. She lifted him up into her arms and studied her youngest. He was a placid child, chubby and healthy-looking with the face, she thought, of an angel, with his pure white hair and clear blue eyes of his father. She loved him so much. She squeezed him and he howled in protest so she let him down onto the floor where he made for the living room to find Catherine who was playing with her dolls. Esther smiled at them and thought sadly of Molly.

She glanced at the clock on the mantelpiece. Edwin, as usual, had gone out with Frances and they were due back any time now. She made herself a cup of tea and sat down to wait for her sister-in-law, her thoughts drifting to Harry who was doing so well in his new job. In the six months since he'd been at the Dockyard he'd found the money to furnish the new house. There were now curtains at the windows and lino on the floors, and he'd managed to get hold of a settee and chairs for the front room. He'd bought a dresser and a couple of wooden rocking chairs for the sitting room, and a large table with six chairs for the kitchen. All second-hand of course but Esther didn't mind that. The garden was only half-finished but he'd grown a few vegetables, and Esther hadn't had to buy any from the Co-op for ages. The trouble was, she thought, he worked too many hours and it bothered her that, when he did come home, he always fell asleep in the chair. Still, he was almost middle aged now and she supposed that was only to be expected.

The arrival of Frances with Edwin broke into her thoughts. 'I won't stop for a cup of tea,' Frances said. 'My mother's coming round this afternoon.'

Esther's face darkened at the mention of her mother-in-law. 'I don't know why she won't come here,' she said. 'It doesn't seem right that Daniel is almost a year old and she's never once seen him. And she's only seen Catherine a couple of times and that was because I happened to be shopping at the Co-op at the same time as her.'

'I know,' Frances said. 'I've tried talking to her but it's no use. In fact, she isn't very well at the moment so I was wondering if you could tell Harry because he hasn't been to see her in ages.'

Esther was annoyed. 'I suppose I'd better, though I don't see why I should. If your mother wants to see Harry, she should come here.'

After Frances had left, Esther couldn't decide whether or not to pass on the message to Harry. If she did, then the visits to his mother might start all over again, but if she didn't and something happened to the old lady, he'd hold Esther responsible. She made up her mind she'd better tell him. It was about four o'clock when there was a knock at the front door and she opened it to stare open-mouthed into the stony face of her mother-in-law.

'I've just had a telling-off from my daughter,' Lydia Cartarett announced as Esther held the door open and invited her in. 'She said I was to come and see my grandchildren and that if I didn't, she would personally bring the lot of them to see me.'

'And that wouldn't do at all, would it?' Esther said.

'Well, I certainly wouldn't want *them* charging around all over the place in my flat,' Lydia replied, as if she were talking about a pack of wild dogs. 'And besides, my cats don't like children.'

The two women moved into the sitting room, Lydia peering into the kitchen as she went. 'David and Alex are at work but this is Edwin, Catherine and Daniel,' Esther said, trying her best to be polite.

Lydia gave them a cursory glance then took in the scene, with disapproval written all over her face. Toys all over the place, the kitchen in a mess with the tablecloth still laid and covered in crumbs, and the children looking as if they needed their faces wiped. Not only that, there was a layer of dust on the mantelpiece, and Esther herself looked as if she'd been dragged through a hedge backwards.

'What time does my son get in from work?' she asked, ignoring the children, and her eyes everywhere.

'I never know when to expect him,' Esther said. 'He sometimes works late but if not, just after five o'clock. Would you like a cup of tea?'

Lydia declined. 'No, I can't stay. I only called because Frances made such a fuss about it. But would you ask Harold to call in on me. *That's if and when he can manage to find the time, of course.*'

'Yes,' Esther said, thankfully showing her mother-in-law to the door.

As Lydia Cartarett walked away from the house, she congratulated herself on being right about the poor choice of wife her youngest son had made.

Harry seemed pleased that his mother had paid a visit but when Esther complained that she'd ignored the children, and spent the few minutes she was there inspecting the place, he accused her of never being satisfied. 'She can't do anything right, can she?' he said.

Esther raised her eyebrows. 'Here we go again. Whenever it's anything to do with her, we end up having an argument.'

'Well, since she's been here and she's not well, I shall have to go and see her whether you like it or not,' he said.

Esther marched off into the kitchen. 'Please your bloody self,' she called out, picking up an enamel plate and throwing it at the wall. It fell to the floor with a clatter, and Harry picked it up.

'One of these days,' he said, unable to recall the number of times a piece of flying china had whizzed past his ear, missing him by inches, 'you're going to hit someone, doing that.'

'*Good,*' she said, 'as long as it's *you.*'

The silence between them lasted until late in the evening when Harry, who hated drawn-out quarrels, caught hold of Esther's hand. 'Don't let her come between us,' he said. 'And I don't like to hear you swear. It's not like you.'

'I'm sorry,' Esther said. 'I was angry that she couldn't even be bothered to speak to the children. She never said one word to them.'

'Well, I shall have go and see her sometime or other. She's an old lady now and won't be around forever.'

Esther nodded. 'By the way,' she said, changing the subject, 'Chad Garnett moved out this morning. I saw the removal van there.'

'Yes I know. He told me the other day that he was moving on.'

'You didn't tell me.'

'It must have slipped my mind.'

'Did he mention Molly?'

'Yes. Molly is staying with her mother.'

'And what's happened about the children?'

'The youngest is with Molly,' Harry said, 'and the others are with their Aunties until Molly's mother can find a bigger house. Then Molly and the children will move in with her. The old lady's well off, so Chad said.'

'I hope he's right, but I do think you could have told me all this. After all, Molly was a sort of friend, even if I didn't see much of her.'

Harry stood up. 'I didn't think,' he said. 'And now, as you seem to have had a lousy day, I'll make the Cocoa for a change. How's that?'

Esther smiled. Whenever they had a quarrel, Harry always, in his own quiet way, managed to smooth things over and make her feel better. 'Go and see your mother this Sunday,' she suggested, not quite knowing why it suddenly seemed important that he should. 'Get it over with.'

'Thanks Esther.'

He went to Southsea on Sunday morning and spent an hour with his mother. She seemed very quiet and said nothing about her visit to Kestrel Road so Harry decided not to mention it. On Monday afternoon, Esther had an unexpected visit from Frances. 'I went to see my mother yesterday evening,' she said, 'and she told me that Harry had been in to see her.'

'Yes,' Esther said. 'I suggested it myself as Sunday's the only day he doesn't have to go into work at the moment.'

'Well, I'm glad he did, because she passed away early this morning in her sleep.'

'Oh.' Esther was so shocked she couldn't think of anything to say, except to ask if the old lady had been alone.

'No,' Frances said. 'I knew she wasn't well so Albert suggested I stay the night with her.' She began to cry and Esther was filled with a mixture of guilt, compassion and another emotion she couldn't describe. Almost like relief it seemed, which made her feel terrible. What sort of a person was she to feel almost glad to hear that someone had just died? She made a pot of tea and the two of them sat for a while, not saying much. There was nothing much to say really. It would have been hypocritical to express a sorrow Esther didn't feel, although she was thankful that she'd persuaded Harry to make that visit on Sunday. It was almost as if she had known it would be the last.

Later that night, when Harry had taken in the news of his mother's death, he and Esther sat together and talked about what was left of their own future. 'I will never,' Esther said, 'cut myself off from any of our children, no matter who they choose to marry.'

'I'm glad to hear it,' Harry said. 'My mother missed out on so much through being such a silly woman, didn't she.'

'I suppose you could say that, but at least she did get to see you before she went.'

'Thanks to you, Esther.'

In her Last Will and Testament, Lydia Josephine Cartarett left almost £6,000; £1,000 to her son Charles, the same to her daughter Frances, £250 to her Grandson Walter and the remainder, together with the proceeds of the sale of her flat, divided equally between three animal charities. To her son Harold and his family, she left nothing.

Chapter Eight

The day before he was due to go out with Alex and the two girls, David discovered that he'd outgrown his only pair of decent trousers. He'd not been anywhere socially since the disaster at the Mission Hall two years' earlier, and it came as a shock when he tried on the grey flannels, to find he'd grown a good six inches since then. Esther offered to alter them. 'I could let the bottoms down about two inches,' she said, surprised that she hadn't noticed how much her son had grown. 'You need a new pair but there's no time for that now.' She was pleased that at last David was going out with a girl, which might help to put paid to the rumours about certain aspects of his character.

Alex, who kept a fair slice of his wages to himself, was always buying new clothes and when he saw David getting ready, offered to lend him a pair of his own trousers. 'You can't go out in those,' he said, laughing and pointing to the flannels Esther had tried to alter. 'They're still miles' too short. You look stupid in 'em, an' I'm not much taller than you, so try these.'

When at last the two of them were ready to go, Alex took it into his head to offer some advice. 'Here's what you do when you're with a girl,' he said, lowering his voice in case their mother was anywhere about.

'I'm not doing any of those things to a girl,' David said, remembering Belle Summerford and her unbuttoned blouse. 'Anyway, I thought you said she was a nice girl, this Sally.'

'She is, but even nice girls like a bloke to try. Otherwise, they think there's somethin' wrong with 'em. Take my word for it.' Alex grinned and David thought how good looking his younger brother was. No wonder all the girls were after him.

Sally was very attractive, with blonde, curly hair and blue eyes, her figure trim in the blue suit she was wearing. She didn't have much to say but that suited David because if there was anything he hated more than a girl wearing make-up, it was one with a loose tongue. There were only three girls in the office at work, and they talked a load of rubbish non-stop from start to finish of the working day and it nearly drove him mad sometimes.

They entered the foyer of the Regal and, before David could do anything, Alex had swaggered up to the cashier to pay for all their tickets. 'I'll pay for mine and Sally's,' David said, but Alex brushed him aside and the four of them went into the cinema where an usherette showed them, at Alex's request, into the back row. After about five minutes of organ music, the lights dimmed and, to a fanfare of trumpets, the film credits began to roll. David's eyes were beginning to smart a bit with all the cigarette smoke but apart from that, he was surprised to find that he was enjoying himself. In the seat next to him, Alex had lost no time in canoodling with Mary and the two of them were all over each other, oblivious as to what was happening on the screen.

Out in the aisles, the usherettes were wandering up and down with their torches, on the lookout for any trouble. David thought about the advice Alex had given him and wondered whether Sally would object if he were to put his hand on her knee. He waited for a few minutes then, unsure of Alex's advice about a girl liking a boy to try, he slipped a hot, sweaty hand underneath her skirt. He could feel the silkiness of her stockings and as she didn't object, his fingers moved up a little until they touched her suspender. As long as he lived, he would never forget what followed, and the next few moments were to be forever etched on his memory. With a squeal, Sally leapt from her seat and at the top of her voice yelled, 'Eeek! What d'you think your doing. Take your hands off me, David Cartarett, you dirty little devil.'

David became aware of a sea of faces turning to stare at him, and the beam of a torch shining in his eyes, then the shrill voice of one of the usherettes ordering him to get out of his seat and out of the cinema. He managed to scramble as far as the aisle, treading on everyone's toes as he went, and then he was grabbed by his collar and frogmarched to the foyer by some Amazon of a woman, who threw him, with some force, out onto the street.

'Dirty little pervert,' she screeched as he landed in the gutter.'We don't want *your* sort in here.'

Stunned, he lay there for a few minutes and then picked himself up from where he'd fallen to find Sally standing on the pavement watching him. 'What did you want to go and do a thing like that for?' he said, trying frantically to brush the dirt from Alex's trousers.

She was half-laughing, half-crying. 'I didn't think you were like all the others,' she said. 'Alex told me you were ... well ... *different*.'

'Oh, I'll bet he did,' David said, knowing exactly what Alex would have told her. 'Well now you know I'm as normal as any other bloke, so you can go and tell him and all your friends if you like.'

She put her hand over her mouth to suppress a giggle. 'It was funny though, wasn't it. I mean, you being thrown out on the street and that.'

'Glad you think so,' David said, then caught her eye and started to laugh. It *was* funny, he supposed. Fancy him, the Nancy Boy, being thrown out of the cinema because he'd got fresh with a girl. He couldn't wait for that lot at work to hear about it ... and they would, once Alex told Sam Totter and he in turn told his Dad. Perhaps they'd leave him alone after that.

'Where's Alex?' he said, wondering why his brother hadn't come to his rescue.

'Still wrapped around Mary I shouldn't wonder.'

David caught hold of her hand. 'Let's go for a walk over Bransbury Park,' he said. 'It wasn't my kind of film anyway.' She hesitated a bit until he promised to keep his hands to himself.

'If you like.'

They strolled through the park in the lengthening shadows of a warm September evening and David, for the first time since he could remember, felt happy. He did nothing more than hold Sally's hand as they wandered along, talking about their work and the things they liked. She told him she was coming up for fifteen, and worked at the Landport Drapery Bazaar. 'I love it,' she said. 'I'm on the linen counter and it's so exciting to serve all the young brides who come in with their new husbands to buy things to set up their first home. It's really romantic.'

'Can't see what's romantic about a few sheets and tablecloths. It sounds boring to me.'

'Well, that's 'cos you aren't a newly-wed.'

'And don't want to be either,' David said. 'I just want to be a great furniture designer and have my own business. I don't want to get tied down with some girl and have loads of children. I want to be rich, and children keep you poor.'

'You'll soon change your mind when you meet someone and fall in love.'

David laughed. 'What rubbish you girls go on about,' he said. 'You're as bad as the typists where I work. All they can talk about is boys, and getting engaged, and all that soppy stuff. Drives me mad, it does.'

'You *are* funny.' Sally stopped walking and turned her face to his. 'You can give me a kiss if you like.'

It seemed the most natural thing in the world to kiss a girl like Sally. Her mouth was soft and warm on his and he put his arms around her and drew her closer. 'You're sweet,' he said as they drew apart. 'And I'm sorry for what happened in the Regal.'

She smiled back at him. 'It's all right,' she said. 'I know that boys like to try it on but I don't want to start doing things like that yet. Well, not until I'm married really. And I shouldn't have screamed and made such a fuss. A slap across the face would have been enough.'

They both laughed and walked on. 'Shall I see you home?' David asked as they came to the far end of the park. 'We can't go any further, unless you want to end up in the sea.'

'I live at Fratton,' she said. 'It's quite a long way from here but I don't really want to walk it on my own and Mary's not around to walk with me. Still canoodling with your Alex I suppose.'

'I know where Fratton is,' he said. 'I used to live not far from there.'

She linked her arm through his. 'All right then. And thanks.'

He left her, with a brief kiss, at the corner of her street and asked if she would like to go out with him again. He was taken aback when she said that maybe she would but she'd have to think about it.

'Don't you like me?' he asked.

'Of course I do. It's just that my Dad doesn't like me going out with boys. Says I'm too young. And he doesn't know I had a date with you tonight.'

Disappointed, as he'd enjoyed the short time they'd spent together, he suggested that when she'd made up her mind, she could ask Mary to tell Alex. 'Then he can pass the message on to me,' he said, not liking the arrangement but unable to think of any other way.

'All right, I'll do that, but I don't know when it'll be as my Dad watches me like a Hawk.'

They parted company and David set out for home, his mind in turmoil. His plans didn't include a girl friend just yet. He wanted to get on with his work without any distractions. Despite the tormenting he'd had to put up with at work, which had been less frequent lately, he liked his job now that he was actually working on something. He'd decided to make a coffee table for his first year's project and it was coming along nicely. The fashionable turned legs were a bit difficult to do but it was good practise for woodcarving and Jim Dangerfield was pleased with it. 'You're doing well, Cartarett,' he'd said the other day, when on a tour of inspection of the shop floor. 'Keep at it.'

As he walked back along Goldsmith Avenue towards Eastbrook, David thought about the consequences of having a girlfriend. He'd have to take her out at least twice a week and probably on Sunday too and he'd need more money and some decent clothes of his own. He still handed over his unopened wage packet to his mother, and although she gave him back a bit more these days, it still wouldn't be enough. He couldn't take Sally to the pictures without offering to pay for her seat as well as his own, and in any case, going against a girls' father was something he'd rather not do. By the time he reached home, he'd decided that having a girlfriend would cause him more problems than he needed and he wasn't ready for it yet. He would speak to his mother though, about letting him sort out his own wages, the way Alex did.

On Monday when he arrived for work, all eyes were turned in his direction, and a wall of silence met him as he walked across the shop floor to hang up his coat. 'Totter's after your blood,' one of the men said eventually. 'E's 'oppin' mad about summat.' David needed the lavatory and was almost at the door when someone grabbed him from behind and pushed him up against the wall.

'Wot you doin' tryin' to rape my daughter eh, you dirty little bugger.' It was Totter.

David struggled to break free. 'Let me go. I don't know what you're talking about,' he yelled. 'I don't know your daughter so take your hands off me.'

'Why should I? Couldn't take your filthy 'ands off my Sally the other night, could you.'

David went cold. Sally was Totter's daughter and he, David, was in it up to his neck. 'I never did any such thing,' he said, scared out of his wits. 'Who says I did?'

Totter, who was twice David's size, lifted him off his feet with one hand. 'Never mind who said, I'm goin' to teach you a lesson you won't forget in a hurry, you little bastard. Never did like you from the day you set foot in 'ere.' His grip tightened and David thought he was going to choke to death. Totter turned to the men who were watching from the benches. 'Come an' give us a hand, Charlie,' he called to a small, frightened looking man who ran over to where David, his teeth chattering, was still pinned against the wall. 'Take 'is trousers down.' Charlie looked around in desperation at the passive faces of the other men, and not having the courage himself to put a stop to this abuse, did as Totter said. David's trousers fell to the floor, leaving him exposed from the waist down, for everyone to see. 'Pass me that pot of varnish, and that brush,' Totter demanded.

David almost fainted. He knew what Totter intended to do, but was no match for the older man and, his knees buckling, he sank to the floor, only to be hauled up again by his collar. 'No you don't, you little pervert,' Totter said, waving the brush in the air, before dipping into the tin of varnish. 'This'll put a stop to your tricks.'

At the same time as David let out a scream, the voice of Jim Dangerfield boomed across the workshop. 'What the hell d'you think you're doin,' Totter. Let go of that boy at once.'

'Bin messin' about with my daughter, Mr Dangerfield,' a startled Totter said, dropping the brush and letting go of David, who fell in a heap to the floor. 'And I was about to give 'im summat to teach 'im a lesson.'

'You'll do no such thing. And I'll see you in my office in five minutes. Is that clear?'

'Yes Mr Dangerfield.'

'An' as for the rest of you,' Jim Dangerfield said, turning to the others, 'you oughta be ashamed of yourselves fer not puttin' a stop to these shenanigans.'

David scrambled to his feet, snatched his trousers and made his escape into the lavatories, then went back to his workbench. Alex had set up the date with Sally, that was obvious, but what part she had played in it, David had no idea. He couldn't believe she'd do a thing like that but then he'd learned, over the past months that you couldn't trust anyone no matter how nice they appeared to be. And he'd make sure Alex was sorry for what he'd done. As for Sally, well she'd better keep out of his way too.

David never found out what transpired that morning in Jim Dangerfield's office between him and Totter. But whatever it was must have worried Totter because from then on, although he never spoke to David, except to give instructions through one of the other workers, there was no more bullying from him or anyone else and he was left to get on with learning his trade in peace.

Alex at first denied knowing Sally was Sam Totter's sister but in the end, admitted that he and Sam had set it up between them just for a laugh. 'We knew Sam's Dad didn't like you but we didn't mean it to 'appen the way it did. An' Sally had nothin' to do with it, honest. I'm sorry.'

For a long time afterwards, David couldn't bring himself to speak to Alex, and he made no attempt to contact Sally. Then events no one could have foreseen took over from everything else, and the episode forgotten, at least for the time being.

As the year 1933 ended, Esther began to worry about her family. There was David who, apart from his weekly visit to Joe Rigby, never went outside the door once he'd finished work. Since his date with Sally Totter, he'd become more withdrawn than ever but when Esther asked him what was wrong, he just said the he didn't have time to go anywhere and there was nowhere to go anyway. He said nothing about the episode at work, but asked to be allowed to sort out his own wages and Esther had agreed to that. Then there was Alex, who had been going into public houses even though he was under age. Sometimes he came home the worse for wear, was smoking heavily, and swearing too much for her liking.

Harry was working long hours now and didn't seem to want to do anything about either of the boys, or was too tired to be bothered. 'They'll both grow out of it in time,' he told Esther when she tried to share her worries with him.

With money more plentiful, they'd all had a good Christmas but on New Year's Day, she felt as if a huge black cloud had settled over her head. She couldn't shake off the feeling of depression or fathom out why she felt like she did when, apart from the two eldest, the others were no problem at all. Edwin had settled down well at school, and she couldn't wish for two more contented children than Catherine and Daniel. Harry was happy in the Dockyard and earning good money, and although she didn't see as much of him nowadays, they were still happy. So what was it that was making feel almost frightened to face the New Year? It was almost as if she was having a premonition that something dreadful was about to happen.

CHAPTER NINE

In March, an epidemic of measles hit Edwin's school. He came home one afternoon covered in a rash, his face flushed with a high temperature, and Esther put him to bed. Both David and Alex had caught it when they were small so she knew exactly what it was and what to do. Lots of drinks, and the windows shaded so as not to let in any light, which could damage his eyesight. Within a week, he was on the mend and Catherine went down with it. She recovered quickly and Esther kept her fingers crossed that Daniel wouldn't have caught it. Although if he had, she reasoned, he's more robust than any of them, and in any case, it might not be a bad thing to get it over and done with.

On 1ˢᵗ April, he woke up covered in the familiar angry red rash. He was also very hot and lethargic and Esther thought it looked as if he might be in for a more severe dose than the other two. After two days, when he didn't seem to be getting better and had developed a chesty cough, she went across to see Phyllis who had done a bit of nursing before she married Jack.

'Don't come over,' Esther said, 'in case you take it back to Sarah, but I am really worried about Daniel and don't know what to do.'

Phyllis insisted on looking at him. 'The boys have all had it,' she said, 'and Sarah's bound to catch it sometime or other. She's asleep in her pram at the moment so I can leave her here for a few minutes.' She was shocked when she saw how ill Daniel was. 'You'll have to try and get a doctor to call,' she said. 'Daniel has a very bad chest by the sound of it, and measles can lead to pneumonia which is dangerous.'

Esther only knew of one doctor she could call on. 'How am I going to be able to get a message to him?' she said, close to tears. 'He lives across town and I can't leave Daniel and Catherine by themselves.'

'I'll go,' Phyllis said. 'Just give me his address and I'll take Sarah in the pram, and on the way back, I'll pop in and tell Frances if you like.'

When Frances arrived, she took one look at Daniel, her face registering dismay at his condition, and insisted on staying until the doctor finally turned up two hours' later. Esther noticed that the man was unsteady on his feet and smelled strongly of whisky. He examined Daniel. 'The child has pneumonia in both lungs,' he said and gave Esther instructions on how to make a steam tent to relieve his breathing. He also suggested she sent to the local chemist for some special powders for children, which would bring down his temperature. He closed his bag. 'There's nothing more I can do. That'll be half-a-crown.'

Esther found her purse, handed him the coin and saw him out.

'Charlatan,' Frances said, in disgust. 'And he'd had a few by the look and smell of him. I hope he falls off his bike.' She reached for her coat. 'I'll pop round to the chemist for some of those powders he was on about.'

Daniel slept for the best part of two days. The steam tent helped with his breathing and on Sunday morning, Esther was relieved to see him open his eyes and smile at her. She lifted him from his cot, wrapped him in a blanket and rocked him gently in her arms, singing his favourite tune, "The Teddy Bears' Picnic." He looked up at her, smiled and closed his eyes. At first, Esther thought he was snoring gently. 'You sound just like your father,' she said, and went to lay him down in his cot when he made a funny little noise in the back of his throat, his body stiffened then went limp, and she sensed that something was wrong. He'd stopped breathing and all the colour was draining from his face. She screamed at the top of her voice for Harry, who was outside working in the garden, and the sight that met him when he burst into the house, told him all he needed to know.

'He's gone.' Esther was hysterical. 'He's gone, he's gone. Our baby's gone. Oh, *do* something. For God's sake *do* something Harry.'

Harry took one look at the lifeless little body in his wife's arms, and gently guided her into a chair. 'There's nothing we can do love,' he said, 'it's too late.'

He tried to take Daniel from her but she clung to her child as if by holding him against the warmth of her own body she could bring him back to life. She was crying, her tears falling softly on the face of the child she had just lost … *they* had just lost. This was Harry's child too and she reached out to him and took his hand. 'Why has this happened to us?' she cried. 'What have we done to deserve this?' But Harry couldn't think of anything to say to his distraught wife so he knelt down beside her, buried his head in his hands and cried with her.

David, who had been helping Harry in the garden, had followed him indoors and now stood in the doorway, his face white at the sight that greeted him. He knew what had happened and, leaving them to the privacy of their own grief, he crept quietly through the sitting room to the hall and up to the bedroom where Alex was lying on the bed reading a comic. 'Our Daniel's just died,' he said.

Alex threw his comic to the floor. 'That's not funny.'

'It's true though.'

'Oh my God, it *can't* be.' The two brothers looked at one another. 'Poor Mum and Dad,' Alex said, his eyes filling with tears. They sat together, side by side on the bed, the two brothers who disliked one another so much, arms around each other, and cried for the little brother who'd been taken away from them.

They buried Daniel at Milton Cemetery on a warm, spring morning, in a tiny grave on a plot especially for children. As the little white coffin was lowered into the cold ground, Esther was reminded of their other two children buried there; the baby Harry had never seen, whose short life had ended, with no known cause, the coroner had said, at only six weeks, and Robert who had died at eight months. She clung to Harry as they walked back to the funeral car, her faith in God in ruins. 'If there really was a God, he wouldn't take little children like Daniel,' she'd said over and over again to him, since that dreadful Sunday when they'd lost their little boy.

Harry had said nothing to that. He'd never been a believer himself and was less inclined than ever now to accept that there was such a being as a God in Heaven. Daniel's death had hit him hard and, just when Esther needed him the most, his own grief got in the way of the support she needed. She wanted to talk about it constantly but he couldn't stand it, and the atmosphere in the house became unbearable.

They were both worried about Catherine, who wouldn't eat properly and showed no interest in food, her toys or anything else. Every so often, she'd start crying and asking for Daniel. 'Where is he?' she kept saying, for she was too young to understand the meaning of death and thought he'd gone away somewhere to be made better. 'I want to see him Mummy. Take me to see him, *please*.' When Esther tried to explain that he'd gone to a lovely place called Heaven, and it was too far away for Catherine to go there, the little girl would run to the corner of the room where she used to play with her brother, and rock back and fore, staring into space and sucking her thumb.

Every day of the week, all through that summer, rain or shine, Esther wrapped Catherine in warm clothing, and, holding her hand, walked along Milton Road, through the cemetery gates and up the little path leading to Daniel's grave. There, she'd placed fresh flowers in a pot and sit for a while talking to him as if he were right there beside her.

'She's going out of her mind,' Frances said to Harry, one evening in July when she'd called in to see Esther who was upstairs putting Catherine to bed. 'Do you know she goes up to the cemetery every day? She told me so herself.'

Harry knew what Esther had been up to, and that she had changed. If he went anywhere near her in the bedroom, she'd curl up in a tight ball with her back to him and more often than not, pretend to be asleep. He'd noticed the shadows under her eyes darken over the weeks following the tragedy, and she was getting thin because she didn't eat enough to keep a bird alive. 'What can I do, Frances?' he said. 'She's in a world of her own these days.'

'Would you like me to talk to her?' Frances said. 'She might just want someone to listen, and it's no good her asking you. You're just as grief-stricken as she is except that you've just had to get on with life, and she can't.'

Harry looked beaten.'You can try, but I don't think it'll do any good.'

When Esther appeared, Harry made an excuse to go out into the garden, leaving the two women alone together. Frances came straight out with it. 'It's been three months now since Daniel died,' she said, 'and it's not doing you or Catherine any good sitting up in that cemetery in all weathers, is it.'

Esther shook her head. 'I know,' she said, 'but I can't face up to the fact that he's gone.' She began to cry. 'I'll never get over it Frances,' she said. 'It seems as if there's nothing left for me any more.'

'That's nonsense,' Frances said, more sharply than she'd intended. 'I'm sorry but you've three boys, and Catherine to think of, not to mention Harry, who seems to have to cope with his own grief all by himself. And on top of everything else, he's worrying himself silly about you.'

'Tell me what I can do, Frances,' Esther pleaded. 'I know how Harry must be suffering and the boys too, but I don't know how I'm ever going to get back to normal again. Even when I *can* manage to get off to sleep, my dreams are full of Daniel. I sometimes feel as if I'm going mad.'

Frances caught hold of her hands. 'You're not going mad,' she said, 'and what you are feeling *is* normal but somehow or other we've got to help you out of this depression.'

'But how?' Esther asked.

'Well,' Frances said, 'the reason I came round this evening was to tell you that the owner of the little shop on the corner of my road is looking for someone to go in a couple of mornings a week to help out. Serve behind the counter and that. Albert won't hear of me doing it and I thought you might like to give it a try.'

'I can't leave Catherine,' Esther said. 'As it is, she seems to be fading away before our eyes.'

'You won't have to,' Frances replied. 'She can come to me. Before Edwin went to school, I often looked after him, and I miss doing that.

And the change would be good for her. So that's that little problem out of the way.'

'Would it help, do you think?' Esther said. 'I really do want to feel better Frances but somehow or other, I don't seem to have the willpower to do anything about it.'

'You could stop going to the cemetery every day of the week for a start,' Frances said. 'It's not helping at all. And it's not fair to keep dragging Catherine along with you, especially when it's pouring with rain.'

'She misses Daniel,' Esther said. 'She's always crying for him to come back and wanting to know where he's gone when he doesn't.'

'She's too young to understand, that's all. Now what do you think about this job?'

'All right, I'll give it a try,' Esther said.

'And cut down on your visits to the cemetery?'

'Yes Frances, I will. Perhaps every other day and see how it goes.'

'Good,' Frances said. 'Tomorrow morning, I'll pop in and see Mr and Mrs Sherlock who own the corner shop and tell them to expect you sometime during the next day or two.'

'Thanks Frances. I'll go and see them tomorrow afternoon.'

After Frances had gone outside to say goodbye to Harry, Esther thought about the conversation they'd had. It was all very well for her. She didn't have any children so who was she to dish out advice to someone whose little boy had just died. She couldn't possible know what it felt like. The guilty feeling of wondering whether she could have done anything more to save him, or whether she'd given up on him too soon. Maybe if she and Harry had tried to bring him round. The terrible sense of loss, the longing to turn the clock back and have him running around the house, making a mess, laughing, climbing onto her lap when he wanted a cuddle. She wept into her apron and rocked back and forth on the chair. 'I want my little boy back.' she cried aloud to herself, repeatedly. 'I want him back. I want him here … with me … in this house where he belongs.' So distraught did she become that she didn't hear the back door open.

'Oh *Mum.*' David had just come in after working overtime. 'Oh, *Mum.*' He was across the room in two strides. He put his arms around her and let her cry, then made her a cup of tea.

They sat in silence together for a while until she told him about his Auntie Frances's visit. 'Sometimes', she said, 'your Auntie Frances is too bossy for her own good. What does she know about anything, anyway?'

'She's only trying to help,' David said, 'and I think you should listen to her. She's about the most sensible person in this family.'

'Whatever is it that's bothering you Jack?' Phyllis said as the two of them settled into their armchairs one Sunday evening after tea. 'You always seem to have something on your mind. Can't you tell me about it?'

Jack shook his head. It was over a year now since Maisie had taken her own life because of him ending their affair, and he still couldn't stop blaming himself for what she'd done. He knew that one day he would blurt the whole sorry story out to Phyllis and be done with it, even though Harry had advised him not to. This evening, with the boys playing out in the street and Sarah in bed, was as good a time as any, he thought. Sarah would be a year old soon, their eldest boy Luke had a job as a delivery boy at the Co-op Grocery in Southsea, Terry had just left school and was looking for work, and Robert happily studying so that he could pass the exams for the Grammar School. There were no problems at all except for Jack's guilty conscience, which never gave him any peace. Far better to bring it out into the open, and then perhaps he could get on with his life and put it all behind him.

Phyllis's world fell apart when he told her. Although she'd been suspicious all along, when it came to hearing it from Jack's own mouth, she was stunned. 'Why have you waited until now to tell me?' she said presently, fighting back the tears. 'Why didn't you tell me when it was going on? I did ask you once, if you remember.'

'I didn't want to hurt you,' Jack said lamely.

'Well what d'you think you've just done then?'

'I'm really sorry Phyllis. You've no idea how sorry I am.'

'If you ask me,' she said, 'the only reason you're telling me after all this time is because you can't stand the burden of it yourself and thought if you shared it, you'd feel better.'

Jack left his chair and started pacing the room. 'Have you forgotten,' he said, 'that for five years you would have nothing to do with me. Night after night we lay together in that bed an' you wouldn't let me do more'n give you a peck on the cheek. What was I supposed to do, eh?'

Phyllis fell silent. That was true of course and what had happened no more than she deserved. But that didn't excuse leaving it until now to tell her when they'd settled down and were happier than they'd been for years. She couldn't even share her misery with Esther now, whose whole life had been shattered into pieces when she'd lost Daniel. *She* wouldn't want to hear about anyone else's troubles.

'I don't know what to say Jack. I suppose I half suspected something was going on, but for this woman to commit suicide over it is terrible and I don't know how you've managed to keep it to yourself for so long.'

'Harry knows,' he said. 'I had to tell someone in the end as I was going out of my mind with worry.'

'So you told Harry but not me. And I suppose it was Harry who told you to confess?'

'No. He said it would be best if I didn't.'

'He was right then.' Phyllis said. 'You should have kept your sordid little affair to yourself after all this time. And does Esther know?'

'No, I don't think Harry's ever told her.'

Phyllis closed her eyes, trying to imagine her Jack in bed with someone else. It was terrible. Yet she herself was partly to blame, and at least Jack had finished the affair when Sarah had been on the way, or so he'd said.

'I'm going to need time for all of this to sink in Jack,' she said. 'I don't know if I'll ever be able to forgive you, and I know I won't ever be able to forget but I suppose I'll have to try, for all our sakes. If you'd only told me before, we might have been able to work something out.'

Jack bent and kissed the top of her head. 'Don't let's lose what we have, Phyllis,' he said. 'I know it won't be easy for you but I'll do whatever it takes to make it up to you.'

They sat in silence for a while.

'What was she like, this Maisie?' Phyllis said presently.

Jack sighed, hoping this wasn't to be the first of many inquests into the affair. 'I hope you're not going to start tormenting yourself about her,' he said. 'She was just ordinary. Not a bit like you.'

Phyllis had to smile at that. She'd always looked upon herself as pretty ordinary. 'I just wondered that's all.'

'Have you seen much of Esther lately?' he asked, changing the subject.

'No. She works a couple of mornings a week for the Sherlocks, in their shop, and she still goes up to that cemetery most days. I don't know where it's all going to end.'

'Has she said anything about the people who've moved into Chad and Molly's house?'

'Only that they seem pleasant enough, and like to be called Mr. and Mrs Cheswick,' Phyllis said. 'They're a bit stuck-up, she says. They have two children but Esther never sees them and doesn't even know how old they are. Not that she wants to see anything of anyone these days.' She stood up and looked at the clock. 'Time our lot were in and getting ready for bed,' she said. 'And I think I'll have an early night myself. I feel worn out.' She averted her eyes and started doing some unnecessary tidying up.

'I'll get the boys in and sort them out,' Jack offered.

Later, upstairs in their bedroom, Phyllis looked at the bed she and Jack had made love in so many times over the past two years. Ever since, in fact, she'd gone to that clinic Esther had told her about. Now, everything was in ruins. She would never be able to bear Jack touching her again without seeing him making love to some other woman. If only he hadn't told her. She climbed into bed, buried her face in the pillow and let the tears come, until much later when she heard the creak of his footsteps on the stairs. He came into the room and slipped into bed beside her, but she lay very still with her back to him, closed her eyes and pretended to be asleep.

Esther was busy scooping sugar into blue bags and weighing them on the scales when, the following morning, Phyllis walked into the shop. 'I've run out of soapflakes,' she said. 'And I wanted to know when we are going for one of our walks again. I need someone to talk to.' She thought Esther looked ill. 'And you look as if you need to see a doctor.'

'I'm all right,' Esther said. 'And I'm sorry I've not been over to see you lately. This job seems to take up most of my time.'

Not to mention all those trips to the cemetery, Phyllis thought to herself. She took the box of soapflakes Esther offered, and paid for them. 'Well, how about tomorrow then?' she said. 'It's going to be a warm day and we could walk along the seafront or wander down Highland Road and look at the shops.'

'I … I have to go up to the cemetery tomorrow,' Esther said, 'and isn't it Sarah's first birthday? Won't she be having a party or something?'

'Well, the cemetery won't take all day, will it,' Phyllis persisted. 'Go there in the morning and we'll have a walk after dinner. And since when did we give our children birthday parties?'

Esther looked away. 'I'll see,' she said.

Phyllis was angry. Although she knew how devastating the loss of Daniel must have been, she felt that it was time Esther began to face up to it. Jack had already said that he'd talked to Harry, who was going through hell, what with trying to come to terms with Daniel's death *and* Esther's obsession with the cemetery. 'She doesn't care about anything or anybody,' he'd told Jack. 'Doesn't bother to make herself look tidy any more, and half the time there's no dinner ready for the boys and me when we get home from work. All she thinks about is sitting at that little grave, talking to someone who can't answer. It's not natural.'

'Tomorrow afternoon,' Phyllis said. 'I'll be ready at about two o'clock,' and refusing to take "no" for an answer, she left the shop, slamming the door behind her as she went.

The following day turned out to be even warmer than Phyllis had predicted. In fact it turned stifling hot as they wandered along Highland Road, looking in the shop windows, before carrying on to the Canoe Lake.

'It's quiet here,' Phyllis said, 'so let's find a seat and talk about things.'

'What things?'

They parked Sarah's pram and Catherine's pushchair and sat under the shade of a tree, in one of the iron seats facing the lake. 'Your problems, and mine,' Phyllis said. 'Who's going first?'

Esther picked up a stone and threw it into the water. 'You can,' she said.

Phyllis related the story of Jack's affair. 'I don't know if I can ever trust him again,' she said, 'and as for ... you know ... I just don't want him anywhere near me, and I know from what happened before that it's wrong to turn away from him.'

'Can't say I blame you though,' Esther said, listening with only half an ear. Had Phyllis told her all this before Daniel had died, she would have been shocked and full of sympathy, but now nothing mattered to her any more and Phyllis's problems seemed trivial compared to those that she and Harry were trying to cope with.

Phyllis fell silent for a minute. She shouldn't be burdening Esther with all this. It wasn't fair. 'I'm sure we'll sort it out in the end,' she said. 'What about your problems Esther?'

'To tell the truth,' Esther replied, glad to have someone to talk to, 'I feel as if I'm going out of my mind and am never going to be able to get over losing Daniel. Everywhere, I see little boys who look just like him, with fair hair and blue eyes, and just about his age too. Then there are the dreams. Vivid they are, with Daniel still alive and doing all the things he used to do. I'm so happy again but then I wake up in a cold sweat and realise he's not here any more and that it was just that; a dream that will never come true.'

'I'm so sorry Esther,' Phyllis said. 'I shouldn't have unloaded all my troubles onto you. You've enough as it is.'

'People keep telling me that time heals,' Esther went on, 'but it doesn't. And I've been told that another baby would help, but that's not likely because, just like you with your Jack, I can't bear Harry anywhere near me since it happened.'

'Oh, Esther, I never thought I'd hear you say that,' Phyllis said. 'You and Harry have always been so, well ... *loving* towards each other.' She thought for a minute. 'I've an idea that might help you,' she said. 'I don't know if it'll work but it's worth trying.'

'What's that?' Esther wiped her eyes with a handkerchief.

'Jack's mother told me about it, some years' ago. When Jack's four-year old brother Sam died, his mother put together what she called a Memory Box. She filled a small box with bits and pieces belonging to her little boy and, when she felt the grief coming on, she would open it and take out each thing, one at a time, and hold it close to her for a while. She said that it brought her closer to him and reckoned that it helped her through the darkest days after his death.'

'I suppose I could try.' Esther said. 'There are still some of Daniel's bits and pieces around which I haven't had the heart to do anything with and it sounds like a good idea.'

'And in the meantime,' Phyllis said, 'we should both do something about keeping our husbands happy, shouldn't we?'

Esther nodded. 'Better get back now,' she said, 'before the little ones come in from school.'

As they walked back through Highland Road, Phyllis sniffed the air. 'Can you smell something burning?' she said.

'Yes, I can,' Esther replied. 'It's probably only a bonfire somewhere.'

Phyllis took in a deep breath. 'Smells like more than that to me,' she said.

As they turned the corner into Kestrel Road, they saw one of Phyllis's neighbours, Mrs Mc Andrew, hanging over her front gate eagerly awaiting someone to whom she could impart the latest piece of local gossip.

"Ave you 'eard?' she said, as they drew level. 'It's the Co-op down Fratton Road. Burnt to the ground this morning an' not a thing left of it.'

'Not the big Co-op?' Phyllis asked, her heart sinking. She'd recently seen a nice sideboard in their window and was waiting for the right moment to approach Jack to see if he would buy it. It would look lovely in their front room, she'd thought.

'Yeh,' Mrs Mc Andrew said. 'The very same. Awful, aint it.'

'How did it happen?' Esther asked.

'Aw, the police don't know yet,' Mrs Mc Andrew said. 'Too early to say but I wouldn't mind bettin' it was one of they scallywags what lives around there. Broke in an' lit a few matches I daresay.'

Phyllis and Esther exchanged glances. Mrs Mc Andrew 's own two sons were always in trouble with the law.

'Anyone hurt?' Phyllis asked.

'Hundreds, I should think,' Mrs Mc Andrew said. 'An' loads more dead, I shouldn't wonder. There's nothin' left of the place an' it were full of customers when it started.'

'Pots calling kettles black,' Phyllis said as they walked on and she and Esther parted company. 'How she can talk about other people's children like that when her own two are always in trouble, I don't know.'

Later that evening when David was visiting Joe Rigby, Alex had gone to the pictures and Catherine was in bed asleep, Esther told Harry about Phyllis's idea for a memory box. Harry agreed that it was worth a try. 'Anything, if it helps you,' he said. 'I'll see if I can find a box. There might be one in the store at work.'

'Did you hear anything about the big fire at the Co-op this morning?' Esther said.

'Yes,' Harry replied. 'It's been burnt to the ground, but by some miracle, no-one was hurt or killed.'

'Thank heavens for that.' Esther sat on the rug at his feet and rested her head in his lap. 'I'm sorry for the way I've been lately,' she said, as he stroked her hair, 'but when we lost Daniel, a part of me went with him. It's not been fair on you, though has it?'

'No,' Harry agreed. 'But I do understand how you feel, even if you think I don't.'

They sat in silence for a while until Esther said she was ready to go to bed. She stood up and reached for his hand, pulling him out of his chair. When she asked him to go with her, he needed no second bidding and that night she conceived her tenth and last child.

CHAPTER TEN

Two important things happened to David at the beginning of 1935. First, he was called into Jim Dangerfield's office one Friday morning in February to be told that he'd be getting some extra money in his wage packet from next week. David was so surprised he didn't know what to say. He'd taken great pains with his project but never imagined it would earn him a pay rise. 'I'm very grateful Sir.'

'And so you should be my boy,' Jim Dangerfield said. 'I know things haven't been easy for you here but that's all in the past now I hope, an' you've the makin's of a good carpenter. My ole pal Joe Rigby'll be pleased to hear you're doin' well so get along as soon as you can an' tell 'im the good news.'

'Yes, Sir, I will.'

David knew his mother would be pleased, especially now she had to buy things for the new baby. He'd be able to give her a bit extra and keep some for himself.

'Off you go then,' Dangerfield said, 'an' get on with whatever project it is your doin' now.'

'Thank you Sir. I'm making a crib for the baby my Mum's expecting.'

'Well done, Cartarett. T'won't be long before you'll be making furniture for the business.'

Back on the shop floor, David became aware of the interested looks shot in his direction. Totter, who still only spoke when he had to, made a crude comment about little creeps who sucked up to their bosses but was told by Tom Fletcher to shut his big mouth. 'Leave the lad alone,' he said. 'Haven't you already done enough to him? And how do *you* know why he was in the Big Man's office anyway?'

Totter fixed his bloodshot eyes on David. 'P'raps the sneaky little bastard'll tell us eh? On the other 'and, p'raps 'e don't want us to know what went on in there.'

David, who since the episode over Sally, no longer feared Totter or anyone else on the shop floor for that matter, had learned the hard way to stand up for himself. 'None of your business,' he said, staring boldly into the other man's face. 'I'll tell you when I'm good and ready and not before, or maybe not at all.'

A cheer went up from the benches. David had discovered some time ago that no one really liked Totter. There were those who went along with him out of fear, but even some of them joined in the laughter that followed.

'Good for you, David,' one of them shouted, and David, with a smile on his face, went back to his bench to start work on the baby's crib.

Harry and Esther were overjoyed to hear the news. David rarely, if ever, said anything about the work he'd been doing, and they were pleased that he'd done so well *and* sorted out the problems of the men on the shop floor for himself. Esther still worried about the lack of friends of his own age, and that he never went anywhere except to see Joe Rigby, but she kept her thoughts to herself and lived in hope that, sooner or later he'd find himself a girl friend and settle down a bit.

David viewed the second series of events with mixed feelings. It was bitterly cold, with a keen North Easterly wind cutting through him like a knife when, the following day, he made his way across the stretch of open ground at the top of Bransbury Park. He was on his way to visit Joe Rigby to tell him the good news, and to see if the old man was any better after a bad bout of bronchitis. Pulling his coat tighter around his body, he shivered and tucked his hands under his armpits. Perhaps with the extra money he'd be earning, his mother would get him some warm clothes from the weekly club she belonged to and he'd give her the money from his share of the wages. Thoughts about his mother made him feel angry that she was once again going to have a baby. Since working for Dangerfield, he'd learnt a thing or two about the facts of life, mainly from the men on the shop floor, and the thought of his mother and father doing what these men loved to talk about in lurid detail, disgusted him. Surely, at their age, his parents shouldn't be doing *that* sort of thing. Sometimes, late at night, he could hear the goings-on in the next room and had to put his hands over his ears, and his head under the covers to shut it out. But if Alex heard it, he'd laugh and say things like, 'Do you hear what I hear? They're at it again,' and David would feel more disgusted than ever. There was also the question of feeding the baby and David hoped that this time his mother would feed it from a glass bottle, like those he'd seen babies sucking from in prams outside shops sometimes. He never wanted to see her bare her breasts in front of him again.

So deep in thought was he that he didn't see the branches of a tree, brought down in recent gales and now lying across the path leading out of the park. The toe of his boot caught in one, and he went sprawling on his face across the pavement.

'Do you make a habit of falling about in the gutter?'

He picked himself up and met the amused gaze of Sally Totter. 'Are you all right?' she said.

'Yes, nothing broken,' David said, feeling ridiculous.

She eyed him thoughtfully. It had been all her fault, that "do" at the Regal a few months' back. She'd heard that her father had threatened David over it, and was sorry because she'd quite liked him and knew he wouldn't want to risk asking her out again. In any case, Totter had forbidden her to have anything more to do with that "creepy little queer Cartarett", as he called David, and she hadn't bothered to try and fix another date.

'How are you?' David asked, brushing the dirt from his jacket.

'I'm all right. I've changed my job though. I'm doing some clerical work for a local Accountant and he's paying for me to go to night school to learn shorthand and typing.'

'That's good.'

'And you?'

David puffed his chest out. 'Won a pay rise, I have,' he said, 'for my first project, a table with turned legs. The boss thought I'd done a good job.' He found himself enjoying boasting to Sally. It made him feel good. 'In fact, I'm just on my way round to see my benefactor to tell him the good news.'

Sally stared at him open-mouthed. 'What's a benefactor when it's at home?'

David told her about Joe Rigby. 'I'm really grateful to him,' he said. 'If it weren't for him I'd still be mending shoes for a living.'

'Well, I suppose you'd better get going then,' she said, fixing her soft blue eyes on him. 'I don't suppose you'd be going to ask me out again?'

David thought of Totter and the tin of varnish, and his mouth went dry. He didn't fancy any more of that. 'I don't know.'

'Frightened of my Dad are you?'

'No. I am *not* frightened of your Dad, so how about tomorrow night? We could go to the pictures if you like,' David suggested, fighting back the feeling that he could be doing something he'd live to regret.

'I'll be outside the Regal at seven o'clock. Don't be late.' She turned to wave at him and he thought how pretty she was. 'Bye.'

'Bye.'

Joe Rigby lived in two rooms in a house owned by a very large Irish woman called Mrs Donovan, a retired nurse who thought of herself as a latter-day Florence Nightingale and treated her three elderly tenants as if they were the children she'd never had. She cooked for them, washed and ironed their clothes and cleaned their rooms. But she really came into her own when they were ill and she could put her nursing experience into practice. On more than one occasion, her expertise had resulted in a life being saved but all these services came at a price, which Joe didn't mind paying as he was well set up financially.

David rang the Gorgons Head doorbell and one of Mrs Donovan's helpers let him in. 'Mrs D's just been in to see Mr. Rigby,' the girl said. 'He's been ever so poorly today. Wait in the front room and I'll tell her you're here.'

Joe was sitting propped up in bed, a glass of whisky in one hand, a cigarette in the other. 'What are you doing smoking, Mr Rigby?' David said. 'That's not going to do your chest any good, is it?'

'No, boy, it aint, but as I see it, there's not much point in me deprivin' meself of a few fags, seein' as I'm not goin' to be around much longer, now is there.' Joe drained the glass and handed it to David, who was alarmed when the old man started to cough and gasp for breath, his faced turning a dark shade of purple. He shouted for Mrs Donovan.

'To be sure,' she said, removing the cigarette from between Joe's fingers, 'you're as daft as a brush, smoking with such a bad chest. Now if Oi I had any sense at all, Oi'd ban the habit altogether in this house. Never have been able to see how anyone could enjoy filling t'emselves up with smoke.'

Joe lay back on the pillows exhausted while Mrs Donovan fussed over him until he'd recovered. 'Now Oi'l leave you in the good hands of your friend David,' she said. 'And leave them coffin nails alone, will ye.'

David stayed just long enough to tell Joe about the wage rise. 'I thought the news would cheer you up,' he said and Joe nodded.

'Always knew you'd do well. You're a good lad, David.'

'I'll be going now, Mr. Rigby, and I'll call in again soon,' David said, but the old man was fast asleep. He crept out of the room and down the stairs to where Mrs Donovan was waiting to have a word with him.

'Oi'm real worried about your friend,' she said, opening the front door. 'Won't let me call a doctor … says they're all quacks … and as for those fags he keeps puffin' away at,' she shrugged her massive shoulders, 'shouldn't be surprised if he don't kick the bucket before long.'

As he walked home, David's thoughts turned to Sally Totter. He wondered whether she would tell her father about their date on Sunday and, if so, what would happen at work on Monday. He didn't want to start all that again with Totter, and by the time he reached home, he'd almost convinced himself that it would be best if he didn't show up. On the other hand, why shouldn't he take Sally to the pictures? After all, she was old enough to go out with who she liked, and he'd be very careful this time not to do anything to upset her.

His mother was in the kitchen when he let himself in through the back door and, after asking about Joe Rigby, gave him her own piece of news. 'It's our Alex,' she said.

'What's he done now?'

'He's thrown up his job at the factory and gone and signed up for the Merchant Navy,' she said, despair written all over her face. 'Did you know anything about this?'

'No, I didn't, and he can't Mum,' David said, 'he's too young.'

Esther wrung her hands together as she always did when agitated. 'He's nearly seventeen, and they've taken him on as a Bell Boy. Goodness knows what'll happen to him in some of those faraway places you hear about. And what about this war everyone's talking about. Alex'll be in the thick of it if it happens.'

'What war?'

'There are terrible things going on in Germany at the moment,' she said. 'I've seen Dad's Daily Herald, and it's on the wireless too.'

'Well, if there *is* another war, we'll both have to go and fight, so it won't make much difference will it. I've heard the blokes at work talking about it and they all reckon it won't happen anyway. Does Dad know? About Alex I mean.'

'Yes. But he seems to think it's the best thing that could happen. Make him grow up, he says.'

'Well, he's right Mum. It'll do him good and he'll be well looked after, so don't worry. You know what our Alex is like. He can take care of himself.'

Later, as David lay wide-awake, waiting for Alex to come in, he couldn't help but feel glad that his younger brother was leaving home. The only time they'd been close, as brothers should be, was when Daniel had died and that hadn't lasted. In any case, it would be nice to have this room all to himself. When Alex finally came to bed, bringing with him the smell of beer on his breath, David asked him why he'd decided to join the Merchant Navy.

'I want to see a bit of the world,' Alex said. 'An' there aint very much goin' on round 'ere, is there. Look at you. Never go anywhere, an' always got your nose in some woodworking book or other.'

101

'I'm happy enough,' David said, not sure whether or not it was the truth. Just lately, he'd had some misgivings about his life, and had tried to push to the back of his mind the feeling that he'd prefer to be doing something different from what he'd chosen. What, he didn't know. He was tempted to tell Alex about the date with Sally but decided not to, just in case he thought up any more tricks. 'What does Mary think?' he asked.

'I 'aven't seen her since that night you made such an ass of yourself at the Regal. She guessed I'd set it up with Sam and thought it was a rotten thing to do, an' said she didn't want to go out with someone who could do that to his own brother.' He climbed into bed. 'Anyway, I've met another girl and we've bin goin' out. She's a bit older than me, so don't tell Mum.'

David thought that was odd. 'Not married or anything, is she?' he said.

Alex didn't answer.

'You'll end up with a knife in your back, you will,' David said, 'and the sooner you leave here the better.'

Sally was already waiting outside the Regal when David arrived at five to seven on Sunday. 'Been waiting long?' he said.

She shook her blonde curls and took hold of his arm. 'No. About five minutes.'

They went inside and David bought two tickets, hoping that the usherette who threw him out before wouldn't recognise him. They found two seats in the back row and settled down to watch The Bride of Frankenstein. All the way through the film, Sally clung tightly to his hand, and David kept his free hand in its place. 'I'll have nightmares tonight,' she said, as they left the cinema. 'Did *you* enjoy it David?'

'It was all right,' David replied. 'I've only been to the pictures once before, except for when I took you last time and got thrown out, and that was a Western. I liked that better.'

'Well,' she said, linking her arm in his, 'perhaps we could go and see a John Wayne film sometime.'

'Yes,' he said.

They walked on in silence, Sally wondering if she'd been too bold to suggest another date. 'By the way, did you tell your father you were coming out with me tonight?' David said.

'No. And I didn't tell Sam or Mary either.'

'So, we're to have secret meetings are we?'

'I thought it best not to say anything,' Sally said. 'Not after what happened last time.'

David felt relieved. Although he was no longer frightened of Totter, he still wasn't sure what would happen if the man found out that his daughter had been going against his wishes. Things had been quiet in the workshop lately and he wanted them to stay that way.

'Perhaps we should leave it like that for the time being,' he said. Sally nodded. 'Yes.'

'Did you know our Alex has joined the Merchant Navy?'

'Yes, Sam told me.'

'Best place for him if you ask me,' David said as they reached the corner of Sally's road. 'He's given my Mum a lot of headaches with the way he goes on.'

They stopped to say goodnight. 'I know' Sally said. 'And I shouldn't tell you this but he's been going out with a married woman from the factory. She's twenty-two and her husband's a sailor, or so Sam told me.'

'I guessed as much.' David said. 'He'll get himself into real trouble one of these days. Still, if he's at sea, he won't be able to get up to much. And your Sam seems to tell you a lot of things.'

Sally held her face up to his. 'You can kiss me if you want,' she said.

He smiled. 'You said that the last time we went out,' he said, and brushed her soft lips with his. It made him feel good and when he put his arms around her and pulled her close to him, she responded by placing her arms around his neck and moving up against him, but unlike when Belle Summerford had done the same thing, he didn't push Sally away. He didn't know why, but with Sally it was different and seemed right somehow. He became aware of the strength of his feelings and desperately wanted to go a bit further, but knew that if he tried anything more, she'd make a fuss which would probably bring people out into the street to see what was going on, and he'd had enough of making an exhibition of himself.

Gently, he moved away from her. 'You'd better go,' he said, 'before your Dad comes out looking for you. It's getting late.'

'Will we go out together again?' she asked.

'Yes.'

'When?'

'Next Saturday if you like,' David said. 'There's a John Wayne film on at the Plaza in Southsea if you want to see it.'

Sally smiled up at him. She'd taken a liking to David Cartarett, and would have gone to see any old film so long as it was with him. 'I'd like that', she said. 'Where shall we meet?'

'On Fratton Bridge if you like. It's not far from the Plaza.' He gave her another brief kiss. 'Sure you'll be all right now?'

'Yes. 'Bye David.'

'Goodnight.'

They parted company and as he walked home, David thought again about what it would mean having a regular girlfriend. It wasn't what he had planned, yet he'd enjoyed being with Sally and would like to see her again. After all, he was coming up for eighteen and it was time he started going out and having a bit of fun. And he still had to convince himself that he was as normal as the next bloke.

Harry was still up when he arrived home. 'I bin waiting up for you son,' he said. 'Bit late aren't you?'

'I took a girl to the pictures and had to walk her home,' David said, wondering why he should have to offer an explanation, when Alex came and went as he pleased. And why was his father was waiting up anyway? 'She lives at Fratton.'

Harry shifted uneasily in his chair. 'Sit down,' he said. 'I'm afraid I've some sad news for you. One of Mrs Donovan's helpers came round to see you earlier on to say that Joe Rigby passed away this afternoon. Very peaceful it was in the end, she said. He went in his sleep.'

David couldn't take it in for a minute. 'I only saw him yesterday,' he said, a hard lump forming in his throat. 'He didn't look too good then. I shall miss him. He's been so good to me.'

'Yes son, he has. Still, you must be thankful he died the way he did. Best way to go I've always said. And you'd best go round to see Mrs Donovan sometime tomorrow to find out about funeral arrangements and that.'

'I will.'

'Goodnight son.'

'Goodnight Dad.'

After Harry had gone to bed, David paced the room. He was ashamed of himself for thinking about such things just now, but wondered if Joe Rigby had remembered to instruct whoever was in charge of his money, to carry on paying for him to stay at Jim Dangerfield's. If he hadn't, then that would be the end of his career in cabinet making because there was no way his father could support it. And if he had to leave there, what would he do for a living? On the other hand, would that be a bad thing? His mind was in such a tangle that he found it difficult to sleep that night.

The following evening after work, he went to see Mrs Donovan. She invited him into the kitchen and made a pot of tea. 'He went very quietly,' she said. 'Sure an' the old divil passed on with a fag still in his hand. Small wonder he didn't catch the place alight.' She sighed and David noticed that her eyes looked a bit red and watery. 'Still,' she went on, 'Oi'l miss him, so I will. An' I daresay you'll find it strange too, not coming round here to visit.'

'Yes, I will,' David said. 'Do you know about the funeral yet, only he didn't have any relations or anyone, so I don't know who's going to make the arrangements, and my Dad wants to know.'

Mrs Donovan promised to see to all that. She was used to it, she said. In her line of business, she often came across the elderly with no one to see to things for them. 'Tis very sad,' she said. And now, would David like to see his old friend, as she'd had him laid out in the parlour? 'The funeral people haven't put him in his box yet but they've put him on a trestle table and he looks so peaceful.'

Apart from baby Daniel, David had never seen a dead person, and no matter how much he'd liked the old man, he didn't fancy seeing him all cold and stiff, and laid out on a plank of wood. 'No, I won't thanks,' he said. 'I'd best be going.'

'Oi'l let ye know when the funeral is,' she said. 'Probably end of the week I daresay.'

As he went down the passageway to the front door, David glanced sideways at the parlour door. He felt awful not wanting to pay his last respects to a man who'd done so much for him but he couldn't face it. It had been different with Daniel. David thought he would rather remember Joe Rigby as he was, puffing away at a Woodbine and complaining about the weather, his shortness of breath and the cost of everything.

The funeral was on the following Friday morning at Milton cemetery and Jim Dangerfield, who had decided to go, said David could go along with him. As he stood shivering at the graveside in the chill wind, David was reminded of the last time he was here to watch Daniel being buried. His mother still grieved over her loss, but everyone was hoping that the arrival of the new baby would help. Trouble is, David thought, she says she only wants a boy, but surely, as long as it's all right, what does it matter? For himself, he'd prefer another sister.

As Joe Rigby's coffin was lowered into the ground, David found himself wondering why people had to fill their heads with strange notions, which were so hard to understand. Why couldn't his mother just be happy that she was going to have another child? After all, she was luckier than Auntie Frances who couldn't have any at all. He picked up a handful of earth and threw it onto the coffin, and as he did so, experienced the first feelings of the depression that was to haunt him for much of his life.

The letter from Joe Rigby's Solicitors arrived ten days' later. It was addressed to David and invited him to attend their offices in Southsea at ten o'clock the following Monday when he would be seen by a Mr Alastair Browning to hear the reading of Joseph Rigby's Last Will and Testament. Jim Dangerfield said he could have an hour off work provided he made the time up at the end of the day, and Esther said she'd like to go along to the Solicitors with him.

'Thanks Mum,' David said, 'but I'm old enough to do things for myself now.'

At ten o'clock sharp on Monday morning, David presented himself at the Solicitors where a receptionist showed him into a dark, musty-smelling office filled with Victorian furniture and heavily framed oil paintings. Behind a large, leather-topped desk, Alistair Browning sat puffing away on a pipe and leafing through some papers.

It was a simple Will, and Joe had done everything he'd promised to do. He'd left all his money to David to be held in trust until his twenty-first birthday when it would be transferred over to him. The regular sum paid each week to make up for the shortfall in David's wages would continue, and any time he needed books or tools, he could apply to the Trustees for the money.

'You're a very lucky young man,' Alistair Browning said. 'With careful investment, the inheritance which, after certain expenses have been deducted, amounts to two-thousand pounds will, by the time you are twenty-one, have increased in value substantially.'

David was surprised. He'd no idea Joe had been that well-off. 'That's a lot of money Sir,' he said.

'Yes, it is. And I hope that when the time comes, you will use it wisely.'

David assured him that he would. 'I hope to start my own cabinet making business,' he said. 'That's what Mr Rigby would have wanted me to do.'

As he cycled back through the streets of Southsea, David thought about all that money. Mr. Browning had said that in three years' time, it was possible to add perhaps another thousand pounds to the original sum, provided the markets were good. Three-thousand pounds would be more than enough to set David up in business, with plenty left over to buy a nice house somewhere. His thoughts immediately turned to Sally Totter.

Chapter Eleven

Frances and Nurse Mary Williams exchanged glances before they both looked towards the bed where an exhausted Esther lay with her eyes closed. It had been a long, hard labour followed by the birth of her baby, who was now crying lustily.

'Will you tell her or shall I?' Frances whispered, cuddling the child in a warm towel.

'It might come better from you,' Mary Williams said. 'You're family.'

Esther stirred and opened her eyes. 'Can I hold my son now?' she said reaching out to take the baby from Frances.

Frances placed the child in Esther's arms. 'It's a girl, Esther,' she said. 'You have a lovely, perfect little girl.' She and Mary Williams waited for some reaction but there was none. Esther just stared at them both in disbelief.

'She's beautiful,' Frances said, perching on the side of the bed. 'Look at her Esther, with all that lovely golden hair, and not a wrinkle to be seen.'

Esther looked at her new daughter and, with tears streaming down her face said, 'I wanted another boy Frances. Another little Daniel, that's what I wanted. Oh, where's Harry?'

Frances wiped Esther's face with a damp flannel. 'No other child can ever replace Daniel,' she said, 'but you have a little girl who needs you to love her. Be glad that she's perfect, just like all your other babies. And Harry's downstairs. I'll fetch him if you like.'

Mary Williams reached out to take the baby from Esther's arms. 'This little mite needs to be washed and made comfortable,' she said. 'Would you like to ask Mr Cartarett to come up Frances?'

Frances went downstairs. 'Just to warn you,' she said to Harry, who had only just come in from work. 'It's a girl, and you know what that means.'

'Is it all right to go up?'

'Yes. And see what you can do. She's a lovely little baby. Well, not so little really, almost ten pounds she was. Esther certainly doesn't do things by halves.'

When Harry went into the bedroom, Esther was staring blankly at the ceiling. 'I didn't want a girl,' she said. 'I wanted Daniel back again. Why has everything gone so wrong?' She clung to him and cried as if her heart would break.

He didn't know what to say or do to make things right for her. 'You'll love this little one same as you do all the others,' he said. 'You need time, that's all.'

Mary Williams brought the baby to Esther. 'She needs a feed,' she said, 'else none of you'll get any sleep tonight.'

'I'm too tired,' Esther said, turning away.

The nurse lost her temper. 'You've a baby here needs a feed,' she said, placing the child on the bed at Esther's side. 'And just to let you know how lucky you are,' she went on, her voice shaking with anger, 'last night I delivered a little boy to a woman whose husband collapsed and died suddenly only last week. She already has five children, and this one is a Mongoloid with a bad heart. The poor woman can't even go to her own husband's funeral, she is so weak. And there is no Frances to give her a hand. So I suggest you stop feeling sorry for yourself and give this little mite the feed she needs.'

'Now just a minute …' Harry wasn't prepared to hear anyone talk to his wife like that, especially after what she'd just been through.

'Leave it Harry,' Frances said. 'The nurse is right, and Esther will have to feed the baby if only until the morning when I can get to the chemist for a bottle and some dried milk.'

Between them, they managed to coax Esther into putting the baby to the breast but as soon as she'd finished, she handed her back to Frances who placed her in the crib David had made. 'Albert's due in for his tea,' Frances said to Harry. 'I'll have to leave you to it but I can come back later this evening if you like.'

'No, that's all right Frances, but thanks all the same. You go home and get some rest yourself.'

'I'll be back first thing in the morning then,' she said, 'and don't worry, Esther will come round.' She looked longingly at the crib. 'I'd give anything to have a lovely child of my own like that.'

Apart from waking up for a feed twice in the night, the baby slept well, and by morning Esther was looking, and feeling much better. Frances arrived early followed soon afterwards by Mary Williams. 'And how are we today?' the nurse said, breezing into the bedroom, bringing with her a whiff of fresh air. 'You're looking much better Mrs Cartarett. What sort of night did you have?' She lifted the infant out of her crib and handed her to Esther, determined that there would be no repeat of yesterday's nonsense.

Esther took the baby without protest, put her to the breast and said that they'd all had a fairly good night, and the baby had only woken up twice.

'That's pretty good for a new baby. Have you thought of a name for her yet?'

'No.'

'Well don't take too long. We can't keep calling her "it" now, can we?'

'I thought April would be very nice,' Esther said.

'Perfect, I would say,' Mary Williams said. 'Now, would you like Frances to bring Edwin and Catherine up to see the new arrival?'

'Yes please.' Knowing how jealous children could be, Esther asked Mary Williams to put the baby back in her crib, and gave Edwin and Catherine a cuddle before she introduced them to the newcomer.

'What do you think of your new sister then?' Frances said.

Edwin glanced briefly at the bundle in the crib. He didn't think that babies were very interesting things. They were always either being sick or messing their napkins. And they cried a lot. 'She's all right I suppose,' he said.

'And you, Catherine?'

Catherine pulled the blanket away from the baby's face and had a good look. 'She's pretty,' she said. 'She has lots of hair, and she looks like Daniel.'

Esther felt a huge lump come up in her throat. Whatever had she been thinking of last night to behave like a spoilt child who hadn't been given what it wanted. She thought about the poor woman who had no husband and all those children to bring up on her own, and felt ashamed of herself. She gave Edwin and Catherine a smile. 'Auntie Frances is taking you to school today Edwin,' she said. 'And you, Catherine will be going across the road to play with Auntie Phyllis's little girl. Give Mummy a big kiss and off you go.'

Later, just after Mary Williams left, Esther heard Frances come back and let herself in through the front door. 'Anything you want before I climb those stairs?' she called out.

'A cup of tea would be nice,' Esther shouted back. 'Mary Williams didn't have time to stop.

'I'm really sorry for the way I behaved yesterday,' she said, as she and Frances drank their tea. 'I overheard what you said to Harry about giving anything to have a baby. And it must be awful for that woman who's lost her husband. She has all those children, and now a baby with so much wrong with it. I'm such an ungrateful cow.'

Frances smiled. 'You've been through an awful lot this past year,' she said, 'and lots of women would have felt the same I daresay.'

'By the way,' Esther said, 'I've lost track of the time. What was yesterday's date?'

'It was 27th April.'

'Ah, that's what I'd like to call her then, if Harry agrees. April.'

The baby stirred and Esther asked to hold her. She studied her new daughter closely and realised just how right Catherine had been when she'd said the baby looked like Daniel.'Yes,' she said, 'I think we'll call her April. It sounds just right somehow.'

'Have you heard anything from Alex?' Frances asked as she moved about the room tidying up.

'One letter in six weeks,' Esther said.

'Well, knowing Alex, that's more than can be expected I daresay. Do you think he's all right?'

'Yes, as far as we could tell.'

'Oh, he'll survive. It's always seemed strange to me how different he is from your David. Alex, strong-minded and brash, and David … well, a bit on the weak side if you don't mind my saying so.'

'He's been seeing a girl,' Esther said. 'David, I mean. He's taken her to the pictures a couple of times.'

'And not before time,' Frances said. 'Anything you want from the shops?'

'No thanks Frances. Phyllis is coming over later and she said she'll get the shopping in. You've done enough already and I'm very grateful.'

Phyllis arrived just after Frances left. 'You certainly have some bonny babies,' she said when Esther told her how much the new arrival had weighed. 'And that is definitely the last?'

Esther smiled. *'Definitely,'* she said. 'I'll have to tell Harry to find another hobby. And that reminds me, I know I shouldn't ask, but is everything all right now between you and Jack?'

Phyllis wandered over to the window and looked down onto the empty street. 'Not really,' she said. 'I just can't seem to forget what happened and when he wants some loving, I just lie there like a piece of stiff cardboard until it's all over.'

'You've got to give it time.'

'I know.'

Esther felt sorry for both Phyllis *and* Jack but there was nothing anyone could do to help. They had to sort it out for themselves. 'So, what have you been up to lately?' she said, changing the subject.

'Helping to organise the street part for the King's Jubilee next month. There's so much to be done, but everyone along the road has been giving a hand.'

'All except me,' Esther said. 'I forgot all about it.'

'Well no one expected you to do anything, in your condition, so don't worry.'

'When is it?'

'6th of May.'

Esther's eyelids felt heavy. 'I'll ask David to come over and see you. He could give a hand.'

'You're just about to drop off,' Phyllis said, 'so I'd better go.' She picked up a list of things Esther needed from the shops. 'I'll get these for you when I go out this afternoon.'

A week later, to the despair of Mary Williams who said it was too soon, Esther insisted on getting up and, to everyone's relief, she doted on April so much that the child was in danger of being spoilt and over protected. Phyllis offered to look after the baby if Esther wanted to go back to her job in the shop when she was fit enough but she wouldn't hear of it. 'I'm not leaving her,' she said, 'if anything went wrong, I'd never forgive myself.'

David said he would give a hand with the Jubilee party arrangements, and spent his spare time going from house to house, collecting names and arranging to borrow tables and chairs from everyone. Almost every house in the road contributed something in the way of food, and the music for a singsong and dance would be courtesy of Billy Foreman and his two sons from number forty-two. They were popular in Eastbrook where they often performed on their accordions at some of the local public houses.

Esther felt guilty that she wasn't fit enough to help, but Phyllis said there were more than enough people doing things, and as it was a public holiday, there would be plenty of men around to give a hand. Although if she really wanted to feel useful, she could write out all the names David had collected, onto cards for the tables.

Jubilee Day dawned warm and sunny, and David and Harry were up at six o'clock to set all the tables out in the middle of the road. Most houses had been decorated with red, white and blue flags, and excitement among the children mounted as, early in the afternoon the tables were laid with sandwiches, cakes, jellies, blancmanges and jugs of home-made lemonade. By three o'clock, everything was ready and the party began with the children sitting down to eat, and the adults serving the food. Afterwards, there were games, which much to Phyllis's surprise, were organised by Harry, who was in his element sorting the unruly bunch of excited children into some sort of order.

'I didn't know he was so good with children,' Phyllis said.

'Oh, yes.' Esther said. 'Harry seems to have the knack of getting them to do exactly as he wants. Except of course, when it comes to dealing with one of his own wayward sons.'

The younger children went home to bed at six o'clock, and it was time for the adults to have their bit of fun. They danced until midnight to all the latest tunes, although Esther had to sit on the sidelines and watch, as she was still too weak from the birth of April to take part in anything so energetic.

The nicest thing about the party, Esther later said to Phyllis, was that they were able to meet and talk to some of the other people who lived in Kestrel Road, which was something that rarely happened. 'Most of them do no more than pass the time of day,' she said, 'and I daresay they will go back to being like that as soon as the Jubilee is forgotten.'

'Your next door neighbours, the Cheswicks, didn't put in an appearance', Phyllis said.

'No they didn't. Strange that.'

The following day Frances called in. 'Thought I'd drop by to see if there's anything you need down the town. Albert's taking me shopping to buy some new clothes and he's some business to attend to,' she said. 'How did your party go Esther?'

'It was very good, except that I had to sit and watch everyone else doing the work, and enjoying the fun.'

'Ours wasn't too bad,' Frances said, 'but I'd sooner have been here.'

Esther had a feeling that Frances was ill at ease for some reason or another. 'Are you all right?' she asked.

Frances studied her sister-in-law closely. Esther looked happier and more at peace than for a very long time. She'd made her Memory Box and it had helped her face life without Daniel. Every now and then, when the black cloud came down and settled over her, she would open the box and spend half an hour or so going through the contents. It held a pair of his shoes, the last he'd ever worn, his teething ring and dummy, the piece of blanket he wouldn't go to sleep without, and some pencilled scribblings he'd done on the back of an old envelope, one wet afternoon when Esther had wanted five minutes to herself. Now, with April sleeping soundly in her arms and Catherine sitting at her feet playing with her dolls, the woman who, a few months' ago was in the depths of a terrible depression, appeared the picture of contentment.

'Yes,' Frances replied. 'I'm just a bit preoccupied with things at the moment, that's all.' She'd come here to break her own piece of news to Esther, but knowing what a shattering effect it would have, decided that there was no urgency. Now wasn't the right time. It would have to wait for another day.

It took a long time for Esther to recover from the birth of April. She was always tired these days and found it difficult to cope with a baby and the demands of the rest of the family. Phyllis helped as much as she could but Frances didn't come round anywhere near as often as she used to. She seemed always to be busy doing other things, and Esther had a feeling that she was keeping her in the dark over something.

What worried Esther the most was all this talk of another war. Harry kept on about it until in the end she lost her temper with him. 'Why *do* you have to keep going on about this war?' she said, one evening when he'd been reading aloud snippets of news from the Daily Herald. 'I don't want to hear about it. In any case, it's not likely to happen. It's just a lot of rumour spread about by the newspapers with nothing better to talk about.'

Having changed his opinion about the possibility of another war, Harry was now convinced that it would come, and in the not too far distant future either. Sometimes, when his thoughts drifted back to the last one, his eyes took on a haunted look, brought about by the things he'd witnessed in France when he'd fought in the trenches in the war that was supposed to end all wars. Things he recalled, mostly at night when sleep wouldn't come, and all he could hear were the cries of his comrades as they died in the mud at Passchendael. And all he could see was the sightless eyes of his friend Jimmy Styles, staring up at him from what was left of his once handsome face. Things he'd kept to himself for more than seventeen years, never having spoken of them to anyone, not even to Esther. He prayed constantly that nothing like that would ever happen again.

'The way things are going my love,' he said, 'it's only a matter of time. There are terrible things happening all over Europe. That madman Adolph Hitler is hell bent on occupying every country within striking distance of Germany and he'll be after England next, mark my words.'

'Well, I don't want to mark your words, thank you,' Esther replied, 'so could we please talk about something else. Like, what is going on with your Frances and her Albert? She hardly ever visits these days and it's not because we've fallen out or anything. When I do see her, it's as if she wants to tell me something but doesn't know where to begin. Do you know what's going on?'

Harry averted his eyes. He knew very well what was going on but Frances had begged him not to say anything until she'd plucked up the courage to tell Esther herself. 'No. I don't,' he said.

Esther eyed him quizzically. 'I'll bet you do,' she said. 'I can usually tell when you're not telling the truth. Your face gives you away every time.'

'Well, this time, you're wrong. If I knew, I'd tell you.'

'All right. I'll find out for myself soon enough I suppose.'

Esther fell to thinking about Alex. Only one postcard they'd had since he'd left home, and that hadn't told them very much. She was surprised how much she missed him. He may have been a bit of a scallywag but, for all his faults, he'd brought a whiff of fresh air into the house with his lively personality, and the house seemed dull without him around. And David ... well, she couldn't make out her eldest son at all. He'd been taking this girl out once a week for the past couple of months but it didn't seem to be going anywhere, this friendship. Not that she expected him to announce any wedding plans or anything like that but he hadn't even asked to bring her home to tea. He was a strange one and no mistake. Not like anyone else she knew on either side of the family, except perhaps Harry's brother Charles. God forbid, she thought to herself, that he should turn out like him.

As December approached, she began to feel better physically but emotionally down. This was the second Christmas without Daniel and she still couldn't get used to the idea that he wasn't around any more. She only visited the cemetery twice a week now and, on what would have been his third birthday she had bought a Rose bush and planted it on his grave. April had given her a new lease of life it was true, but there was nothing could ever replace her little boy.

She was busy making the Christmas cake one afternoon when it struck her that she could ask David if he'd like to bring his girlfriend to tea on Boxing Day. Esther would love to meet her, and after all, Christmas should be all about families and friends getting together.

'Thanks Mum but no,' he said, when she asked him.

'But we haven't met her David. And she'd probably like to meet *us.*'

David shook his head. 'I don't want her getting ideas,' he said. 'Meeting families is another way of saying you're serious about someone. And I'm not serious about Sally.'

'Have you met any of her family yet?' Esther asked.

David could hardly tell his mother that the man who had tormented him at work for the past two years was Sally's father. 'No, I haven't,' he lied. 'And that's the way I want it.'

'Well, please yourself, but if you change your mind …'

'I won't.'

When she told Harry about the conversation, he laughed. 'For God's sake woman,' he said, 'he's only eighteen. Give him chance.'

She smiled. 'I was only seventeen when I married you.'

'That was different,' he said.

For the first time since they married, Harry was able to afford a turkey for Christmas dinner. Frances and Albert came, and Esther noticed that they both seemed on edge all through the meal.

'What's wrong Frances?' she asked, when the two of them were alone in the kitchen clearing up. 'Something's been the matter for ages and I wish you'd tell me what it is.' Frances didn't answer for a minute then she said that Christmas Day wasn't the right time and that she'd tell Esther once the festivities were over.

On Boxing Day, Harry, Esther and the children went across the road to Jack and Phyllis's for tea and Esther told her of her worries.

'You don't think she's ill or anything, do you?' Esther said.

'It's hard to say. Although I'd have thought she would have confided in you if that were the case,' Phyllis said. 'No, I'm sure it's nothing to worry about, and if there *is* anything, she'll tell you soon enough.'

It was another week before Frances called in to tell Esther her news and she came straight out with it. 'We've bought a small-holding,' she said, 'and I'm afraid it means we'll be moving.'

So that was it. Esther felt as if she'd been hit in the face with a brick. Albert and Frances had probably not wanted to say anything until it was all cut and dried but all the same, it would have been less of a shock if they'd said something sooner. At least then, she would have been prepared.

'Oh, Frances you *can't*.' She was close to tears.

'I'm sorry love, but it's just what Albert has always wanted. It's on the edge of the New Forest and there's enough ground for us to grow things, and there's a lovely cottage goes with it so we don't even have to worry about searching for another house.' Frances felt terrible, dropping this bombshell at the start of a new year. Albert had been fed up with the trams for a long time now, and when he'd read in one of the daily papers about Riverside Cottage being up for sale, he jumped at the chance to make an offer on it. Having been brought up on a smallholding owned by his parents, he'd had considerable experience of gardening. He would have taken over the business had it not been for the war, and the death of his father in 1917 when he, himself had been away doing his bit in the Navy. His mother, who sold up shortly afterwards, had died within months of his father and Albert, their only child, had inherited everything. At the end of the war, he and Frances were married, and it had been at her suggestion that they buy a house with the inheritance. At the time, work had been scarce and he'd been glad of a job driving the trams. Always, though in the back of his mind was the plan to return one day to what he loved best ... working on the land.

'You and Harry will be able to come and stay,' Frances said, with a mixture of guilt and irritation. 'It might be called a cottage but it's really big, with three bedrooms and a huge kitchen. You'd all fit in and it will be lovely for the children to have a holiday in the country.'

Esther stared at her sister-in law as if she'd lost her mind. 'And how do you suggest we get to this wonderful place you're moving to?' she said. She knew she sounded bitter but Frances had always been there for her and she couldn't imagine how she would manage without her.

'There are such things as trains,' Frances replied angrily. She and Albert were entitled to a life of their own after all, and Esther should be wishing them well, not making it look as if they were following their own path with no regard for her feelings. 'And you still have Phyllis.' She took hold of Esther's hand. 'Please be happy for us,' she said. 'This move means such a lot to Albert. It's what he's wanted for years.'

Esther gave Frances a hug. 'Of course I'm happy for you,' she said. 'It just seems so sudden that's all. I'll miss you so much Frances. You've been like a rock to me.' She rubbed at her eyes. 'When are you going?'

'In two or three months if all goes well.'

'As soon as that?'

'Yes,' Frances said, 'that's when we have to sign all the papers.'

'What's happening to your house?'

'It's been sold, and the new people want to move in as soon as possible.'

Esther went over to the window and stared out into the garden. 'I suppose you're right,' she said, 'I do have Phyllis and she's a good friend, but she's not family, is she.'

'No,' Frances agreed. 'But you've got to know each other, and you'll soon get used to not having me around.'

'I doubt that very much,' Esther said.

Later that evening, she spoke to Harry about it. 'What is it,' she said, 'that we seem to be losing everyone. First Daniel, then Alex going away to God knows where, and now Frances and Albert. It makes me wonder who's going to be the next.'

Harry set aside the Daily Herald he'd been trying to read. 'It's the way things are,' he said, pulling her onto his lap. 'Nothing ever stays still, and we have to accept changes as they come along.'

'Well, I don't like changes. I want things to always stay as they are.' Esther knew she sounded like a petulant child.

Harry pushed her gently from his lap and stood up. 'There's one thing'll never change,' he said, 'and that's the way I feel about you.'

119

Esther felt so ashamed. 'Oh, Harry,' she said into his shoulder, 'I'm a miserable little cow, aren't I?'

He lifted her chin with one finger and smiled into her eyes. 'Well, even if you are,' he said, 'I wouldn't have you any other way.'

Chapter Twelve

One afternoon, about three weeks' later, Esther was on her way home from the shops when she learned of the death of King George V. Mrs Mc Andrew, who always managed to find out things long before anyone else was, as usual, hanging over her gate waiting for someone to whom she could relate the latest bit of news or gossip, and as Esther drew level, the older woman's multiple chins wobbled from side to side as she shook her head. 'The King's dead,' she said. 'My Stan came in for 'is dinner an' told me his boss saw it in the Times newspaper and announced it to the workers.' She gave a deep sigh and dabbed at her eyes with the corner of her apron. 'Late last night it was. Who'd 'ave thought it. 'E only 'ad a chesty cold, so we was given to believe. 'E was a lovely man.'

Esther wasn't an ardent follower of royalty, and thought they were a load of parasites living off the backs of the likes of ordinary people. All the same, she felt a pang of sadness at the passing of King George V. As Mrs Mc Andrew had said, he was a good man, and one of the few members of the Royal Family who seemed to be in tune with his subjects. He was very popular with the British people and those who were fond of Royalty would probably miss him.

'I suppose that means the Prince of Wales will become King?' Esther said, not bothered that much about who would follow George V to the throne.

'Yeh. Trouble is, e's not like 'is father, and t'won't be the same,' said Mrs Mc Andrew. 'A bit of a playboy 'e is, so I've 'eard.'

Esther pushed April's pram forward. If Mrs Mc Andrew was looking for the chance to air her knowledge about the Royals, she was in for a disappointment. 'I have to go, Mrs Mc Andrew,' she said. 'Lots to do, you know.'

Mrs Mc Andrew stayed put. Someone else might come along in a minute and perhaps be a little more willing to stop and have a good yarn. 'Well, take care Mrs Cartarett,' she said, waving to April. 'Lovely little girl you've got there.'

Thankfully, Esther moved on. It's always sad, she thought, when someone dies, as she knew to her cost, but at least the King had lived to a good age which was more than could be said of the three children she and Harry had lost. She went indoors, unpacked her bits of shopping, then lifted April from her pram and strolled across the road to see Phyllis.

'Trust that nosey old biddy to find out before anyone else,' Phyllis said when Esther told her the news. 'There's nothing gets past her.'

Esther laughed. Everyone knew about Mrs Mc Andrew always keeping her ear to the ground, but the woman had never been malicious about anyone and was harmless enough.

'I suppose,' said Phyllis, 'that this means another street party to organise.'

'Phyllis.'

'Well, it's something to look forward to isn't it?'

'Yes. But the poor man's hardly cold yet,' Esther said, 'and I doubt if it will be this year, anyway.'

They lapsed into silence for a few minutes then, as if she could read Esther's thoughts, Phyllis asked if there was any news of Alex.

'You must be a mind-reader,' Esther, who had been thinking of her son, said. 'He should be on his way home by now, and knowing him, he'll probably just turn up one day out of the blue.'

'I'm sure he will. That's your Alex all over.'

Esther lifted April from the floor where she'd been playing with Sarah. 'Must go,' she said. 'Harry likes his dinner to be on the table when he comes in from work.' She rolled her eyes. 'I sometimes wonder what these men would do if they had to look after themselves for a while.'

Back in her own house, she put April down for her afternoon nap and sat in Harry's armchair. Just lately, the day-to-day round of domestic chores had been getting her down. Why, she asked herself, did women have to be so subservient to men. She was as bad as any for pandering to her husband's likes and dislikes but would it really hurt if just for once he came home and *didn't* expect his dinner to be put in front of him immediately? And as for David ... well, he was forever out in the garden giving Harry a hand, but ask him to wash a dish and you'd have thought the world was coming to an end.

She took hold of the poker and prodded the fire viciously, sending sparks flying up the chimney and bits of half-burnt log spattering onto the hearth. She wondered what it was that was making her so angry about everything lately when up until recently she'd been happy to be just another housewife, looking after her family. Surely, at her age, she was too young to be on the change, and yet, these were some of the signs she'd read about in the woman's magazine she bought each week. Of course, there was Frances moving away and that didn't help. She'd be gone in a couple of months to that God-forsaken place in the New Forest and Esther felt sure that they wouldn't see each other as often as Frances had promised. Albert was buying a car and they would be able to visit Esther and Harry at least once a month, she'd said. 'That was a load of rubbish just to shut me up,' Esther said aloud to herself.

She almost died of fright when a voice from behind said, 'Talking to yourself Mum?' It was Alex.

She flew out of the chair and flung her arms around him. 'Oh, son,' she cried, squashing him in a bear hug, 'you frightened the life out of me. I didn't hear you come in. Oh, how glad I am to see you.'

He'd grown taller and even more handsome. He had a deep tan and looked well. Esther was in tears. 'I don't know what to say,' she said. 'This must be the best surprise I've had in my whole life.'

'It's lovely to see you again Mum.' Alex was touched by the warmth of his mother's welcome. He hadn't known what to expect. He'd gone off to sea without asking permission, and only once had he sent a postcard and that hadn't told his parents much. If they'd turned him away, he couldn't have blamed them.

'How long are you home for?' Esther called from the kitchen where she'd gone to put the kettle on.

'Only for a couple of days, then I have to report back to the ship.' He began searching through his case. 'Look at what I've bought you, all the way from India.'

Esther took the blue, pure silk scarf from him and held it up against her. 'It's beautiful,' she said. 'Though I don't know when I'll have the chance to wear something as glamorous as this.'

'I bought it 'cos it matches the colour of your eyes,' Alex said, and Esther felt a surge of love for this son of hers she'd never before felt close to. No wonder he was so popular with the girls. Even Harry wouldn't have thought of saying a thing like that.

Over a cup of tea, she sat listening to the tales of his first trip abroad. He'd been to some fascinating places although, as he said, he didn't get much time ashore as once the passengers had disembarked, he and the other Bell Boys had to clean up after them. 'You'd be surprised Mum,' he said, 'how untidy some of them are. They leave their cabins in a terrible mess, and you'd think they'd know better seeing as they're what we call the Posh Nobs.'

Esther sat mesmerised while he described the sunsets and sunrises he'd seen. 'Like nothing you would ever see in this country,' he said. 'The Temples and the beautiful gardens. And, Mum, it was so *warm* everywhere. Malta, Gibraltar, the Suez Canal … the sun never stopped shining. And when we got to India we were allowed ashore to see the Taj Mahal by moonlight, and oh Mum you've never seen anything like it.' His face was animated, his eyes alight with the wonder of all the things he'd seen, and she knew then that he was lost to her forever because he'd never come back to settle in England. Then he told her of the other side of India he'd seen. The real poverty he'd witnessed everywhere. 'You've often told us about Wimple Street but this was different. Pitiful little children, covered in scabs and flies, begging for food in the streets. And blind old men sitting on filthy pavements, moaning to themselves as they pray to die.' He almost choked on his words. Esther took hold of his hand. This was not the Alex she knew … this was a young man who, because of the dreadful things he'd seen, had suddenly grown too old for his years.

'It must have been awful for you, seeing all that,' she said. 'But there's nothing any of us can do about it. It's happening all over the world and we just have to think ourselves lucky to have what we have.' The words sounded trite but what else was there to say?

So engrossed was she in listening to him describe his voyage to India that she forgot the time and it was only when April stirred in her pram and started to grizzle that she realised there was no dinner in the oven. She gave the baby her tea and set about the cooking, leaving Alex to dream in front of the fire.

Harry was the first to come in, just after six o'clock. His face, when he saw Alex, lit up like a beacon as he strode across the room and took his son's hand. 'Good to see you son,' he said. 'You're looking well on it.'

There was no such welcome from David, who arrived shortly afterwards. He took one look at Alex and his face dropped a mile. 'So you've decided to come home, have you?' he said. 'Pity you couldn't keep our Mum informed of your whereabouts. She's been worried sick.'

Esther threw him a dark look. 'Alex is only home for a couple of days,' she said, setting out the table, 'so I suggest you be a little more friendly to your brother while he's here.'

'He's not sleeping in my room.'

'Oh, yes he is,' Esther said. 'I'll say who sleeps where in this house.'

'I'm used to roughing it Mum,' Alex said. 'I'll sleep on the settee. It's all right.'

'You won't do any such thing,' Harry put in, ashamed of the behaviour of the older boy. 'As your mother says David, Alex'll be sharing your bed for the next couple of nights. And if you've anything to say about that, then say it.'

David stared sullenly into his dinner and said nothing. After the meal, he disappeared in a mood up to his bedroom and Alex repeated his story to Harry while Esther cleared up.

'Did you know the King has died?' she asked, having forgotten, in all the excitement, the day's most important piece of news.

Harry nodded. 'Yes it's on all the placards down the town.'

'Our captain told us this morning before we disembarked,' Alex said.

Esther told Alex about his Auntie Frances and Uncle Albert moving to the New Forest and suggested he might like to pop round and see them before he went back to sea. He was surprised to hear that they were leaving Portsmouth. 'Of course I will,' he said. 'You'll miss her won't you Mum.'

'Yes,' Esther said.

Later that night, when a weary Alex climbed into bed next to David, he wondered whether to tell his mother and father about the plans he'd heard about the future of the ship he was on. Maybe not at the moment, he thought as he closed his eyes. His mother would worry herself silly and his father would dismiss it as speculation about something that may not even happen. His last thoughts before falling into a dreamless sleep were of the welcome he'd received from his mother, and how nice it was to be home again, even if only for a couple of days, and despite David's resentment at him being there.

Alex's visit had an unsettling effect on David. Esther had told him her own version of his brother's trip to India and it left him wondering in which direction his own life was going. He was bored with taking Sally Totter to the pictures every Saturday. It was the same thing every blessed week. Meet outside the Regal or on Fratton Bridge, watch the films then walk her to the end of her road before giving her a swift goodnight kiss. Since their first date, he seemed to have lost the urge to go any further with her, whether in the cinema or out of it and this brought back memories of the name-calling episodes he'd hoped to forget. Maybe there *was* something wrong with him if, at his age, a pretty girl like Sally couldn't excite him.

In the end, Sally it was who put an end to their friendship. Although she didn't want to start any messing about, David's indifference was about as welcome as being on the receiving end of a bucket of cold water. 'I don't think this is going anywhere,' she said one evening when they met outside the Regal. 'I like you David and I don't want to do anything that's wrong, but kissing you is like kissing my mother before I leave for work in the morning.'

'Well,' David said, 'you want to make your mind up. You had me thrown out of here once for getting carried away, in case you've forgotten.'

'I know. But that was back last year. And all I want is a kiss with a bit of warmth in it. Not too much to ask, is it?'

David supposed not but he was secretly relieved that she wanted to finish with him. It saved him having to find the right words to end their meetings without hurting her feelings. For some time he'd thought about telling her he didn't want to carry on but each time he made up his mind to say something, he'd not been able to find the courage. That evening, they parted company the best of friends, without even bothering to see the film.

The other thing that had troubled him lately was the thought he often had that he was going out of his mind. There were the longings he sometimes had of almost wishing he could go to sleep and not wake up again, and the enormous black cloud that seemed to settle over him when, after a restless night, he'd open his eyes to face another day. He'd told no one of his troubled mind since it would have given his mother yet another thing to worry about, and by the way she'd been behaving lately, she already had enough on her mind.

On the last Saturday in March, he awoke early as usual, to what he now called his "Black Cloud" hanging over him. It was a sunny morning, and he slipped out of bed before anyone else was up, dressed and went outside for some fresh air where, apart from some birdsong in the Rowan trees next door, it was as quiet as the grave. As he surveyed the garden his father had created from nothing, he suddenly realised that making fancy chairs, tables and china cabinets for people with more money than sense, was not what he wanted to be doing at all. He'd made a mistake in his choice of work and that was what was causing these black moods he'd been having. Of course he liked making things from wood, but, after spending much of his spare time helping his father, he discovered that it was gardening he really loved. Sowing tiny seeds and watching them grow into food for the table or flowers for the house. Digging and hoeing and making bonfires … all out in the fresh air instead of being shut up in a stuffy workshop for eight hours' a day listening to the filthy jokes and swearing from the men on the benches.

His spirits rose, then fell again as he remembered Joe Rigby's legacy. Was there anything in the Will that said David could only inherit the money if he finished his apprenticeship? He didn't want to lose the money but the thought of another three years working at Dangerfield's troubled him. Not that he'd had any more problems with the men since Totter had tried to do that terrible thing to him, and Jim Dangerfield had put a stop to it. Since then, most of the men looked upon David with a certain amount of respect. No, it wasn't anything to do with that. It was all to do with the mistaken belief that he'd thought he wanted to spend his life making things from wood, and now that he'd had the chance to do that, he'd not found much satisfaction from it.

He heard his mother moving about inside the house and went back into the kitchen where she was preparing breakfast. 'You're up and about early, David,' she said, setting out the porridge bowls.

'Yes Mum. I was wide awake and it looked like a nice morning so I thought I'd take a look at Dad's garden.'

Esther smiled. 'Yes,' she said, 'your Dad has worked hard getting it up together. And do you know, I cannot remember the last time I had to buy fresh veg from the shops.'

'When is he going to buy some chicks?' David asked.

'I think he's changed his mind about that. Says it would be extra work for me, feeding them and keeping the runs cleaned out.' Esther handed him a bowl of porridge. 'Anyway, Jack over the road keeps chickens and he supplies us with eggs in exchange for fresh veg and fruit. It works very well.'

'*I'd* like to be a gardener,' David said, keeping his eyes down on his dish of porridge.

Esther stared at the back of his head in surprise. 'I thought you wanted to be a cabinet maker,' she said. 'That's what Joe Rigby's money is paying for.'

'I know Mum.'

'Well I hope you're not thinking of leaving Dangerfield's or any nonsense like that.'

David fell silent. He'd already decided to make an appointment to see the Solicitor about Joe's Will, but didn't see any sense in telling his mother or his father about it at the moment, just in case nothing came of it. 'Of course not,' he lied.

On Monday, he slipped out of the workshop during his lunch break and called the solicitors office from a telephone box on the corner of the road. Yes, Mr Alistair Browning could see him at ten o'clock the next day if David could manage that. Without even thinking about how he'd be able to get away from the benches to keep the appointment, David said he would be there, and he spent the rest of the afternoon wondering what excuse he could make to Jim Dangerfield for wanting an hour off work. In the end, he decided on the truth, or rather a slightly twisted version of it. 'Mr. Rigby's Solicitor wants to see me,' he said. 'Tomorrow at ten o'clock. Is it all right if I take an hour off, Sir? I'll make the time up at the end of the day.'

Jim Dangerfield, who could spot subterfuge from a mile away, closed the order book he'd been studying. Not many people were buying furniture these days it seemed, and the orders were not coming in as fast as he would have liked. It looked like he'd have to make cuts somewhere if the business were to remain solvent. 'I thought you'd sorted all that out ages ago, Cartarett,' he said, his sharp eyes noticing the flush on David's face. 'Not my business, but why's 'e want to see you after all this time?'

'I don't know Sir,' David said. 'It's something to do with the money that's held in trust, I think.'

Jim Dangerfield sighed. 'Oh, all right then,' he said. 'But you make the time up. I aint runnin' a blessed charity y'know.'

David thanked him and went back to his bench.

The following morning, he presented himself at the Solicitors offices just before ten o'clock, where the receptionist showed him into the same waiting room as before. 'Mr. Browning won't be long,' she told him, wondering why someone as young as David Cartarett needed the services of a legal man. 'He's just finishing with another client.'

'Well, young Cartarett,' Alistair Browning said from across the desk, when at last David was shown into his office. 'What can I do for you?'

David explained why he was here. 'I was wondering,' he said, 'if there was anything in Mr. Rigby's Will that says I must stay with Dangerfield's for another three years. Only I want to do something else. I want to do gardening.'

'You do?'

'Yes Sir.'

The older man studied his young client for a minute or two. 'If I remember correctly,' he said, 'the last time you were here, you couldn't wait to learn the cabinet making business. Am I right?'

'Yes. And I still like making things from wood.'

'Then why do you now want to work on the land?'

David shrugged. He couldn't answer that. 'I don't really know Sir,' he said at last. This conversation was getting nowhere and he was worried about the time. 'I just want to know if I can leave Dangerfield's if I want to, that's all.'

Alistair Browning referred to the file in front of him. 'Well, as I see it,' he said, 'there is nothing to stop you moving on if that's what you want to do. Your Mr. Rigby was a shrewd man and he didn't tie you up with indentures or anything like that.'

'Indentures?' David didn't know what that meant.

'Yes, *Contracts*.' He tapped a finger on the file. 'He must have had some idea that you might change your mind at some point and there is nothing in his instructions to me that says you have to stay put until you're twenty-one. The money will be yours no matter what.'

David sighed with relief. Now he could tell his father and mother, and follow the plan he'd dreamed up last night to ask Uncle Albert and Auntie Frances if they'd give him a job on their smallholding. His mother wouldn't like it, he knew that, but the New Forest wasn't the other side of the world and he would be able to visit home sometimes. He thanked Alistair Browning, left the office and pedalled furiously all the way back to the workshop, not wanting to spend half the night making up for time off.

His way home from work took him past the end of the road where Albert and Frances lived and he decided to call in and see them before saying anything to his father and mother. Frances answered the door and was surprised to see her nephew standing on the doorstep. She couldn't remember the last time he'd paid them a visit. 'Come in David,' she said. 'Nothing wrong I hope.'

'No. Is Uncle Albert in?'

'Yes, he is. Come through.' She showed him into the back parlour where his Uncle was reading the evening newspaper.

Albert's face registered surprise at the unexpected visitor. 'Sit down David,' he said, putting his paper to one side. 'It's not often you come and see us. What can we do for you?'

David explained his reasons for being there. 'I wondered if you would be looking for help on the smallholding and if so, whether you'd give me a job,' he said, his heart sinking as he saw the expression on his Uncle's face.

'We hadn't thought that far ahead,' Albert said, 'and it would mean you living away from home.'

'I know that, Uncle Albert. But it's what I want to do. And I'll be nineteen this year, and wouldn't be any bother I promise.'

Albert and Frances exchanged glances, both thinking the same thing. They would, of course, need help in getting their smallholding running properly but Harry and Esther wouldn't thank them for taking David away from home. They had already lost Daniel, and it wasn't all that long since Alex had left home to go to sea. Esther in particular would be heartbroken at losing David as well.

'Have you told your father and mother about this?' Albert said.

'Not yet.'

'And what'll happen about your apprenticeship with Dangerfield?'

'I've been to see the Solicitor and he said there was no proper contract and I can leave if I want. And I'll still inherit Mr. Rigby's money.'

'Well,' Frances put in. 'You seem to have sorted things out for yourself well enough but I think you should go home and talk this over with your parents before making up your mind to do something you might regret. Don't you Albert?'

Albert agreed. 'Your Auntie Frances and I will have to think about what you say,' he said. 'But we can't make any promises at the moment. It all depends on how much work there is needs doing. We've looked the place over and it's in a bit of a state but we may need to employ someone who's experienced in working on the land.' He stood up and patted David's shoulder. 'And you have think about the effect this would have on your mother,' he added. 'She's very fond of you David, and might not take kindly to you leaving home.'

David was tempted to say that his mother would just have to get over it. After all, he wasn't going to be living at home forever. Instead, he thanked them both, shook his Uncle's hand, gave his Auntie a kiss and left them pondering over the possibility of having their nephew live with them in the New Forest.

'It's not such a bad idea,' Frances said to Albert after David had gone.

'I agree,' he said, 'except that Esther won't like it very much.'

'Well, she can't hang on to her son forever.'

'No, I suppose not. And he's a good lad is David. Not like that scallywag of a brother of his at all,' Albert said.

Frances pulled a face. If she were asked to choose between her two older nephews, it would be Alex she'd favour. He might have been a bit wayward but at least you knew where you were with him. David on the other hand, she had never been able to fathom out. He'd no social life to speak of, didn't like girls very much, and spent most of his time in his bedroom reading books. And, as Esther had told her, his dark moods were becoming more frequent these days, and she didn't know what to do about him. Perhaps leaving home might sort him out, Frances thought.

As David turned the corner of Kestrel Road, he began to feel uneasy. What would his father and mother say when he told them what he'd been up to without their knowledge?

CHAPTER THIRTEEN

'You did all this without even talking to us first?' Harry said as he and Esther stared in disbelief at David. 'What d'you think you're playing at, eh?'

David had expected them to be angry but not as angry as this. He would soon be nineteen and old enough to make his own decisions and should not have to ask permission for everything he wanted to do. Hadn't they in the past, wanted him to stand on his own two feet?

'So,' he said, 'it's all right for our Alex to go and join the Merchant Navy without telling you but I've to ask before I do anything. Is that it?'

'Don't speak to your father like that,' Esther said.

David, having found the courage to stand up for what he wanted, wasn't going to be silenced. 'It's always been the same,' he said. 'Alex can do what he wants and get away with it. Like helping himself to whatever he wanted for pocket money out of his wage packet without permission, while I had to hand mine over unopened. It's not fair.'

'Unlike you, Alex didn't have a benefactor paying for him to do what he wanted,' Harry pointed out. 'And another thing, I don't suppose you've even thought of what Mr. Dangerfield's going to say about all of this, have you?'

'It's nothing to do with him,' David said.

Esther thought Harry would explode. 'So, you think it's nothing to do with him eh? Why, he's only the man who took you on to teach you the trade you said you wanted to learn, and now, because you've changed your mind, it's all right to let him down.' He brought his fist down on the table. 'Christ Almighty,' he said, 'Joe Rigby must be turning in his grave.'

'*Harry!*'

'Sorry Esther, but this ungrateful little bugger, sitting here telling us what he wants to do, needs a good kick up the arse.'

David jumped out of his chair. 'I'm not listening to any more of this Dad,' he said. 'I'm nearly nineteen and if Uncle Albert says I can go with him, I'm going and that's that.'

'We'll see about that,' Harry shouted as David stormed out into the garden, slamming the door behind him.

Esther waited until Harry had cooled down. 'I don't think we can stop him,' she said.

'Oh yes we can,' Harry said. 'He's another two years before he comes of age and can do as he pleases. And you've been through enough already. I'm not having you upset again and David can do as he likes about it.'

Esther was almost in tears. 'I think we should let him go,' she said.

'Let him have his own way you mean?'

'Yes.'

'And what about *your* feelings in all of this?' Harry said. 'You don't really want him to leave home, do you?'

Esther admitted that she didn't want to see David go away but he would be with Albert and Frances, and not going to the other side of the world, like Alex. 'If we don't let him go now,' she said, wisely, 'we'll lose him altogether.'

Harry scratched his head. 'I'll be damned if I'll ever understand you,' he said. 'One minute you're complaining that everyone's leaving us, and in the next breath you're saying we should let David go. What is it you want, woman?'

'First of all Harry,' Esther said, 'what I want is for you to stop calling me "woman". I've put up with it for years and I hate it. I do have a name. And secondly, as I have already said, we could lose

David altogether if we try and stop him and I'd rather send him away with our blessing than not ever see him again.'

'All right, but I want to see Albert before we decide what to do. For all we know, he may not want to take David along. And then what?'

'I don't know.' Esther was tired of trying to keep the family together. She knew that at some point, the children would want to flee the nest but everything seemed to be happening at once and it was becoming more and more difficult for her to cope with it all. 'Let him go, Harry,' she said. 'Just let him go.'

When Albert and Frances finally made their decision to take David with them, they went together to see Harry and Esther. 'He'll be all right with us,' Frances assured them. 'And we'll see to it that he earns his keep.'

'Exactly where is it that you're moving to?' Harry wanted to know. He'd heard of the New Forest but had no idea how far away it was.

'It's about thirty-odd miles from Portsmouth,' Albert said. 'Not far from Southampton.'

'Well,' Harry agreed at last, 'he can go with you but be it on your own heads. He's a bit of a strange one is David, and if at any time he doesn't toe the line or you get fed up with his moods, you can send him packing back home.'

'Oh, I'm sure it won't come to that,' said Frances.

If David was surprised at the angry reaction of his mother and father, the response from Jim Dangerfield to the news that he would be leaving at the end of April astonished him. 'My old friend Joe Rigby must've had second sight,' he said when David told him. 'He said at the time that he didn't want to tie you down to a contract for five years, an' that's why you were never indentured. He must've known this would happen.'

'You're not angry then Sir?' David, who had dreaded the moment he'd have to face his employer to ask him to accept a month's notice, said.

'You're no use to me if you want to be somewhere else, now are you?'

'No Sir.'

135

'Mind you, I'll be sorry to see you go. You've the makings of a fine cabinet maker and I'm surprised you've chosen to work on the land for a living. Bloody hard work that.'

'Yes I know.'

Jim Dangerfield stood up and showed David to the door of his office. 'Well, if it doesn't work out,' he said, 'there will always be a place for you here.' He pulled a wry face. 'That's if I don't go broke in the meantime. Things aren't that good at the moment.'

It was at the beginning of May that David went with Albert and Frances to their new home in the New Forest. Harry had given him some money to tide him over until he would start earning, and Esther had lovingly packed his few clothes and possessions in the suitcase she'd bought him as a leaving present. Albert and Frances turned up in their new Austin Seven to collect him and David hugged Esther until she could hardly breathe. 'I love you Mum,' he said, before climbing into the back of the car, 'and I'll write, I promise.' After a tearful goodbye to all of them, Esther went back indoors, unable to watch as they turned the corner of the road and disappeared from her sight.

She didn't know what to do with herself after they'd gone. Within the space of a few months, two of her children had left home and she felt as if her little family was falling apart. She had asked Phyllis to take Edwin to school this morning, as she hadn't wanted to make small talk with the other mothers who'd be there. Catherine, seeming to sense that her mother was upset, climbed onto her lap and Esther held her close. Soon, this little one would be starting school and then there'd be just April left at home. Catherine, who could never sit still for more than a minute, scrambled back down to the floor, and Esther sat for a while, thinking about her life. She and Harry were approaching middle age and where were they going from here? She was luckier than many, she knew that, but something was lacking and she had no idea what it was. It seemed that the business of being a woman, with all that it meant, was eating into her. Her childbearing days were, she hoped, over and she was thankful for that, as it meant that, once April went to school, she'd be free to do some of the things that she'd always wanted to do. But, she asked herself, what things? What time had she had since marrying Harry to think of what she wanted to do to follow her own interests, even if she'd had any? And why were women expected to give up everything when they married and had a family?

A knock at the front door brought her out of her mood of self-pity, and she opened it to find Phyllis on the doorstep. 'Thought I'd come over and see if you were all right,' she said, following Esther through to the living room. 'I saw them go.'

'I don't know how I'm going to cope with losing David as well as Alex,' Esther said, trying hard not to cry. She'd shed enough tears in recent years and didn't want to go down that path again.

'You haven't lost them,' Phyllis said. 'Most children leave home at some point and we just have to face up to it. But it doesn't mean they'll never come back. And David needed to sort himself out, as you well know.'

'You're right Phyllis. He's a strange boy is that one.'

'Young man,' Phyllis corrected.

Esther laughed. 'Of *course*, I keep forgetting he's eighteen, coming up nineteen. And I was married to Harry by the time I was that age.'

'Well there you go then,' said Phyllis. 'Now, are you going to make us a nice cup of tea or are you just going to sit there all day feeling sorry for yourself.'

'Do you ever feel that you're nothing but some kind of skivvy?' Esther said, as they drank their tea. 'You know what I mean. Never a single minute to call your own and always at the beck and call of everyone else?'

'Yes,' Phyllis said. 'I often feel like that. But that's the way it's always been, and will be until some clever woman stands up for the rest of us and changes things.'

'Will that ever happen, do you think?'

Phyllis stared into her teacup. It had already happened to some extent, with the Suffragettes but not a lot had changed for women, except they were now allowed the vote. 'Someday it will, I'm sure,' she said, 'but not in our time, so we'll just have to make the best of things as they are. Mind you, Jack has been bending over backwards to do things for me since the business of that other woman. He even washes the dishes for me now and again, and puts the washing out, although he won't go as far as hanging my smalls on the line.'

Esther laughed. 'I should think not,' she said.

Phyllis had always had the ability to cheer her up when she was down in the dumps and by the time Harry came home, she was feeling better. 'You should have seen Albert's car,' she said to him as they sat down to their meal. 'Real posh it is and must have cost a fortune.'

'Perhaps it's just as well I didn't,' Harry said. 'I'd have only been jealous, and it's not something we could ever afford to have.'

'One day perhaps?'

Harry shook his head. 'I shouldn't think it's likely,' he said.

It took a long time for Esther to get used to the idea that almost half her family were missing. She had to admit to herself that there was less to do. Less washing and ironing, less cooking and cleaning, but also less money. It had been bad enough when Alex left and his wages stopped but now that David no longer contributed to the costs of running the household, she had to be more careful how she spent Harry's hard-earned wages.

'Could you give me a bit more housekeeping money?' she said to him one Friday night after he'd handed over the usual two pounds, with which he expected her to pay for everything. 'With the boys' money no longer helping out, it's getting difficult to make ends meet.'

One of Harry's vices had always been a tendency to meanness with money and Esther had often wondered where, after he'd given her the housekeeping, the rest of his wages went each week. He didn't drink or go out, and only smoked a few Woodbines a day but whenever the subject of money came up, he either shut up like a clam or said there was no more in the pot.

'Maybe he's saving up for a rainy day,' Phyllis said once, when Esther had confided in her. 'Or perhaps he's going to take you on the Queen Mary for a cruise.'

Esther had laughed at the time but now it wasn't funny any more. 'I really do need more money Harry,' she said, hating having to demean herself by practically begging. 'The girls need new shoes, and the cost of food is going up all the time.'

'Sorry love, you'll have to make do,' he said, tucking the buff envelope containing the rest of his wages into his back pocket. 'Money doesn't grow on trees you know and you'll just have to cut down and make it stretch a bit further. Now, what's for me dinner?'

Esther lost her temper. 'You're just bloody mean,' she screamed at him. 'And all you ever think about is food, and never mind where the money's coming from to put it on the table.'

Harry winked. 'That's not the only think I think about,' he said, trying to humour her.

He caught hold of her hand but she snatched it away and went over to the dresser. She rarely lost her temper but when she did, it was like putting a match to dry tinder. 'Don't touch me,' she said, 'I'm not in the mood for your efforts to shut me up, so leave me alone.' The plate she threw at him smashed against the wall, missing his face by inches, the shattered fragments of white china landing at his feet.

He was across the room in two strides.'I've told you before about throwing things,' he shouted, taking hold of her wrists in a vice-like grip, 'and if you ever do it again, so help me, I'll give you the hiding of your life.'

She tore herself away and glared at him, her flashing, dark blue eyes stirring up the familiar feelings of his desire for her. 'You ever lay a hand on me, Harry Cartarett,' she said, 'and I'll ...'

'You'll do what?' He was laughing at her now and had to fight off the urge grab hold of her, carry her up to their bedroom and teach her a lesson.

If she hadn't felt so eaten up with rage at the injustice of it all, she probably would have laughed with him, and gone willingly with him to satisfy his needs. Instead, she stormed upstairs, slammed the bedroom door and stayed there until the sound of April crying forced her to move.

So incensed was she that she hardly slept a wink that night as, tossing and turning, while Harry snored gently at her side, she mulled over their conversation about money. It wasn't damned well fair that he should expect her to make ends meet on the lousy housekeeping he gave her. And what was he doing with whatever was left over from his wages? She knew he was well paid at the Dockyard, and couldn't see any reason why she shouldn't have a bit more to make life easier. Well, he'd soon laugh the other side of his face when she put less food on his plate and stopped making fancy puddings for him, like the spotted dick and custard he was so fond of. Maybe he'd sit up and take notice when he discovered that she wasn't the subservient little woman he'd always thought, and was quite capable of standing up for what she wanted.

The next morning she went shopping. 'Your usual order Mrs Cartarett?' the man behind the counter at the Co-op said, as she took a seat and handed over her order book.

'No Mr. Simms, I'm cutting down a bit this week. Just half of what I usually have will do thank you. And margarine instead of butter please.'

Mr. Simms raised his eyebrows. Half of what Mrs Cartarett normally had wouldn't feed a scarecrow but if that was what she wanted, so be it.

Esther's next call was at the butchers. 'A pound of scrag-end,' she said, 'and four of those beef sausages please.'

'Gone off the pork then Mrs Cartarett?' the butcher asked. She usually took a whole pound of his best pork sausages, and never bought scrag-end. Well, certainly hadn't since the days when she and Harry had lived hand to mouth in Wimple Street.

'No,' Esther said. 'Just cutting down, that's all.'

She finished her shopping, packed it all at the foot of April's pram, and went home where, after counting the money left in her purse, she discovered she'd only spent about half of what she usually did on a Saturday.

'What d'you call this?' Harry said, eyeing the solitary sausage and meagre pile of mashed potato on his plate. He'd just come in from work and was starving. 'Is this Edwin's plate or mine?'

'Yours,' Esther said, without batting an eyelid as she tucked into her own dinner.

Harry cleared his plate. 'What's for pud?' he said.

'There isn't any.'

'What did you say?'

Esther stood up and cleared the dirty plates from the table. 'I said there isn't any,' she repeated. 'I'm doing what you said I was to do, and cutting down.' She turned her back on him, afraid she was going to burst out laughing at the look on his face. Perhaps she was going too far in her bid for more housekeeping money. Still, if she didn't make a stand, there'd be no choice but to cut down anyway so she might as well see it through.

Harry thought she'd soon tire of her campaign but by the following Friday he'd had enough of coming home to half a plateful of dinner, no puddings, and margarine instead of butter. Even the sandwiches he took to work for his dinner break hadn't escaped. Instead of four slices of bread filled generously with cheese or ham, he had two slices spread with margarine and a thin layer of cheese, with not even a bit of pickle to give it some taste. And not a sign of a piece of fruit-cake either. He knew what she was up to and that he was beaten.

'All right,' he said on Thursday evening after sitting down to one egg, a spoonful of beans and half-a-dozen chips, 'you win. When I get my wages tomorrow, you can have an extra two shillings.'

'Three and sixpence,' Esther said.

Harry was exasperated. 'For God's sake woman,' he said, 'there's no satisfying you, is there.' He brought his fist down on the table. 'I'll give you your bloody three-and-sixpence, but I'll expect to see some decent food for that. And don't buy any more of those beef sausages either. They taste like someone's old boots. And I want butter on my bread in future, and Branson pickle on my sandwiches.'

'Thank you dear,' Esther said, smiling at him sweetly. 'And I've asked you *not* to call me "woman", haven't I.' It had taken all her willpower to go through the week seeing him go hungry but it was worth it if it had made him see sense.

When she told Phyllis what she'd done, they both laughed until the tears ran down their cheeks. 'Serves him right,' Phyllis said. 'Jack's always been generous with money and I don't know how you've put up with the pittance Harry's been giving you all this time.'

'Well,' Esther said, 'it just goes to show that standing up for our rights now and again, is worth it doesn't it. And that won't be the last time, either, although I'm not sure if I could go through all that again.

CHAPTER FOURTEEN

As the year wore on, speculation about King Edward VIII mounted, with everyone wondering when the Coronation was going to be. Esther, who was looking forward to being able to help with the street party this time, asked Harry if there'd been anything in the papers about it.

'Plenty,' Harry said. 'Edward VIII is involved with some woman who's about to divorce her second husband. The Prime Minister doesn't like it, nor does the Church of England, and it might be that he'll never be crowned after all.'

'What would happen then?' Esther wanted to know.

'I suppose he'd have to give up the throne to the next in line, his brother George,' Harry said.

Esther didn't understand any of it. It didn't matter to her if the new King wanted to marry a woman with two heads as long as there was a street party at the end of it. She was feeling much happier these days. Alex had sent just the one postcard from Malta to say that he was enjoying his life at sea and was going to apply for a Steward's post, and there was a cheerful letter from David.

"Dear Mum and Dad," he'd written,

I hope you are well. Auntie Frances says she's sorry we haven't been able to come and see you as promised but there is such a lot to be done. I love it here, although I miss your cooking Mum. Auntie Frances isn't a very good cook. She burns everything. I am sleeping in a caravan in the garden. I asked if I could have it for the summer and I've cleaned it up. It's like having my own home except that I eat with them of course. When it gets cold, I'll move back into the cottage, so don't worry. Uncle Albert has bought two greenhouses and we have been putting them up. He is going to grow flowers in them I think. There is a huge garden and he is going to keep chickens, and grow vegetables for sale. We haven't started to dig it as he says it's best to do that in September so that the frost can break up the earth. See, I am learning things already. There is a farm close by, and twice a day the farmer drives his cows down the lane to the milking sheds. I love to watch them go by. And you should see the foxgloves. They are everywhere. And the wild ponies in the New Forest. They come right up to you if they think you've something for them to eat. I am saving up to buy a camera. I have made a sort of friend. His name's Adrian and he's a bit younger than me. His father is a doctor in the village. That's all for now. I do miss you Mum but I am very happy here and hope to see you soon.

Your loving son David.

'I'm glad he's settled down,' Esther said to Harry, after showing him the letter. 'But I'm annoyed that, in two months, Albert and Frances haven't been able to spare the time to visit us. Especially as she promised they'd come down once a month.'

'Never mind love,' said Harry. 'As long as David is all right, it doesn't really matter, does it. And Albert must have a lot to do to get the place sorted out.'

Esther folded the letter in two and placed it in a drawer. 'I suppose so,' she said.

At the beginning of September, Catherine started school and she went quietly without any fuss when Esther left her making friends with another little girl. Phyllis had been looking after April and when Esther called to collect her, she sensed something was wrong. 'Whatever's the matter?' she said. 'You look as if you've lost a shilling and found tuppence. Is everything all right?'

Phyllis burst into tears. 'No,' she said, 'It's not. Oh, Esther, I don't know what to do.'

'What is it ?' Esther said.

Phyllis didn't answer for a minute. Then, 'I'm in the family way again,' she said, 'and I don't want it.'

'But I thought you and Jack didn't …' Esther began.

'We don't very often, that's the worst of it. It must have been a couple of months' back when he practically forced himself on me one night,' Frances said. 'I suppose I asked for it but now look at what's happened.'

'Well, it's not the end of the world.'

'I'm not going through with it Esther and that's that.'

Esther looked her friend straight in the eye. 'If you're thinking of doing something about it, *don't,*' she said. 'It's illegal, and dangerous.'

'I don't care. Jack and I don't get on any more and I'm not going to tie myself down again with another baby.' Phyllis reached into her apron pocket and pulled out a slip of paper. 'There's this woman,' she said, 'who's supposed to be very good. I'll go to her if I have to.'

Esther was horrified. 'Where did you get this from?' she said, handing it back.

'Oh, I've had it years. Someone gave it to me when we lived in Wimple Street, before I fell for Robert. I thought I was expecting at the time and we couldn't afford another one, but it turned out to be a false alarm in the end.'

'You'll die of blood poisoning or something.'

'No I won't. This woman's done hundreds and she's never killed anyone yet.'

Esther shook her head. *'Please* Phyllis,' she begged, 'don't do it. Not only is it dangerous but it's just not right to kill an unborn child. Not, that is, unless there's a very good reason.'

Phyllis jumped to her feet. 'Well,' she said, 'there's good enough reason for me not to bring another child into this house, believe me. And now, if you've finished preaching, I've things to do.'

'If only that bloody idiot Jack had listened to me and not told Phyllis about that woman,' Harry said, when later that evening Esther decided to tell him Phyllis's news. 'I knew it was a mistake and now look what's happened.'

'I think we should tell him what she plans to do,' Esther said.

'No.' Harry was insistent. 'If Phyllis is determined to go through with this, then it won't make a bit of difference, will it. It's none of our business and we should keep out of it.'

Esther didn't agree with that. If Jack knew what Phyllis was thinking of doing he might be able to persuade her to change her mind. But as Harry said, it was up to her and nothing to do with anyone else. All the same, Esther kept an eye on her friend over the next few days and, even though Phyllis was cool towards her, they still went shopping together, although neither of them mentioned the subject again.

It was in the middle of September that Phyllis finally plucked up the courage to visit the run-down home of the back street abortionist, after slipping away unseen by Esther who, she knew, had been watching her like a hawk. To avoid arousing Esther's suspicions, she took Sarah with her, hoping there'd be someone to keep an eye on her. The hardest part had been finding the ten shillings the woman wanted and she'd had to miss a week's rent in order to rid herself of this unwanted burden.

It was a seedy little house with tattered curtains, and dust and dog hairs everywhere. A young girl of about fourteen, who could have done with a good wash, showed her into the parlour. 'Mum won't be a minute,'she said, scratching her head, 'she's gorn to the lav.'

I hope she washes her hands afterwards, Phyllis thought to herself, parking Sarah's pushchair under the stairs in the hallway.

The procedure took about twenty minutes during which time the young girl watched everything that went on. 'Have a lie down when you get 'ome,' the woman, whose name Phyllis wasn't allowed to know, said. 'An' don't lift anythin' 'eavy for a few days.'

Phyllis set out for Kestrel Road and by the time she reached home, she was feeling faint. She'd lost a lot of blood which, the woman had said, was quite normal, and all she wanted was to sit down with a cup of tea and try to forget about what she'd done. If Jack ever found out, then that would be the end of everything between them, she knew that. Men were funny about things like abortions. It's all very well for them, she thought, they don't have to put up with the endless work and worry of looking after children, especially when, in her case, there were already four to cope with. She made herself some tea, gave Sarah her lunch then dropped exhausted into a chair.

The following morning, Esther was getting breakfast when she heard a knock on the front door. She immediately thought something had happened to Harry, but when she opened it, Robert was standing on the step in his underclothes crying his eyes out. She pulled him inside. 'Whatever's the matter?' she said, knowing it must be something to do with Phyllis.

'It's Mum,' Robert said, shivering with the cold. 'She's ill. Please could you come over?'

Esther dashed back upstairs to ask Edwin to look after April then ran across the road with Robert. Jack and the other two boys had gone to work, Sarah was standing up in her bed screaming the place down and Phyllis, her face scarlet and wet with perspiration was thrashing about in the bed like someone in a fit.

'Oh, my God, what have you done?' It was a stupid question. Esther knew exactly what her friend had done. 'Put something warm on,' she shouted to Robert who was trembling with fear outside the bedroom door, 'and run to the Police station and ask them to fetch an ambulance. Tell them where your Dad works and that he's needed at home.' She ran downstairs to the kitchen, drew off some water into a bowl and searched around for something with which to bathe Phyllis's face.

By now, Phyllis was delirious and calling out for Jack. Esther dampened a flannel she'd found and sat wiping the beads of perspiration from her friend's burning hot face. When Robert came back with the message that an ambulance was on its way, she sent him downstairs to get something to eat for Sarah. 'Anything will do,' she said. 'A Farley's Rusk or something. Whatever you can find, and you'd better get something for yourself and then get ready for school.'

The ambulance arrived within ten minutes and the driver took one look at Phyllis, who was by now losing consciousness. 'Gawd Missus,' he said to Esther. 'She's in a bad way.' He and another man lifted her gently onto a stretcher and took her away to the Isolation Hospital in Milton Road. As Esther stood on the pavement watching the ambulance out of sight, she shivered, certain that Phyllis was going to die, and all because of some dirty woman whose business it was to make money out of the desperation of others.

Esther took Edwin and Catherine to school, but Robert refused to go. He wanted to stay with Sarah, he said, and wait until his father came home so that he could explain what had happened.

For three days, Phyllis hovered between life and death. The hospital put her on the Danger List and allowed Jack to go in to see her at any time, although they banned all other visitors. He slipped away from the dairy whenever he could, to stay a few moments with her, and spent every evening at her bedside until late into the night.

With Esther's help, Robert and his two brothers looked after everything, and she thought how much the older two had changed since moving away from Wimple Street. Luke was now seventeen, and had moved on from being a delivery boy to work behind the counter at the Co-op in Southsea. He'd never given Jack and Phyllis a moment's trouble since leaving school and neither had sixteen-year-old Terry who had found a job at a local bakery where he was learning how to make bread and fancy cakes. If only Jack had kept quiet about his affair, everything would have been perfect for him and Phyllis. Now it looked as if he was about to lose his wife, and the children their mother.

It was almost a week before Phyllis began to show signs of recovery. 'It's a miracle,' the Ward Sister told Jack when, on one of his evening visits, Phyllis opened her eyes and spoke to him. 'Septicaemia was what she had, and we all know what caused it.' She straightened Phyllis's bedcovers. 'I'd like to see these back-street abortionists shut up in prison for a very long time. The damage they do is appalling.'

147

Jack looked at her in amazement. No one had told him the reason for is wife's sudden brush with death, Esther having decided not to say anything about it. All he'd been told was that she had blood-poisoning, but he knew nothing about any abortion. Phyllis hadn't said a word to him about another baby on the way. 'Why didn't someone tell me?' he said. 'I had no idea.'

'I'm sorry Mr. Martindale,' the Sister said, 'we were all too busy trying to save your wife's life to wonder whether or not you knew what she had done.'

'Yes, of course Sister,' Jack said. 'And I'm very grateful for what you've all done believe me, but I knew nothing about her condition. If I had, I would never have allowed her to do what she did.'

'Well, she'll need a lot of looking after for a while, and what she won't need is anyone telling her what a wicked person she is to have done such a thing.'

After a week, Phyllis was off the Danger List, which meant that Esther could visit for an hour in the afternoons. After that, she was allowed to get out of bed and walk up and down the ward to get her strength back, but it was another week before she was able to go home. Esther didn't mention the abortion, having been asked by Jack not to say anything about it at all. 'It's best not talked about,' he said. 'It's all my bloody fault anyway. If I hadn't done what I did, then none of this would've happened and I'll never forgive myself for what she's been through because of it.

Esther didn't know exactly what Jack was blaming himself for; having an affair in the first place, or being daft enough to tell Phyllis about it. 'Well,' she said, 'she's on the mend now and the best thing you both can do is to put it all behind you and start afresh.' My God, she thought to herself, I sound just like one of those busybodies in the women's magazines, who are paid too much money for telling other people how to run their lives.

'We can only try,' Jack said without conviction.

Towards the end of the year, stories regarding the King and his mistress had spread worldwide. No one seemed to know what was happening, and the papers were full of wild rumours about his affair with Mrs Wallis Simpson. The Government, the Head of the Church of England, and the General Public were against any marriage between the couple, mainly because she was a divorcee twice over and considered unfit to become Queen. Finally, by the 10th of December, and under pressure from the Prime Minister, King Edward VIII had decided to abdicate. The following day he made a speech on worldwide radio announcing his reasons for discharging his duties to the throne and naming his brother George as the new King of England.

'Thank goodness for that,' Esther said to Harry, after listening to the abdication speech on the wireless. 'Now, perhaps we can organise a street party.'

Harry laughed. 'You and your street party,' he said. 'That's all you've been thinking about since the old King died.'

'Not the only thing,' Esther said.

'What else then?'

'This.' She handed him a letter. 'It's from Frances.'

He read the hastily scrawled pages then handed it back. 'So, she wants us to go down to the New Forest for Christmas,' he said. 'Would you like to? That's if we can find the ways and means of getting there.'

Esther was emphatic. 'No, I do *not* want to spend Christmas in the New Forest,' she said. 'I want to spend it here, in our own home.' She poked the fire angrily. 'We've seen neither hide nor hair of Albert, Frances or our David since they went last May and I don't see why we should traipse all the way down there to see them. They've a car, and we haven't.' She swallowed on the lump that had come up in her throat, and stabbed viciously at the dying embers of the fire. 'No, I won't go and that's that.'

'You'll poke that thing through into next door if you're not careful,' Harry said, taking the poker from her and laying it on the hearth. 'Don't get yourself all upset about it. David does write every week after all and things for Albert have turned out differently from what he expected. They just haven't had time to visit us.'

'All the same, I'm staying here,' Esther said, clamping her lips firmly together, which meant the subject was closed.

Later, as she lay in the big double bed listening to Harry snoring gently, she reflected on the last few months. She still missed David, and looked forward every week to his letters, which were always cheerful and full of the things he'd been doing. He and Albert had dug the plot over for the winter and David couldn't wait for the spring when they'd be able to start growing things. It was hard work but he loved it. They had fixed up some heating in the new greenhouse and David had been sowing some early vegetable seeds into boxes. He was still friends with the Doctor's son, who had offered to teach him to fish in the local river once the season started. In his letters, he always said that he loved his mother and was looking forward to visiting as soon as it was possible, but nothing ever came of it and Esther had to accept that he was growing away from his own family. As for Alex, she'd no idea where he was. A couple of postcards during the year to say he was well and having a good time, and that was it.

She slipped out of bed, put a cardigan on over her nightdress and went downstairs to make herself a cup of tea, and as she was passing the landing window, she looked across the road and noticed a light on in Phyllis's house. Poor Phyllis was taking such a long time to recover, both physically and emotionally, from her ordeal. No one had ever dared mention the abortion, although sometimes Esther felt that it might have been better if Phyllis could have talked about it to get it out of her system. But Jack, who had kept his own feelings on the matter to himself, had been adamant that he didn't want any discussions on the subject. 'She'll get over it in her own time, without anyone delving into the whys and wherefores,' he'd said. 'There's no point in holding an inquest on what's over and done with.'

Esther wrote back to Frances, thanking her for asking them down but saying that she wanted to stay at home for Christmas for the sake of the children. It wasn't much of an excuse but brought forth a response from David which cheered her up no end. In his next letter, he said that as they couldn't visit the New Forest, he'd decided to come home for Christmas. Uncle Albert would drive him to Southampton and there were plenty of trains from there so, all being well, he'd see them on the twenty-third. And to add to Esther's joy, there was a postcard from Alex to say that he couldn't make Christmas but would be home for the New Year. She breathed a sigh of relief that the two of them wouldn't be home at the same time.

She spent the next couple of weeks in a frenzy of planning, icing the cake she'd already made, wrapping presents and, with the help of Edwin and Catherine, making paper chains for the sitting room, although she decided to wait until David was home before decorating the tree Harry had bought. She couldn't remember being so excited and, in the end, Harry had to force her to stop for a rest.

'You won't be fit for anything if you carry on like this,' he said. 'Sit down for five minutes and have a breather.'

David arrived just after midday on the twenty-third, and Esther couldn't believe the change in him. In just a few months, he'd grown taller and filled out. His face was brown with working in the open air so much, and even his voice had deepened. Her favourite son had grown up. She gave him a hug.

'It's lovely to see you David,' she said, close to tears. 'You look well.'

'And you Mum,' he said, patting the top of her head. 'I'm taller than you now.'

She laughed. 'So you are. Makes me feel quite old, it does.'

He looked around the room. 'Where are the others?'

'April is asleep in her pram in the hall, and Edwin and Catherine are still at school. They break up today and I'll be going to fetch them shortly. Meantime, I've saved you some dinner, and when you've eaten, you can tell me all about life in the New Forest.'

Esther thought it was the best Christmas she had ever known. Frances had sent some pies filled with fruit from the orchard, a hock of cooked ham, and a bag of apples. 'She'd have sent more if I'd been able to carry it,' David said, as he unloaded it all onto the kitchen table. Harry had bought a Turkey and two bottles of white wine to go with it, and Esther wondered where the money had come from to pay for it all, but didn't spoil the surprise by saying anything.

The meal was perfect, and as David mopped up his gravy, he made them all laugh with stories about Frances's attempts at cooking. 'Everything gets burnt,' he said. 'She puts things in the oven and forgets about them. Uncle Albert goes mad at the waste of good food, although we usually manage to eat most of it.' He caught the look on his father's face. 'Oh, she won't mind me telling you,' he said. 'It's a family joke.'

Esther cleared the dinner table, Harry fell asleep in his chair, and Edwin and Catherine, having already tired of their new toys, had a fight. She asked David to keep an eye on them and April, while she popped across the road to see Phyllis.

'Am I glad to see you,' Phyllis said, as she let Esther in through the front door. 'Jack bought Robert a train set for Christmas and you'd think he'd meant it for himself. Poor Rob hasn't had a look in yet, and the other two haven't stopped arguing over how it should be set up. I could do with a bit of female company.' She lifted Sarah from the floor. 'Let's go in the front room out of it,' she said.

Esther had found it difficult these past few weeks to find something to talk about without asking Phyllis how she was feeling or how things were between her and Jack. 'What do you think of the abdication?' she said, searching for something to say.

'Look Esther,' Phyllis said, 'I'm sorry if you feel awkward but never mind about what Jack says, if you want to know how things are, ask me and I'll tell you. As for the abdication, I couldn't care less if they crown King Canute at the moment.'

'All right then, how *are* things with you and Jack?'

'A bit chilly.' Phyllis replied. 'I think he feels guilty and blames himself for what happened to me, but on the other hand, he can't accept that I went ahead without telling him and got rid of our baby. He seems to think I did it to get my own back, which of course, isn't true.'

'So what are you going to do about it?'

Phyllis sighed. 'I honestly don't know. He's told me how he feels about it, but won't discuss it any further. I suppose we'll just have to carry on as best we can. We can't afford to divorce, or even separate so there's not much we *can* do, is there.'

Esther was shocked to hear the word "divorce" mentioned. She hadn't realised things were that bad. 'You still love each other, don't you,' she said.

'Well, I still love Jack but how he feels about me is anyone's guess.'

'I'm sure he does,' Esther said. 'It will just take time, that's all.'

'Do you really think so?' Phyllis said, doubtfully.

David went back to the New Forest the day after Boxing Day with a promise to visit again as soon as he could get away. 'It's coming up to a busy time,' he said, as Esther and the younger children walked with him to Fratton station. She thought how grown-up he sounded, although during his stay over Christmas, she realised that he was still the same David ... quiet, and moody, with a tendency to shut himself away in his old room with the carpentry books he'd left behind. He and Harry hadn't said much to one another all through the holiday, and Esther sensed a bit of tension in the air between them, although why that was she'd no idea.

The massive engine let off an ear-splitting jet of sooty smelling steam as it heaved itself out of the station, and Esther and the children waved to David, who was hanging out of a window, until he and the train disappeared from view. Her heart felt like a lump of lead in her chest but she turned April's pram around, and with Edwin and Catherine trotting alongside, marched resolutely towards home.

Alex arrived home on New Year's Eve, breezing in like a breath of fresh air. He hugged Esther. 'Here I am again, Mum,' he said. 'Your prodigal son returns to the fold.'

She laughed, wondering why it was that her two eldest living sons, born just a year apart, were so different from each other, both in looks and temperament. She looked up at him and smiled. 'If you get any taller,' she said, 'we'll have to alter all the doors in this house.'

Harry, who was in the kitchen mending a pair of his boots, stuck his head round the door. 'Hello, son,' he said, between a mouthful of nails, 'be with you in a minute.' If he had been happy to see David go back to the New Forest, he was even happier to see Alex come home. There was something about his eldest son that he didn't like very much but couldn't quite work out, and even though Alex had been a bit of a problem in the past, he was by far the easiest to get along with.

Esther had kept Alex a dinner and when he'd finished, and the others were in bed, he told her and Harry about his latest voyage, which was not so very different from the last one except that he'd applied to train as a Steward. 'I don't know whether I'll be accepted,' he said, 'but I love the sea, and can't think of anythin' I'd rather be doing. An' Stewards earn good money, what with tips an' things.'

'That's good,' Harry said, secretly wondering what would happen to Alex if, as everyone seemed to think, there was going to be another war. During the last lot, the Government had requisitioned most of the liners for use as hospital or troop ships.

As if reading his father's mind, Alex said that rumours were flying all over the place about the possibility of another war, and that his ship would be among those that would have to be used as part of a convoy escorting troopships to wherever they were needed. 'So if it comes, then I'll be right in it from the beginning,' he said.

'I don't believe all this nonsense about Hitler, and what he's doing,' Esther said. 'It's all a lot of war mongering, if you ask me.'

Alex and Harry exchanged looks. 'We'll see Mum,' Alex said.

They talked between themselves for the remainder of the evening until Harry glanced at the clock on the mantelpiece. 'It's almost twelve o'clock,' he said, leaving his chair to pour each of them a drink of the wine left over from Christmas. 'Nearly nineteen thirty-seven, and what a lot has happened over the last twelve months. Two of our children flown the nest, one King dead and another given up the throne. Still Esther, you'll get your street party at last.' As the clock struck twelve, the three of them raised their glasses. 'Happy New Year,' they each said in unison, with Harry adding a silent wish of his own that the rumours of another war would turn out to be just that ... rumours, although he had his doubts.

CHAPTER FIFTEEN

'I've written to your Mum and Dad inviting them to stay with us for a few days,' Frances said to David one morning towards the end of March. 'The change will do them all good so I hope that this time they'll be able to come.'

David treated his Auntie to one of his rare smiles. 'I hope so too, Auntie,' he said, 'because we are going to be so busy over the next few months that I won't be able to leave Uncle Albert to do everything on his own, and I know Mum misses you.'

'Yes, I know she does. And I feel so awful that we haven't been to see your family in all the ten months we've been here.'

'Oh, I expect Mum understands,' said David.

Frances walked down to the village to post the letter. Although not regretting the move to the New Forest, she missed popping in and out of her brother's house, and missed the children more than she cared to admit. This was a lovely place to live, but since they'd moved, she had never made any close friends. She wasn't a church-going woman, and the few social events in the village seemed geared towards those who belonged either to that, or some club or other, which she'd neither the time nor the inclination to join. Albert and David spent most of their time outdoors, setting up the smallholding, and Albert had promised that once they'd got it going, he'd be free to spend more time with her, although when that would be, he'd no idea.

As she crossed the road to the Post Office, it came to her that she was lonely. Surely, she thought, Harry and Esther would come this time if only out of curiosity to see Riverside Cottage, and of course, their son. It surprised her, the way in which David had settled into his new life away from home. First up every morning, he couldn't wait to get out into the fresh air and start work on the land.

'It seems he was born to it,' Albert said, one evening when David had gone over to see Adrian, and he and Frances were enjoying a cup of tea after their meal. 'I hardly have to tell him what to do next and he's been a great help in getting things going.'

'He's like his father,' Frances replied. 'Harry could never bear to be shut indoors, which is why he didn't do what Mother wanted him to and study for what she always called "a respectable profession".'

'I'm glad that we brought David with us,' Albert said, 'for I don't know what I would have done without him.'

When Esther received the letter, she didn't know whether to feel angry that Albert and Frances *still* wouldn't be coming to Portsmouth, or pleased to have the chance to see where David was living. She no longer worried about him and he'd written so much about his new life in the New Forest that she couldn't wait to see for herself.

'We *can* go, can't we?' she said to Harry as soon as he came in from work.

'You've changed your tune a bit,' he said. 'Last time we had an invitation, you were quite determined not to go.'

Her face fell. 'But that was Christmas.'

'And this time it will be Easter.'

'Oh *please* let's go Harry,' she begged. 'It will be so lovely for the little ones to see their Auntie Frances again, and you and I need a change.'

He folded the letter and handed it back to her. 'All right. Write back and tell Frances we'll come. But I warn you Esther, no matter how much you fall in love with the New Forest, it'll be no use you asking if we can move there.'

'Don't be daft,' she said. 'I'm happy here, with you and the children and wouldn't want to live anywhere else.'

Since Harry had given her a rise in her housekeeping, she had managed to save a few shillings, which she kept in an old tin on the top shelf of the larder. At the end of each week, however much was left of her housekeeping money, she put away, although Harry knew nothing about this. She took the tin down and had a look to see how much was in it. Ten shillings and sixpence; enough to buy some chocolates for Frances, a pair of white ankle socks for Catherine, and a straw Easter Bonnet for her and April. She felt quite pleased with herself although Harry had never really forgiven her for what he said was nothing more than blackmail.

She wrote back to Frances and told her they'd visit over the Easter.

"It's Good Friday on April 7th," she wrote, "so Harry thought we'd come down the day before. He's allowed some holiday time so we could stay until the Tuesday if that's all right with you. It will be lovely to see you all again. The little ones have missed their Auntie Frances.

They decided to walk to Fratton Station. Harry carried April on his shoulders, Edwin and Esther between them, managed the two small cases borrowed from Phyllis, and containing all they would need for the holiday and Catherine trotted alongside with a bag of toys. They were to catch the train to Southampton to meet Albert who would take them to Riverside Cottage in his car. It took over an hour from Southampton to reach the cottage, during which time Albert had to stop twice for Catherine who was car sick, and for Edwin to relieve himself. Esther, with a fretful April on her lap, was almost fainting with the heat by the time they arrived, to find Frances hanging over the garden gate waiting for them. There was no sign of David.

'He's gone over to see his friend Adrian,' she told Esther when she asked where he was. 'He said he'd be back before you arrived but when those two get together they forget the time of day.'

Esther was annoyed but not wanting to start off on the wrong foot, asked if she could see over the cottage. She loved it, except, as she said to Harry later, for the low, beamed ceilings and tiny windows which made her feel shut-in. 'It's a lovely place,' she said to him, 'but I don't think I'd like to live in it, would you?'

'No,' he said, 'and I'm pleased to hear it.'

David arrived just as Frances was getting the tea ready. He said he was sorry for being late, gave Esther a hug, had words with the children then went out into the garden where Albert was showing Harry the greenhouses.

'Don't mind David too much,' Frances said, seeing the look on Esther's face when he disappeared. 'He's always outside doing something or other. Never wants to be indoors. To be honest, I don't know how we'd have managed without him.'

'Does he have a girl friend?' Esther wanted to know.

'I don't think so. He spends all of his spare time with Adrian. They go fishing quite a lot during the season, or looking for butterflies.'

'Is he all right … this Adrian?'

Frances could almost read what was going through Esther's mind. 'Now, if you think there's anything "funny" about those two young men, then forget it,' she said. 'I remember you telling me a couple of years' back, how worried you were about David and the names the men were calling him at work. Well, there was no truth in it then and there isn't now, so you can stop fretting and eat your tea.' She put the kettle on and asked Esther to call everyone in to sit at the table.

Esther couldn't believe her eyes when, once the meal was finished, David cleared the table and did the washing up. 'However did you manage to get him to do that?' she asked.

'Easy,' Frances said. 'I just told him that if he wanted to live with Albert and me, then he'd have to do his share in the house. And when he said that he'd never had to do things like that at home, I offered to let Albert take him to Southampton to catch the train back to Portsmouth.'

Esther laughed. She envied Frances her modern way of thinking. There was no man on earth who would treat *her* like a skivvy and get away with it. Albert had always done his share in the house even though he'd never allowed Frances to find a job and she was there all day, with plenty of time to do everything herself. 'Albert thinks,' she'd once told Esther, 'that most women get a bit of a raw deal, and he doesn't see why they should act like unpaid servants and have to do everything.' Esther had told her how lucky she was.

'Are you having any street parties in the village, for the Coronation?'

'Yes,' Frances said. 'Well, not street parties exactly. I believe there's going to be one big "Do" on the village green. I haven't been asked to help yet, but it's a bit too soon.'

Esther sensed a note of sadness in her sister-in-law's voice. 'Are you happy living here?' she said.

'Oh, yes,' Frances replied, 'it's lovely, but I don't seem to fit in very well with the locals. And of course I miss you and the children.'

'It's a bit primitive,' Esther said. 'You know, the lav having to be emptied every day, and no gas or electric. Not a bit what you're used to, is it.'

'No,' Frances agreed, 'but Albert says that when the smallholding starts to pay its way, we'll be able to afford to have the cottage modernised, although I don't know about running water and the like. Still, we may be able to get electricity put in.

'I hope so,' Esther said.

On Good Friday, when they had all recovered from the journey the day before, Albert and Frances took them for walk through the forest where Edwin and Catherine fed the wild ponies, climbed trees and gathered some wild flowers to give to their Auntie Frances. It's an idyllic place for children, Esther thought, although she still wouldn't swap her modern house for the cottage with its oil lamps for lighting, its well water and its lavatory, which was in a shed in the garden and had to be emptied into a pit every day. Only someone like Albert could deal with that.

David showed his mother the caravan he'd made into a place of his own, and she was surprised at how clean and tidy it was. 'I'll sleep in the cottage when it's winter,' he said, 'so you don't have to worry about me catching a cold or anything.'

Esther asked whether he and his friend Adrian ever went out with girls.

'No. Mum,' he said, 'Adrian's too busy with his studies and I have too much to do here to help Uncle Albert.' He gave Esther a puzzled look. 'Girls are a nuisance anyway,' he added.

'What is he studying for?' Esther asked. 'Is he going to be a Doctor, like his father?'

'Yes, he'll be going to Medical School soon to train.'

'Well, I'd like to meet him before we go home on Tuesday,' Esther said. 'Could you bring him round here do you think? I'm sure Auntie Frances wouldn't mind.'

'I'll see,' David said. 'And Auntie Frances won't mind a bit. She makes Adrian welcome when he comes here, and she doesn't ask as many questions as you either.'

Adrian didn't put in an appearance until about an hour before Harry and Esther were due to leave for Southampton with Albert on Tuesday morning. Esther spotted him when she was in the bedroom tidying up and he walked past the window and round the side of the cottage. She saw him tap at the open kitchen door and walk in, just as if he'd lived here all his life. She left what she was doing and went through to the living room where he was sitting in Albert's armchair talking to David.

'Ah,' David said, 'this is Adrian, Mum.'

The young man stood up and shook hands. He was tall, blonde and very handsome and just a bit too smooth for Esther, who was used to the men in her life being just a bit, well ... *unpolished.* 'Lovely to meet you Mrs Cartarett,' he said.

'And you Adrian. We, that is, David's Dad and I, have heard such a lot about you.'

Adrian smiled. 'And David has told me all about you.'

Esther took an instant dislike to him. For a start, he was far too self-assured for a seventeen-year-old, and she didn't like the way he looked down at her. What had happened to David that he should have chosen for a friend, someone so different from that of his own class?

'I'm afraid we're just off home,' she said, trying not to sound like the disapproving mother she was. 'Perhaps we'll see you again next time we come down.'

'I shall look forward to that,' said Adrian, sounding more like a thirty-year-old than someone not long out of nappies, she thought.

They were on the train before she had the opportunity of talking to Harry about their son's friend. 'Pity you didn't meet him,' she said.

'I did,' Harry replied. 'I was in the garden with Albert when he came round to see where David was, and Albert introduced us. Quite a pleasant young man, I thought.'

'Well, I didn't like him one little bit,' Esther said. 'He's far too big for his boots.'

Harry laughed. 'There isn't a young man or woman on this earth who'd be good enough for *your* boys. Come on, admit it.'

'All right, have it your own way,' Esther said, 'but this Adrian's not suitable for our David. They're different as chalk and cheese, and I don't want to see David getting big ideas above his station.'

'David can look after himself,' was Harry's only comment.

After his family and Adrian had left, David went for a walk in the forest to clear his head. His thoughts, as he wandered through the narrow pathways between the trees, centred on his mother. She didn't like Adrian, he could tell. She was a strange woman sometimes, and he'd often thought she was gifted with some kind of mystical power that enabled her to read other people's minds and see things there that others couldn't. Not that he cared whether she liked Adrian or not. It didn't matter to David one bit. Adrian was his friend and nothing was going to change that, and in any case, he, David, would soon be twenty and was old enough to make his own mind up about who he wanted as a friend. He was troubled to think that maybe she'd sensed what appeared to be an *attraction* he felt for Adrian which was more than just liking him, and a feeling he'd never experienced for anyone else. To him, happiness was just being with his friend. He'd told no one of this yet and as nothing other than some playful sparring had happened between the two young men, David had, until now, felt it best not to say anything. All the same, he couldn't stop thinking about the name-calling at Dangerfield's and wondered if those men had been right about him all along.

There had been times recently when he'd awoken to the early morning depression of a year ago, although nowhere nearly as often as in the past, and today, as he walked back to Riverside Cottage, he made up his mind to speak to Albert about his problems. There was no one else he could turn to. Adrian's own father, in his capacity as a Doctor, would probably have been the best man to approach but, because he *was* Adrian's father, that would be out of the question.

Albert was in the greenhouse when David returned. 'Ah,' Albert said, 'I wondered where you'd got to. I need some fertilizer. D'you fancy a walk as far as the village?'

'Could I to talk to you about something first, Uncle Albert,' David said, not wanting a couple of bags of fertilizer to get in the way of his resolution.

Albert looked at his pocket watch. 'Plenty of time,' he said, 'the shop doesn't shut until five o'clock. And now that you're nearly twenty, David, why don't you drop the Uncle bit and call me Albert.' He sat down on an upturned wooden box. 'So, what is it you want to talk about?'

David was surprised how easy it was to talk to his uncle. He went right back to the night he'd gone to the Mission Hall and met up with Belle Summerford, the name-calling he'd had to put up with at Dangerfield's, and the dates he'd had with Sally Totter. 'I just don't seem to like girls, uncle,' he said, 'and some of the men at Dangerfield's said I was a Nancy Boy. I didn't know then what it meant but I do now.' His face reddened as he stumbled over the next few words. 'I ... I think they may have been right.' He went on to try to describe his feelings for Adrian but it was difficult to put into words, although Albert seemed to understand.

'So,' Albert said when David had finished, 'you think the way you feel about your friend is wrong. Is that it?'

'Yes.'

'Have you said anything to him?'

'No, I haven't.'

Albert scratched his head. Never having had any children of his own, he was a bit out of his depth here. He'd always known David was a bit of a strange lad but this was something which could have serious consequences. 'I think,' he said, 'that you're worrying about nothing. Put it this way. You came down here to live, away from all your friends.'

'I didn't have any friends.'

'Well then, away from everyone you knew. And you met up with Adrian and the two of you get along well together. Now what is wrong with that?'

David shrugged. 'I don't know.'

'There's *nothing* wrong with it,' Albert said, 'but I think I should tell you that, even if you're right about your feelings, there's nothing you can do about them. Loving someone of your own sex is illegal and you would be in a lot of trouble if you broke the law. Did you ever hear about a man called Oscar Wilde? He ended up in prison because of his love for his friend, who also happened to be a man.'

'So, what should I do?'

Albert smiled as he recalled his own youth. 'Although there were some lads who had what we called a "crush" on one or other of the Masters at school, most of us spent our spare time chasing the girls,' he said. 'The best thing you can do to get over this infatuation, for that's what it is, is to find yourself a nice young girl to go about with. Or better still, *two* young girls ... one for you and the other for Adrian.'

'He won't be here much longer,' said David. 'He's going to Medical School soon to start training to be a doctor, like his father. And I don't seem to get on with girls.'

'Ah,' Albert said, 'that's because you haven't met the right one yet. It'll be different when you do. And if Adrian's going away, then the problem is solved, isn't it.'

'No, it isn't,' David said miserably. 'I don't know what I'll do with myself when he's gone.'

'I shall keep you so busy working for me,' said Albert, 'that you won't have time to fret about him. Now, let's get going for that fertilizer, shall we.'

'You won't say anything to Frances, will you,' David said as the two of them, walked towards the village, along the towpath by the river. 'I don't want her to know.'

'Of course I won't,' Albert said. 'I'll not tell anyone.'

Esther was glad to be home at last. It had been a lovely change to see Albert and Frances again and, of course, David but there was no place like your own home. Among the letters on the doormat was a card from Alex to say that he would be home for the Coronation of King George VI, and that he had some good news to tell them. After dinner, she took the suitcases back to Phyllis. 'It's lovely to be home,' she said.

'Nice to have you back,' said Phyllis. 'I missed you all. What was it like?'

'It was all right,' Esther said, 'but I wouldn't want to live there myself. Frances seemed rather lonely I thought. Even after a year, she hasn't made any real friends, and Albert's always busy. They never go anywhere and I think she was glad of some company.'

'And David?'

'He's just the same as ever. Quiet, moody, and he still hasn't grown up. He's made friends with this Adrian, the local Doctor's son but I wasn't keen on him. Nice looking young man, but not David's type at all. And I think David spends far too much time with him. He should be looking at girls now that he's nineteen, and I sometimes wonder if there was any truth in the names the men at Dangerfield's used to call him.'

'*Esther*, that's a terrible thing to say of your own son'.

'I know,' said Esther, 'and I just hope my suspicions are wrong. Harry would disown him if he turned out to be one of *those*.' The subject turned to the street party. 'By the way,' she said, 'Alex'll be home in time for the party if you need a hand with anything, and I'll be able to help this time around.' Her eyes took on a glazed look. 'It doesn't seem five minutes' since the last one.'

'Two years almost to the day,' said Phyllis.

Alex arrived home the day before the party. Esther was in the kitchen cleaning the vegetables for dinner when she heard the back door open and in he walked. She swung round and her mouth dropped open in surprise at the sight that met her eyes. There he was, this handsome young son of hers, standing with his arms folded, a great big grin on his face, all dressed up in the uniform of a ship's Steward. She wiped her hands in her apron. 'Oh my God,' she said, flinging her arms around him, 'just *look* at you.'

'Hello Mum,' he smiled down at her. 'How d'you like the uniform?'

She swallowed hard on the lump in her throat. 'You little devil you,' she said. 'You didn't let us know you'd been made a Steward, did you.'

'I wanted it to be a surprise,' he said.

She held him at arms' length. 'Well, it's certainly that. And you look very smart I must say. How long are you home for this time?'

'Five days.'

'Your Dad will be pleased to see you. He'll be in shortly.' She gave him another hug. 'Would you go and say "hello" to Edwin and the little ones. They've been looking forward to you coming home. And your old bedroom's ready if you want to take your stuff upstairs.'

Alex went through to see the children, then up to the room he used to share with David. It seemed strange to be in a proper bedroom after the cramped cabin he had to share on board ship with two other Stewards. He unpacked his case and was about to change into his civilian clothes when Esther called up the stairs. 'Don't get out of your uniform yet Alex,' she said. 'Let your Dad see you in it first.'

Harry could hardly believe that the tall, good-looking young man in uniform was his own son. 'Sea life suits you,' he said. 'And congratulations on your promotion.'

'Thanks Dad. Can I now go back upstairs and change into me civvies?'

After the children had gone to bed, Alex settled down with Harry and Esther and told them about his new job. 'I'm on the Queen Mary now,' he said, 'and it's much better, except that it goes to America and not India, an' I used to enjoy that trip. It gets full of rich an' famous people an' I've met quite a few film stars and sportsmen. Most of them give good tips so I've bin able to put some money aside.' He reached in his trouser pocket and pulled out a wad of bank notes. 'Here you are Mum,' he said, 'take it towards me keep while I'm home. An' buy an ounce of baccy or some Woodbines for Dad when you go shopping.'

'You don't have to,' Esther said.

Alex pressed the money into her hand. 'I know that, but I want you to have it,' he said. 'Now what about this party tomorrow?'

They were all up early to put up the flags and set the tables, just as they had two years' before for the Jubilee, only this time it was Alex helping instead of David. And as before, once the children had eaten, and played their games, they were all put to bed and the adults had their bit of fun. Neither Harry nor Jack could dance a step so Esther and Phyllis sat on the side and watched the others enjoying themselves.

'Who's that girl your Alex's been dancing with all evening?' Phyllis asked, pointing to him and a young woman with long, blonde hair who was resting her head on his shoulder as they smooched to a waltz.

'Blowed if I know,' said Esther. 'She lives along here somewhere I think as I've seen her flying by on a bicycle first thing in the morning. They're getting pretty close together by the looks of it. And I didn't know our Alex could dance.'

'I think,' said Phyllis,' that Stewards on board ship are expected to be able to dance with the passengers if asked. These luxury liners are usually full of lonely, rich old ladies, who like to be seen in the arms of handsome young men like Alex.'

'As long as they keep their hands off my son,' Esther said. 'Hey, look, he's bringing her over to meet us.'

'Mum, this is Barbara Tracey,' Alex said. 'She lives at number eighty, right up the top of the road.'

Esther smiled at the young girl on Alex's arm. She looked a decent sort, and Alex seemed taken with her. 'Pleased to meet you Mrs Cartarett,' Barbara said.

'And this is Mum's friend Mrs Martindale who lives opposite.' Alex was all smiles as he introduced Barbara to Phyllis. 'D'you mind if we carry on dancing Mum?' he said, not waiting for an answer as he guided Barbara into the road for a Foxtrot.

'He's got it bad,' Phyllis said with a laugh. 'And your face is a picture.'

Alex spent the rest of his leave taking Barbara out in the evenings. She worked, he told Esther, in a Solicitors office in Southsea, her father was a Fireman and her mother a part-time Nurse at St. Mary's hospital.

'Does she have any brothers or sisters?' Esther asked, wanting to know all she could about the girl who had suddenly come into her sons' life.

'None,' Alex said. 'And that's all I know about her. She's nice though, isn't she, and we're goin' to write to each other when I go back.'

'Tell her,' Esther said, 'that if she wants to call in any time and have a cup of tea with us, she's welcome.'

'Thanks Mum.'

On 20th May, King George VI, Queen Elizabeth and their two daughters visited Portsmouth for a Review of the Fleet. 'How about we all go to see it together?' Phyllis suggested. 'We missed the one for the Jubilee, and the children will love it.'

It was only a five-minute walk to the seafront, and they all set out just before dark to see it. They took packets of Smith's crisps and some bottles of Tizer and sat on a wall watching the dazzling show of searchlights playing over an Armada of ships festooned with lights, their multicoloured brilliance reflected in a Kaleidoscope of moving patterns, on the sea. It was a breathtaking sight, and none of them had seen anything like it in their lives.

'You can keep your countryside, and the New Forest,' Esther said, when at last they had managed to drag the children away, and were on their way home. 'I wouldn't live anywhere else but here, close to the sea.'

CHAPTER SIXTEEN

Esther's birthday was on the 21st July. Harry went off to work without a mention of it and, as she vented her temper on the breakfast dishes, breaking a cup into the bargain, she was reminded once again of her ever-increasing dissatisfaction with her life. He could at least have wished her a Happy Birthday, even though he'd overslept and had to rush off without having any breakfast. She took Edwin and Catherine to school, called in at the Co-op for some eggs, and on the way home looked in to see Phyllis.

'You look as miserable as sin,' Phyllis said, handing her a Birthday card. 'You're supposed to be happy today. What's the matter?'

Esther told her. 'I don't know why I'm so fed up with everything,' she said, 'but it would be nice if *someone* in my own family showed a bit of appreciation.' She tore open the envelope. 'Thanks Phyllis. At least *you* remembered.'

Phyllis went to the sideboard. 'And here's a little something to cheer you up,' she said, 'and to celebrate Robert's passing for the Grammar School.'

Esther took the glass of sherry. 'Oh, that's wonderful Phyllis. You must be very proud of him. And I shouldn't be drinking at this time of the morning. Whatever would my dear husband say if he knew,' she said, swallowing a large mouthful of the golden liquid in one go.

'Who cares? It's your birthday.'

'So it is.'

Between them, they managed to finish off almost a whole bottle of Sherry and by the time she went home, Esther had had more than was good for her. She left April, who had fallen asleep in Harry's armchair, then went into the kitchen and swilled her face under the cold tap. She wasn't used to drinking at any hour, let alone of a morning, and the fact that she'd enjoyed it worried her a bit. Her own mother had been an alcoholic and Esther didn't want to follow her down that path. Still, as Phyllis had said, it was her birthday and she was entitled to have a couple of drinks if she wanted. Her eyes felt heavy and she stumbled into a chair, her legs like two lumps of lead, and the room spinning. She couldn't keep her eyes open, and had almost nodded off when a loud hammering on the front door brought her unsteadily to her feet.

The man standing on the doorstep was dressed in blue overalls. He took a step backwards. "God, these women who drink when the ole' man's at work", he thought to himself as Esther's breath almost knocked him sideways. "Oughter be a law agin it". He waved a piece of paper under her nose. 'One parcel Madam,' he said. 'Where would you like us to put it?'

Esther stared at him through a hazy blur. 'Parcel?' she said, trying not to fall over. 'I think you've the wrong address. I'm not expecting anything. It must be for someone else.'

'Look Missus,' the man, who had better things to do than stand here arguing with a tipsy woman, said, 'It says here, "Mrs E. Cartarett, 12 Kestrel Road, Eastbrook". Now, is that you, or isn't it?'

'Yes, it's me.'

'Well, could we get on with it then. Where d'you want it to go?'

Esther thought quickly. 'In the front room,' she said, wondering what Harry would say when he came home and found out she'd been so drunk she'd taken delivery of someone else's parcel. There had to be some mistake. If he'd had anything to do with it, he'd have told her, surely.

The man and his mate carried the large, square parcel up the path and propped it up against a wall in the front room. 'Sign 'ere please,' he said, giving Esther the piece of paper. 'I suppose you *'ave* got a pen Missus?'

She found a fountain pen on the dresser, signed where he told her to, and the two men left. 'Makes ya wonder what the world's comin' to,' the first one said to his mate as they went off down the path.

Esther stood looking at the parcel for several minutes. It was heavy, wrapped in thick brown paper, and tied with string. On the back and front, the word FRAGILE stood out in big red letters. The label clearly read "Mrs E. Cartarett" and it was the right address. She didn't hear the door knocker, and nearly jumped out of her skin when someone banged loudly on the window behind her. It was Phyllis.

'It came then,' Phyllis said, as Esther let her in. 'Thank goodness for that.'

Esther stared at her friend in amazement. 'You *knew* about it then?'

Phyllis laughed. 'Of course I did,' she said. 'Who do you think was given the job of going all the way to Southsea to order it for Harry? He couldn't do it himself now, could he.'

'But what is it?' Esther said.

'I'm not telling. If you want to find out, you'll have to undo it. All I know is, Harry came over to see me a couple of weeks ago and asked if I'd go to this particular shop in Albert Road and order whatever it is to be delivered on your birthday. He'd already done all the arranging with someone in the Dockyard.'

Esther was baffled. 'I hope it wasn't expensive,' she said.

'Paid for in cash,' Phyllis said. 'And you're always saying you don't know what he does with his wages. Well, now you do. He's probably been saving up to buy you this present, and I think you're very lucky. Jack's generous to a fault but he wouldn't spend that kind of money on me. Now, are you going to open it or stand there worrying about how much it cost?'

It was very heavy, and Phyllis steadied it while Esther undid the string and removed three layers of paper. 'Oh my goodness.' She took one look at the drawing of Daniel, in its moulded gilt frame, and nearly fainted. 'Oh, Phyllis, it's beautiful. Have you seen it?'

'No,' Phyllis said, 'but I knew what it was. There's this man who works with Harry, and his son is some kind of artist. He has a studio over a shop in Albert Road and paints portraits from photographs.

Harry thought it would be a lovely surprise for you, so he set it all up with the man at work, and I acted as messenger girl if you like.'

The portrait was an enlarged version of a photograph taken of Daniel only a month before he died. He had been sitting on the settee reading a picture book at the time, and Esther remembered Harry taking the snap with his Brownie camera. Later, after Daniel had died and the film developed, Esther could hardly bear to look at it and had put it to one side in a drawer.

'This artist, whoever he is,' Esther said, 'must be very clever. Look at the way he's captured the colour of Daniel's eyes and hair.' She took a closer look. 'It's been done in pastel, I think. Harry must have gone to a lot of trouble to have this done for me.'

'Yes, he did. All the time it was going on, he was scared stiff the photo would be lost and kept asking me to find out when it would be finished. He nearly drove me mad but it was worth it.' Phyllis went out into the hall. 'I must be off,' she said. 'Want anything from the Co-op?'

'No thanks Phyllis. I think I've got just about everything I need.'

She was overjoyed that Harry had taken so much trouble over buying her a present. Usually, birthdays, except for the children's, came and went with nothing more than a mention, and sometimes not even that.

She said nothing to Harry when he came in from work that evening. She laid the table and dished up the dinner just like any other day, and waited. He didn't mention anything until he'd wiped his plate clean, and then asked her what she'd been up to all day.

'You don't usually ask me that,' she said, her voice sharp because she was beginning to feel angry that he still hadn't spoken about her birthday. 'I've not been up to anything, although two men called this morning and left a parcel for me in the front room.'

His eyes twinkled at her across the table. 'Happy Birthday,' he said, getting out of his chair and dragging her from hers. 'Give us a kiss.'

'Not in front of the children,' she said, pushing him away.

'Never mind them. They're too busy with their pudding to see what we're up to.' He pulled her close to him. 'Do you like your present?'

'Yes, it's lovely. I couldn't have wished for anything else.'

'Let's have a look at it then,' said Harry.

They went into the front room but he was more interested in having his own way with her than looking at the picture he'd saved so hard to buy. 'Later,' she protested. 'Someone might come in.' She went over to the portrait that she had left propped up against the wall. 'It would look really nice in here,' she said, 'but I think I'd like it where I could look at it all the time. What made you think of such a thing?'

He put his arms around her. 'I know,' he said, 'that you've never been able to get over the loss of Daniel, and that you've not been very happy with all the things that have been happening lately. Alex and David gone, Frances no longer around the corner, and me working all the hours God sends.'

'Oh, Harry, that's not true,' she said. 'I've been a bit down lately, but it's because I still miss Daniel. Although I only go to the cemetery once a week now, it doesn't mean I've forgotten him. And yes, I do I miss David and Alex, and Frances. Oh, I don't know what it is really.' She burst into tears and he held her close until, scrubbing her eyes with a handkerchief, she stopped crying and smiled up at him. 'Anyway,' she said, 'it was a bit of a shock when that man turned up at the door this morning.' She laughed. 'I'd had a few too many Sherries and I think he thought I was round the bend, the way I carried on. It was such a surpise.'

'Well,' said Harry, looking at his pocket watch, 'that's what I meant it to be and there'll be another one in about five minutes, so go and sit down and wait for it.'

'The dinner dishes ...'

'Never mind about them. Do as you're told.' He led her through into the sitting room and pressed her into a chair. 'I'll be back in a minute.'

Esther, still feeling the effects of the Sherry, sat back and closed her eyes. She really *was* lucky to have a husband like Harry.

'Hello Mum. Happy Birthday.' It was David.

Her eyes flew open, she leapt to her feet and threw her arms around him, almost crushing the bunch of flowers he'd brought for her. 'Wherever did *you* spring from?'she said.

'I caught the late afternoon train. But it's only for one night. I've to get back to the New Forest tomorrow.'

'Never mind,' Esther said, 'it's lovely to see you.'

David handed her the flowers and a brown paper package. She opened it and pulled out a book of poems by Patience Strong, with a hand-written message inside that read, "With love from Albert and Frances".

Harry was standing in the background grinning from ear to ear, and Esther wondered how he could have known that David would be coming down to see her. Later, when she and Harry were in bed, she asked him.

'For the last two weeks, letters have been flying back and fore between Frances, Phyllis and David,' he said. 'That's all there was to it.'

'Seems to me,' Esther said, 'you were all in this together.'

'All in a good cause,' he said, pulling her close to him. 'And now it's time for my reward.'

The next morning as Harry was about to leave for work, David followed him out into the front garden. 'I want to talk to you Dad,' he said, 'but not in front of Mum. It won't take long.'

'What is it?' Harry said, hoping he wasn't about to hear any more of his son's personal problems.

'It's Frances. She's not well.'

'In what way is she not well?'

'She keeps crying. And she doesn't want to go out. Albert's really worried about her, and so am I.'

Harry thought about his sister and tried to remember her age. She was older than he was, but by how many years, he wasn't sure. He was now forty-three so she must be at least forty-seven, or maybe older.

'It might be something to do with her age,' he said, not wanting to go into details about the middle-aged problems of women. He didn't have much idea about them himself but knew that depression was one of the many symptoms of the change of life.

'I don't think she likes living in the New Forest,' David said, burying his nose in a red rose and savouring its heady scent. 'What's the name of this one?'

'There's not much anyone can do if you're right about Auntie Frances. She'll just have to get used to it. But I'll talk to your mother about it if you like,' Harry said. 'And that's a Bourbon rose called Gipsy Boy. Beautiful, isn't it.'

'Yes it is, and thanks Dad. I'll have to be going now else I'll miss my train.'

'And I'll be late for work. 'Bye son.'

David went indoors to say goodbye to everyone.

'Thanks for coming all this way to see me,' Esther said. 'Give my love to Albert and Frances, and see if you can talk them into coming down to see us sometime.'

'I will.'

'Oh, and by the way, would you tell Frances that Phyllis's boy Robert has passed for the Grammar School.'

When Esther returned from taking the children to school, the house seemed empty. She flicked through the book Albert and Frances had given her, then wandered off into the front room and looked again at the portrait. It was so lifelike and seemed almost as if Daniel was there with her, his blue eyes twinkling in that mischievous way he'd always had. Harry had promised to hang it in the sitting room over the fireplace where she could look at it whenever she wanted, and for the first time since Daniel had gone, she felt as if he had never left her.

CHAPTER SEVENTEEN

Every morning, before she left for work, Barbara Tracey waited at the front door to see if the Postman had anything for her. She'd fallen head over heels for the handsome young Steward whose family lived just down the road, and looked forward to his letters which were always full of where he'd been, what he'd been up to and all the famous people he'd met. What she liked most though was the little bit at the end where he always said how much he couldn't wait to see her again. She wished he could come home more often so that they could get to know one another better.

'You'll be late for work,' her mother called out from the kitchen. 'Standing there like some lovesick mopsy. Heavens above, you only met the boy a couple of months' ago. An' he's only a young sprout.'

'Oh, don't keep on at me Mum,' Barbara said, taking the letter in its blue envelope from the Postman. 'I'm going now. See you tonight.' As she cycled past number twelve, she thought about the invitation from Alex's mother to drop in for a cup of tea sometime, and made a mental note to pay her a visit the following weekend.

She waited until her tea break before opening the letter. It was a little different from the usual and her heart sank as she read about how much he loved the sea and could never settle to anything on dry land. He loved her, he thought, but it wasn't fair, was it, to ask her to wait around for him between sailings, and if she wanted to, she should feel free to find someone else. He would be home in two weeks' time, and they could talk about it then. He would understand, whatever she decided to do, but felt it only right that she should know how he felt. The letter finished with him telling her how much he was looking forward to seeing her again.

'Funny kind of love *that*,' she said to herself as she went back to her work.

The following Saturday afternoon, she walked down the road to number twelve and knocked on the front door. Esther, who had been ironing, didn't at first recognise the nervous young girl standing on the doorstep. More than two months had passed since Alex had introduced her at the street party and as Barbara hadn't taken up the invitation to call in, Esther had all but forgotten what she looked liked.

'It's Barbara, Mrs Cartarett,' she said. 'I hope it's not inconvenient to call and see you.'

'Not at all,' Esther said, asking her in. She went through to the kitchen and turned the gas out from under the iron. 'Give me a minute and I'll put the kettle on.'

Barbara recounted almost her whole life story in the space of about fifteen minutes, and Esther, who was anxious to know if there was any news from Alex, sat patiently listening. An only child, she was eighteen and lived with her parents who, she said, were "getting on a bit", having had her late in life. 'My Mum's nearly fifty,' she said, and Dad's fifty-two.' There had been a brother but he'd not survived an attack of Measles, and this brought back memories of Daniel to Esther, who hardly knew of anyone who'd *not* had a child taken from them. She had to smile at the "getting on a bit". Barbara's parents weren't that much older than Harry and her.

'Does Alex write very often?' Esther said.

'Twice a week I get a letter from him,' Barbara replied. 'He loves the sea and talks of nothing else but the ship he's on and the famous people he meets.'

'Yes,' Esther said, 'I can't see him ever settling down on dry land again, can you?'

'No.'

Esther thought there was something troubling the girl. 'Would you like to meet Alex's Dad?' she said, 'and the little ones. They're all out in the garden enjoying the sunshine.'

They went outside, where Harry was pulling some vegetables for Sunday dinner, and Esther introduced Barbara to him. 'This is Alex's young lady,' she said, watching his face closely to see what reaction there'd be.

His eyes lit up. 'Pleased to meet you Barbara,' he said, treating her to one of his roguish smiles. 'My son seems to have the same good taste as his father.' They all laughed, although Esther felt a pang of jealousy when she noticed the admiring looks he was giving this attractive young woman.

'And these two scruffy little scallywags are Edwin, and Catherine,' she said 'And April, who's the baby of the family, is over there making mud pies.'

Barbara stayed for another half and hour then said she'd better be getting back home for tea and would look in again sometime. 'Mum'll be angry if I'm not at the table by five o'clock,' she said. Harry and Esther exchanged glances.

'Nice girl,' he said, later that evening.

'Yes, she is and I could tell you thought she was all right the way your eyes popped out of their sockets.'

'Jealous?'

'Of course I'm not.'

It was several days' later, when Harry and Esther were talking about the New Forest that he suddenly thought of something. 'I forgot to tell you,' he said, 'that when David came down on your birthday, he told me that Frances isn't very well.'

'For God's sake, Harry, that was over a month ago,' Esther said. 'Why didn't you tell me before?'

'I forgot. It's nothing serious but David didn't want to tell you himself,' Harry said. 'He's an oddball is that one.'

Esther ignored that. 'What's wrong with her, or aren't you going to tell me that either?'

Harry repeated what David had told him.

'I had a feeling,' Esther said, 'that she wouldn't be happy moving away from here. She's used to the sea, and living close to us. I don't suppose it's any more than that but I'll ask Phyllis if she'll look after the children for the day while I go down to see what's going on.'

Phyllis would be happy to help out, she said, so Esther wrote to Frances that day and asked if Albert could pick her up from Southampton on the following Monday. She didn't say anything about what David had told Harry but made it look as if she, herself, needed a day off to escape from the family for a while.

She caught the early morning train, and Albert was at Southampton station to meet her. She thought he looked a bit strained and wondered if he'd bitten off more than he could chew with this smallholding. He was older than Harry by a few years, and it did seem a bit silly to try and start up a business at his age. His job on the trams may have been boring but at least it was easy and with regular hours. Frances was pale, and had lost weight, and Esther began to wonder what it was about this place that didn't suit either of them. 'Are you all right?' she asked. 'Only you look a bit under the weather.' They were sitting outside on the verandah, enjoying a cup of tea, and with Albert and David busy in the garden, now was the chance to find out what was wrong.

It all came out at once, with Frances stumbling over her words, and trying not to break down in front of her sister-in-law. She loved the New Forest, but there was nothing for her to do; she didn't want to join anything in the village and, in any case, the locals weren't friendly unless you went to church, which didn't appeal to her. Albert spent most of his time in the greenhouse, and David, if he wasn't with him, was over at the Doctor's house with Adrian.

'But I thought Adrian was going away to Medical School,' Esther said.

'He is. But not until October. And that bloody car Albert paid the earth for, sits on the drive all day not going anywhere.'

Esther didn't know why the idea suddenly came to her but it seemed the perfect solution. 'So, why don't you learn to drive it yourself?' she said.

'Me? Drive a car?'

'Yes. Why not?'

'Oh, I couldn't.'

'Of *course* you could Frances,' Esther said. 'You'd be able to get away from here whenever you wanted. *And*,' she said on a laugh, 'there'd be no more excuses for you not to visit us, would there.'

Frances thought about it. There was no reason why she shouldn't learn to drive, even if she *was* fast approaching her forty-seventh birthday. She'd have to take a test of course but that wouldn't be a problem. Esther was right.

'I'll speak to Albert about it,' she promised. 'And thanks Esther. You've been like a breath of fresh air to me.' They went back into the house and Frances called to David to come in and see his mother before she left.

Esther told him about Alex's girl friend.

'I wonder how long *that'll* last' he said.

Esther lost her temper. 'At least,' she said, 'he's taking a girl out and not spending all his time with another bloke.' She could have bitten off her tongue. David's face turned ashen and, without a word, he turned on his heels and walked out of the cottage. 'Oh, my God Frances, what *have* I done?'

'Touched on a raw spot, I think,' Frances said.

When the train pulled into Fratton station, Esther sighed with relief. Although she'd been able to come up with what could be a solution for Frances, the visit had ended on a sour note. David would probably never forgive his mother for making vague suggestions about a side of his private life he was still trying to sort out.

After his mother had gone, David asked Albert if he could manage without him for a while, as he wanted to go and see Adrian. 'Of course I can,' Albert said, 'I'm just about finished for the day anyway.'

Adrian lived in a large house on the edge of the village, and as David walked along the lane leading up to it, he made up his mind to tell his friend about the feelings he had for him, and see what came of it. One way or another he knew he couldn't go on any longer pretending he was the same as other young men. And if Adrian felt the same way, as David suspected he did, then at least they would both know where they stood. He went down the side of the house to the back garden where he guessed his friend would be larking about with his two dogs. He could hear voices and as he pushed open the side gate, the sight that greeted him brought him to a complete standstill. There on the lawn was Adrian with a girl, and they were laughing and *kissing*. David stood watching them for what seemed a lifetime until Adrian, sensing that he and the girl were not alone, drew away from her and turned to look in the direction of the gate.

He jumped up, red in the face, brushing grass clippings from his clothes. '*David,* I didn't expect to see you this afternoon.'

'So I see.'

'This is Isobel, who has just agreed to be my girlfriend. We met when we were both on holiday with the parents back in July.'

The girl, who was now standing at Adrian's side, held out her hand. She was beautiful, expensively dressed and spoke with a refined accent. 'How nice to meet you at last, David,' she said. 'Adrian's told me so much about you.'

David took the well-manicured hand in his. 'Pleased to meet you too,' he said, feeling awkward, clumsy and sick. Adrian had never mentioned a girlfriend, and all David could think of as he stood there between them was how close he'd come to making a complete fool of himself. Not only that, he was now no nearer to resolving the problem he'd been wrestling with for so long. He stayed for a few minutes then made his excuses and left.

A week after her visit to the New Forest, Esther had a letter from him.

Dear Mum, he wrote,

Uncle Albert is teaching Auntie Frances to drive the car and she is getting on well. She is much better since you came down to see her.

I think you should say sorry for that horrible thing you said to me. Adrian has a girlfriend now so I won't be seeing much of him before he goes away. And I don't go around with girls because, down here they all have fellers of their own. I don't know when I'll be down to see you again. Perhaps Uncle Albert would teach me to drive too.

David

When Harry came home and she showed him the letter, he almost exploded. '*You*,' he said, 'say sorry to *him*. You'll do no such thing, and if he wants to stay away, then let him.'

For once, Esther agreed. The son she had once preferred to her other children, had grown so far away, she hardly recognised him. As Harry said, he could stay away if that was what he wanted. All the same, that night in bed, she couldn't stop herself from weeping into her pillow. It wasn't just that she'd upset David; that had been her fault, and she shouldn't have said what she did, but she still wished he could sort himself out once and for all, even if it meant Harry would disown the boy if it turned out that he *was* different. And disown him he would, she could be sure of that.

In September, Edwin's teacher, Miss Milligan buttonholed Esther one morning as she dropped the children off at the school gates. 'Now that the summer holidays are out of the way, I'd like to have a word with you about Edwin,' she said, as Esther was about to leave. 'Could you spare a few minutes?'

Esther said she hoped he wasn't in any trouble.

'Not at all,' Miss Milligan said in her broad, Irish accent as Esther followed her into an empty classroom. 'He's one of the best behaved boys in my class. I just wondered if you'd ever seen any of his writing.'

Edwin was always doing something with pencils and paper but Esther had to admit she'd not taken too much notice.

'His work is exceptional,' Miss Milligan said, taking an exercise book from the cupboard. 'Take a look at these compositions.'

Esther couldn't believe what she was seeing. The handwriting was in copperplate, and as she flipped through the pristine pages, with not a blot in sight, she could hardly take it in that this was the work of her young son. 'He couldn't possible have done these,' she said. 'He's too young to be able to write like this. Isn't he?'

'They are all Edwin's work, I can assure you,' Miss Milligan said. 'It seems that as soon as he puts pen to paper, the words just flow from him naturally. Do you have any other talent like this in the family?'

'Not as far as I know.'

'Well, I thought you should be told about his gift for writing,' Miss Millgan said. 'He's too young to be thinking of a career but I feel we should keep an eye on him for the future.'

Esther thanked her and left. Edwin had a remarkable talent and those writings were exceptional for one so young. She hoped Harry would see it that way.

'Writing stories and such is for the likes of Charles Dickens and people like that,' he said, 'so just because he's clever at stringing two words together, don't go giving the boy any fancy ideas. He'll work for his living, just like the rest of us.'

'Of course,' Esther said, smiling enigmatically.

'We don't seem to see much of Jack these days,' Esther said to Phyllis one morning as they walked the children to school. 'Is he all right?'

'To be honest,' Phyllis said, 'he's fed up with the dairy. They're expecting him to put in more and more hours, and for no extra money and when he does get home from work, he's too tired for anything. Lately, it's even been left to me to look after the chickens.'

'Would you like me to ask Harry if there's anything going in the Dockyard?'

'Oh, yes *please*,' Phyllis said. 'Although Jack's forty-seven, so I expect he's left it too late.'

'It's worth a try though. I'll speak to Harry this evening.'

Harry said that the Dockyard had been taking on extra workers and training them to do a variety of jobs. 'If the rumours of another war come to anything,' he said, 'they'll need all the men they can get. I'll have a word with Jack myself.'

The mention of another war sent shivers down Esther's spine. The situation on the continent was getting serious, with Hitler ordering the destruction of anything belonging to the Jews or Gipsies. They'd had their homes and businesses seized, and now there was talk of even worse atrocities. No one really knew what was going on but the talk of another war intensified, with not a question of "if" but "when" it would happen.

Towards the end of October, Esther fell to thinking about the events of the past year. Alex's romance with Barbara Tracey seemed to be heading for an engagement, despite his suggestion that she should find someone else. 'I only want you,' she'd told him, when they'd talked about the letter he'd sent about his love for the sea. 'I'd rather see you now and again than not at all.' She visited Esther once a week, and there was always a welcome for her at number twelve. Esther was determined not to follow in the shoes of her own mother-in-law and become an enemy rather than a friend. Alex managed to get home whenever his ship docked at Southampton but Esther didn't see much of him as he spent most of the time with Barbara. As for David, Esther hadn't seen him since her visit to see Frances. He still wrote occasionally but his letters were cool and he never mentioned Adrian. Esther assumed he'd gone away to Medical School by now.

It was in November that Frances wrote to say she'd passed her driving test and would be coming to Portsmouth the following week. There was no mention of David and when, one Sunday morning the car drew up outside, she was on her own.

'I knew you could do it,' Esther said, marvelling at the way she parked the car so neatly against the kerb. 'What was it like? The test I mean.'

'Awful,' Frances said. 'But I wasn't going to have some little pip-squeak of a man telling me I couldn't drive, so I took a few deep breaths and got on with it. And here I am. Where is Harry? And the children?'

'Harry's gone across to see Jack and taken the children with him. They'll be back in a minute.'

Esther pointed to the painting of Daniel above the fireplace, and Frances's eyes filled with tears. 'It's beautiful,' she said. 'I would never have believed Harry could think of something like that for you.'

'Oh, he has his moments,' Esther said.

Harry brought the children across and said he had to go back over the road to help Jack with the new chicken run he was building. He stopped just long enough for a chat with Frances, asking after Albert and how was he getting on with the smallholding.

'It should start making money next year,' she told him. 'But it's hard work and I don't know how he'd have managed without David.'

'Give him my regards. Albert that is, when you get home.'

Frances and Esther exchanged looks.

Esther told Frances all about Alex's girlfriend. 'It looks as if an engagement will soon be forthcoming,' she said, 'although they're far too young to be thinking of getting married just yet.' She then asked after David.

Frances said that, since his friend Adrian had gone away, he'd been seeing a girl from the next village. 'He takes her out once a week, but I don't think it's anything serious. He's a bit *different* from most young men.'

'Yes he is. And I don't think he's forgiven me for what I said when we came to visit you, has he?'

'He's never mentioned it to me, but you're probably right,' Frances said.

'Will he be coming home for Christmas, do you think?'

'He's not said anything about it but I'll ask him. I'm afraid he's not been very happy since Adrian went away, and I don't think he's all that interested in this girl.'

An awkward silence hung in the air between the two women. Then Esther said, 'Frances?'

'Yes?'

'Do you think there was ever any *funny* business between David and Adrian?'

Frances shook her head. 'Not very likely,' she said. 'Adrian's found himself a girlfriend, so I hear, and when he comes home for weekends from Medical School, they are inseparable.'

'Thank goodness for that,' Esther said, still unconvinced.

The day flew by so quickly that she was surprised when Frances said it was time for her to start back. 'It's been lovely seeing you all again,' she said, 'and now that I can drive the car, I'll come more often.'

Alex came home just before Christmas but David wrote to Esther and said he'd be staying with Albert and Frances this year. Esther was both hurt and angry but the news that Alex and Barbara had decided to get engaged took the edge off her disappointment. The young couple went off to buy the ring, and when they came back, Barbara asked if Harry and Esther would like to meet her parents. 'We're not exactly having a party,' she said, 'but Mum thought it would be nice if she and Dad met you, seeing as you're going to be sort of related.'

Harry and Esther met their son's future in-laws on Boxing Day. Esther was worried about taking the children with them but Barbara insisted it would be all right. 'They won't be any trouble, Mrs Cartarett,' she said.

Mr. and Mrs Tracey turned out to be a couple of devout, teetotal, churchgoers, with minds, Esther said to Harry later, as narrow as bootlaces. Mrs Tracey, a small, birdlike woman, with sharp eyes, had a high-pitched voice that grated like a saw on metal. Barbara's father Arnold was, by contrast, a heavily built man with a magnificent moustache, and the habit of finishing off his wife's sentences for her. Otherwise, he had little to say, and when he did speak, it was in a Scots accent and difficult to understand.

Mrs Tracey made a pot of tea but there were no biscuits, for fear, Esther suspected, of dropped crumbs landing on her best rug. 'Of course,' she said, 'we like to keep ourselves to ourselves and don't mix with our neighbours. It doesn't do to get too friendly with people you hardly know.' She leaned forward. 'I hope,' she went on, lowering her voice to a whisper in Esther's ear, 'that your son is … er, *looking after* our daughter, if you know what I mean. We've never had a scandal in either family, and Barbara's a nice, respectable girl who wants a white wedding.' She poured tea into dainty, china cups. 'And I do hope the young man doesn't *drink*,' she went on. 'It's the cause of all sin and damnation.'

Esther didn't know whether to tell the woman to mind her own business, or laugh in her face. 'My son,' she said, 'is a decent young man and knows how to respect a girl. I'm quite sure there will be no reason for Barbara not to have the sort of wedding she wants. As for his drinking, I'm afraid I have no idea but perhaps you should ask him yourself.'

Edwin and Catherine, who couldn't understand why they had each been banished to a chair in the corner of the room, sat silently listening and watching. If they'd hoped to be given a treat, they were in for a disappointment. Mrs Tracey handed them each a half-filled beaker of weak orange squash, with instructions not to spill a drop on her nice Indian rug. 'Or I shall be very cross,' she said, frowning darkly at them both. April slept through it all on Esther's lap, and when she stirred and started to cry, Esther thankfully announced that it was time they went home.

'God Almighty,' Harry said, as they all strolled back to number twelve, 'I hope we don't have to visit *them* very often. I feel sorry for our Alex, having that woman for a mother-in-law. There wasn't one family in this road that escaped her acid tongue.'

'Did you see Alex's face when she asked about his drinking?' Esther said.

'Yes. *And* Barbara's.'

Later, when the subject of the Tracey's was still being aired, Harry remarked that he hoped Barbara wouldn't turn out to be like her mother. 'You know what they say,' he said. 'If you want to see what your wife will be like in the future, just look at her mother.'

'Oh, Harry, I hope not.'

When Alex came home for his supper, he said he was sorry about Barbara's mother, 'but that's the way she is and it's best to take no notice and just let her get on with it.' She was harmless enough, he said, but once he and Barbara were married, he'd make sure they didn't live anywhere near her. 'It's Barbara's Dad I feel sorry for,' he said. 'There's no escape for him.'

Chapter Eighteen

On the 3rd June 1938, David was twenty-one, and came into his inheritance. A week before, he'd had a letter from Solicitor Alistair Browning, suggesting the following Tuesday as a date for a meeting to discuss the legacy.

'We'll all go to Portsmouth,' Albert said, 'then, when you've finished your business, we can go and see your Mum and Dad. After all, it's your special birthday and they'll want to see you, even if you don't want to see *them.*' David had never relented after his mother had cast doubts on his friendship with Adrian, and although he still wrote to her now and again, he'd not visited, even at Christmas.

They left the New Forest early, in order to make the most of a warm, summers day, and dropped David off at the Solicitors just after nine o'clock. Albert asked him how long he thought the meeting would last.

'About an hour I should think,' David said. 'That's what it said in the letter.'

'We'll be back just after ten. And good luck.'

'Thanks.' David went up the steps and into the waiting room. He'd not given a thought as to what he'd do with the money. Once, a long time ago, he'd planned to open up a cabinet-making business, but that was all in the past and he was happier working on the land. He could put some of the money into Uncle Albert's smallholding then his uncle might consider making him a partner in the business. On the other hand, with all the talk of another world war, it might be better to re-invest it until everything settled down. He knew nothing about money matters and would have to rely on the advice given by Alistair Browning.

'The original amount of two-thousand pounds was well invested by the Trustees,' Alistair Browning told David, 'and has attracted a substantial amount of interest.' He consulted some papers on the desk. 'We are now looking at somewhere in the region of three-thousand, which is an excellent return, wouldn't you say?'

'Yes, Mr. Browning,' David said.

'Have you decided what you are going to do with such a handsome sum of money?'

'Not yet. I need to speak to my Uncle Albert first.'

Alistair Browning raised an eyebrow. 'Uncle Albert? What about your own father?'

'He and I don't get on.'

'Yes, but he *is* your father and I think you should at least have the courtesy of telling him about your plans.'

'I don't have any plans yet,' David said.

Alistair Browning studied his client. David Cartarett was now a man but had not yet learned how to behave like one. He was sullen, petulant and immature, but the legacy was now his to do with as he wished, and if he didn't want to involve his own father, that was up to him. 'I will be having a meeting with the Trustees later this week and will write to you with the outcome. In the meantime, I suggest you find yourself a good Bank Manager, and await developments.'

'When will I have the money?

'I can't tell you that at the moment,' Alistair Browning said. 'These things take time but Mr Rigby's Will is straightforward so it shouldn't be too long before you can call yourself a rich young man. There are one or two ends to be tied up and then it's all yours.'

Albert had dropped Frances off at Kestrel Road, and was now sitting in the car outside the solicitor's office. 'How did you get on?' he asked when David appeared.

David repeated everything that Alistair Browning had told him. 'When we get back to the New Forest,' he said, 'I'd like to ask your advice about the money.'

Albert laughed. 'I'm not sure that I am the right person to give out that kind of advice,' he said. 'Frances is better at sums than me but I'll gladly help if I can.'

The atmosphere when David arrived at Kestrel Road was tense. Harry and Esther, even though they could ill-afford it, had bought him a pocket watch for his birthday. He undid the parcel and his face lit up momentarily. 'Thanks Mum,' he said, giving her a brief peck on the cheek. 'I've always wanted one of these.' Albert and Frances had bought him a Gardening Manual, and Phyllis popped across the road to wish him a Happy Birthday and to give him a box Jack had made to keep his fishing tackle together.

'Can't stop,' she said. 'But this is from Jack and me with our best wishes.'

Harry arrived home in time to see them all before they left, and did his best to cheer things up a bit but Esther was glad when at last Albert said they would have to be off. The strain of keeping her face fixed in a smile had made her jaws ache, and after they'd gone, she turned on Harry. 'David's just like your bloody brother,' she said, 'and if I never set eyes our eldest son again, it won't be a moment too soon.'

'You don't mean that Esther.'

'Oh, yes I do.'

'You don't.' Harry dropped a kiss on the top of her head. 'Did he mention his inheritance?'

'Not a word. In fact, apart from thanking me for the watch, he didn't speak to me at all.' She snatched the empty cups and saucers from the table and banged them down with a crash on the draining board.

Harry went up behind her and put his arms around her waist. 'Don't let it upset you my love,' he said. 'And don't break any more of them dishes or we'll have nothing left to drink out of.' She turned round and saw that he was trying hard not to laugh. She kissed him, long and hard, and then burst out laughing herself. What did any of it matter anyway, and of *course* she didn't mean what she'd said about David.

'You're a wealthy young man now.' Albert said, a few weeks' later when all the legal necessities had been settled and there was a little over three-thousand pounds sitting in David's newly opened bank account. He'd taken advice from the Trustees and his Bank Manager, and had decided to have the money invested in an account with the bank until he had made up his mind what to do with it.

'I was wondering,' David said, 'if you'd like some help with the smallholding. I mentioned this to the Bank Manager and he suggested that perhaps we could form a partnership. What do you think Albert?'

Albert was taken aback and didn't know what to think. This had come as a surprise as he'd no idea David had been thinking along those lines. If it were to be a success, the smallholding could certainly do with some extra money spent on it, and an extra pair of hands to help with the heavy work. But a partnership? He wasn't sure. 'Well David,' he said, 'it's a very kind thought, and I'd like to think it over but your Mum and Dad might not be very pleased about it.'

'I don't care *what* they think,' David said, and Albert was shocked at the anger in his voice. 'Mum thinks I'm a Nancy Boy and Dad can't make up his mind whether I am or not. Whatever I do with the money will be wrong anyway.'

Albert thought that the business of whether David had certain unnatural tendencies or not should have been resolved one way or the other a long time ago. Instead, it had festered on until Esther happened to make that unfortunate remark, and David had never been able to forgive her. 'Let's talk about it again at the end of the month when Frances has done the books eh?' he said, 'but with all this talk of another war, perhaps you should leave your money where it is until we know what's going to happen.'

Jack had his interview for the Dockyard but they'd filled their quota of new workers for now, he was told, although there would be vacancies later on in the year. His name would be added to the list of hopefuls and he'd be one of the first to hear when there was a place for him.

'He's a bit down,' Phyllis said to Esther, 'but at least he knows he's not stuck in that damned dairy for much longer.' They were standing at the school gates waiting for Robert, Edwin and Catherine.

'Is everything all right between you now?' Esther said.

'No, it isn't. We've decided that, when Sarah goes to school, we'll separate and get a divorce.'

Esther thought it was some kind of joke. 'You don't mean that,' she said.

'Of *course* I mean it. There's no point in carrying on with a marriage that's as good as dead.'

'But you'll never be able to afford it. Do you know how much it would cost? Besides, you have to have grounds. And it takes *years*.'

'Jack'll give me grounds,' Phyllis said, her face a picture of misery. 'He's done it before so why not again?'

'Oh, *Phyllis,* I don't know what to say. You just can't forgive him for what he did, can you?'

Phyllis didn't answer. She still loved Jack and couldn't understand why she felt the way she did. He didn't want a divorce but the two of them couldn't go on forever living in a sterile marriage the way they were.

'By the time Sarah goes to school,' Esther pointed out, 'you'll both be getting on a bit. How you can even *think* about parting, I don't know. Where will you go? And what, may I ask, will you live on?'

'Something'll turn up,' Phyllis said.

'You sound just like Mr. Micawber in David Copperfield.'

They both laughed at that and the tension passed.

As they turned into Kestrel Road, they noticed Mrs Mc Andrew who was leaning over her front gate waiting for an audience. 'Some man up the road died this morning,' she said in a reverent whisper, as they drew level. 'Found dead in 'is bed 'e was. Awful, innit? The police were there, an' all. Then the ambulance people came an' took 'im away.'

Phyllis asked if she knew who it was.

'Mr. Tracey 'is name was, so I were told.'

Esther turned pale. 'Oh, my God, that's Alex's girlfriend's Dad.'

'You knew him?' Mrs Mc Andrew said, her eyes lighting up.

'Yes. My son is engaged to Barbara Tracey.'

'Well, there's a thing.'

Esther and Phyllis walked on. 'That woman never misses *anything*,' Phyllis said. 'I'm sure she knows what everyone in the road has for breakfast.'

When Harry arrived home, Esther told him, and he insisted that she go along and see if there was anything they could do. 'Mrs Tracey and Barbara must be in a right state, finding him dead like that, in his own bed.'

Barbara answered the front door and invited Esther in. 'Mother's in the living room sorting through some papers,' she said. 'Come through. It's been such a terrible shock. He was all right last night but when Mother got up this morning, he was still lying in bed, which was unusual, so she called me and we discovered that he'd passed away.'

'Is there anything we can do to help?' Esther asked Mrs Tracey who was sifting through a large tin box, looking for some papers. 'Alex's Dad says you've only to ask.'

'Thank you Mrs Cartarett, but there's nothing at the moment. I'm just looking for some Insurance Policies I know my late husband had. I'm afraid he was never one to put anything in its proper place.'

Esther repeated the offer of help then left. 'That woman,' she said to Harry, 'was more concerned with finding the poor man's Insurance Policies than the fact he'd died. I could hardly believe how offhand she was about the whole thing. And not a tear to be seen, even from Barbara.'

A post-mortem held on Arnold Tracey revealed that had died of heart failure. The funeral was private and Harry and Esther not invited. It was not until the middle of that night, that Esther, unable to sleep, suddenly had a thought. Barbara's mother was now a widow and would probably expect her daughter to remain living at home, even if she were to get married. And Barbara, being the sort of girl she was, wouldn't have the heart to refuse. What chance would she and Alex have of making a go of marriage if they had to live under the same roof as that woman?'

In August, Harry and Esther had a steady stream of visitors. First, Alex came home with the news that he was leaving the Merchant Service to join the Royal Navy. He'd had enough, he said, of scivvying for the idle rich, and in any case, with the prospect of war looming larger than ever, all the armed forces were crying out for volunteers. He also told Esther that whenever he'd called to take Barbara out, her mother always put a stop to it by snivelling into her handkerchief and begging not to be left alone, and Barbara was giving in to her.

'I don't know what to do Mum.' he said. 'I was sorry to hear about Mr Tracey but I've been home for nearly a week now and I haven't been out with Barbara once.'

Esther was sympathetic. 'I knew this would happen,' she said. 'But it's only been a few weeks' since Mr Tracey died and I suppose Barbara feels she can't leave her mother on her own just yet. All the same, if she doesn't make a stand now, Mrs Tracey will never let her go.'

'I was wondering,' he said, 'if you and Dad would mind if she came here for a couple of hours so that Barbara and I could go to the pictures.'

'Or I could go and sit with her,' Esther said quickly, not keen on the idea of having the house-proud Mrs Tracey looking down her nose at the untidy, cluttered home that was number twelve. Not that Esther was ashamed of it; it was clean enough, but the springs in the settee were sticking through, the mats threadbare, and April had scribbled all over the walls in the sitting room with some crayons.

The problem solved itself when Mrs Tracey said she had no intention of being treated like a child who needed looking after. In the end, Alex went back to his ship without once seeing Barbara on her own, but not before warning her that he would break off their engagement if she didn't make a stand.

The next day, Frances drove down from the New Forest. She was on her own because, as she told Esther, it was a busy time of the year and David had to stay behind to give Albert a hand. She told Esther about the offer David had made to Albert regarding the money. 'Nothing's happened yet,' she said, 'but they may be going into partnership.'

Esther was angry that David hadn't spoken to Harry about any of this. 'I cannot believe,' she said, 'that this is the same David who, a couple of years' ago was so concerned about *me*. Since he moved to the New Forest with you and Albert, he's grown so far away from us that it no longer feels as if he's our son.'

'Are you blaming Albert and me?'

'No, of course I'm not.'

'Well, it sounds like it to me.'

Esther was close to tears. 'Please don't let us fall out Frances,' she said. 'We don't see you often and I don't want to spend the little time you *are* here, arguing over David. He's old enough now to please himself but I do think he might have come home to see his father before making any decisions.'

Frances agreed. 'And how is Edwin getting on at school,' she said, hoping to lighten the atmosphere.

Esther told her about the writings Edwin's teacher had shown her. 'They're good,' she said, 'and he's having some of them shown in an exhibition of children's work soon. The trouble is though, Harry says I'm not to let him get big ideas, but if he's as talented as his teacher says, then I think we should encourage him, don't you?'

'Ah, well that's just Harry,' Frances said. 'Take no notice. You never know, you may have a future Shakespeare in the family, or maybe even a Charles Dickens. And yes, I think you should at least take an interest in what he's doing. And Catherine?'

'She's a little on the slow side with some things,' Esther said, 'but her teacher says she'll catch up with all the others in her own good time. It's funny that even now she still sometimes asks where Daniel has gone. His death must have affected her far more than we thought.'

Frances stayed just long enough to see the children before she had to drive home. 'Now that the weather's improved, I'll come down more often,' she promised as Esther waved her off.

Two days' later, Esther had the shock of her life when David turned up without warning. 'This is a lovely surprise,' she said. 'I thought you and Albert were busy.'

'We are,' David replied. 'But Frances gave me a good talking to and said I should come down to see you and Dad about the money, so I've taken the day off and here I am. It's good to see you again Mum and I'm sorry for the way I've been lately.'

'That's all right David,' Esther said, 'it was my fault. I shouldn't have said what I did.' She put her arm around his shoulder. 'Dad won't be home until about six o'clock, and you can stay the night if you like. Your old room is empty.'

'Thanks Mum.'

She gave him a meal and they sat and talked for a while, about things Esther considered more important than money. David told her about the girl he was taking out. 'Her name's Bronwen, she's a waitress in one of the hotels in the next village,' he said, 'and lives in. Her mother lives in Swansea in South Wales but there's not much work down that way so Bronwen moved to the New Forest a couple of years' ago.'

'Is it serious?' Esther asked.

'No,' he said. 'We're just good friends, that's all.'

Esther said nothing to that. At four o'clock, she put April into her reins, and went to fetch the other two children from school.

Later that evening, David went with Harry out into the garden so that they could talk. He'd decided to leave most of his money invested for the time being, until the negotiations with Hitler that Neville Chamberlain had been talking about were over. It looked as if the threat of war had receded for the time being but there was no point in doing anything if he was likely to be called up for service. Albert had suggested that the question of the partnership should wait for now and had agreed to accept some money to cover the cost of essentials for the smallholding, David explained to his father.

'That's all right by me son,' Harry said. 'You can do what you like with your own money but I don't like to see you upset your mother the way you did. She didn't mean anything by what she said that time, and if I were you, I'd forget all about it.'

'I will Dad.' David reached inside his jacket, pulled out an envelope and handed it to his father. 'There's some cash in here Dad, for you and Mum to buy something you want for yourselves.'

Harry refused to take it. 'We don't want your money David,' he said. 'We've enough to be getting by on, and you might need it.'

'Dad, I have more than enough for what I want, so please take it and if you don't want it for yourself, let Mum have it.' He was beginning to wonder exactly what it was he had to do to please his father. In the end Harry ungraciously accepted the money and promised that he'd let Esther decide on what it was to be spent.

The next morning, David left early to catch his train and was walking down Goldsmith Avenue towards the station when a familiar voice brought him to a halt. He turned around. 'Sally.'

'Hello, David.' She was standing just behind him. 'I've been following you for ages but couldn't be sure if it really was you. You've grown so much taller. It's lovely to see you again.'

'And you.' David looked at his pocket watch. 'Look,' he said, 'I've another ten minutes before my train's due. Are you in a hurry?'

'No.'

'Come on then. I'll buy you a platform ticket and we can talk while I wait for my train.'

So many things had happened since he'd gone to live in the New Forest, she told him. Her father had died, and her mother then insisted on moving to Milton where rents were a bit cheaper. Sally still worked for the same Accountant, had passed all her typing and shorthand exams, and was now his Secretary. Her brother Sam was in the Army, and up North somewhere doing his training.

David was surprised to hear that his old enemy Totter had died. 'What happened to your Dad?' he asked.

'He had a fall. Hit his head, went into a coma and died in his sleep.'

'I'm sorry,' David said, untruthfully.

He told her about his new life in the New Forest, and how he'd come into his inheritance and was now a rich man. 'I don't feel any different though,' he said, noticing how much prettier Sally was now that she'd grown up a bit. Pleasantly surprised by the strength of his feelings, he asked if they could write to each other. Sally held up her left hand. 'I'm engaged to be married,' she said, 'and I don't think my fiance would like it.'

David's heart sank. 'Lucky man, whoever he is.'

Sally's face turned a deep shade of pink. 'It could have been you David,' she said, 'only you were so cold and distant with me, and a girl likes to think she can stir a man a bit, if you know what I mean.'

Before he realised what he was doing, David pulled her to him and kissed her on the mouth. 'Like this, you mean?' he said. 'Oh, Sally, what an idiot I've been all these years and now it's too late.' He let her go and jumped to his feet as his train came into view. 'Perhaps we'll run into each other another time.'

Sally stood on the platform, waving to him until the train rounded a bend in the track and was gone, and then she turned on her heel and, fighting back the tears, walked away. She'd always loved David Cartarett but there wasn't anything she could do about it now.

CHAPTER NINETEEN

September saw Prime Minister Neville Chamberlain set off to Munich for a meeting with Adolph Hitler to try to negotiate some kind of peace settlement. The fear of war had escalated over the past few months and everyone thought it was now inevitable. Even Esther had come round to the idea that it was only a matter of time. There was talk of gas masks, air raid shelters, re-armament, conscription of all young men of a certain age and mass evacuation of children to safe areas. Nothing had come of any of it yet but with each passing day, the threat of war became closer.

'I can't bear the thought of our boys being dragged into it,' Esther said to Phyllis. 'David and Alex would have to go and so would your Luke and Terry although Harry and Jack are too old, thank goodness.'

'I suppose that's something,' Phyllis said.

They were sitting in Phyllis's back garden enjoying the warm September sunshine. Phyllis smiled as Sarah chased April up and down the path. 'It doesn't seem possible that Sarah will be starting school next week, does it?' she said. 'I can hardly believe how the years have flown by.'

'Nor me. Are you still determined to get a divorce when Sarah's a bit older?'

'It all depends.'

'On what?'

'On whether or not Jack's willing to give me the evidence I need.'

Esther threw her hands in the air in despair. 'How you can sit there and talk about it like that I don't know. You want Jack to be unfaithful to you just so that you can be rid of him. That's it isn't it?'

'Yes, if that's the way you want to see it.'

'Well it serves you right if he refuses because, unless you can prove adultery, you can't divorce and that's that.'

Suddenly, Phyllis burst into tears. 'I don't want any of it,' she said. 'I don't want to lose Jack but he says he's had enough.'

'Of *course* he has,' Esther said, 'but I don't suppose he wants to go through with it any more than you do so why don't the two of you behave like adults and sit down and see if you can work something out.'

'We've tried but it always ends in an argument.'

Esther gave up. She couldn't understand why Jack and Phyllis had let things get so out of hand. 'Perhaps if there *is* another war,' she said, 'you'll have something else to think about other than your own feelings.'

Towards the end of the month, Neville Chamberlain flew back to England from one of his peace missions, and waved a piece of paper at the press reporters who were waiting for him at the airport. His speech to them appeared in the papers the following day, and Harry read a bit of it out to Esther from the Daily Herald.

"My good friends", it said, "for the second time in our history, a British Prime Minister has returned from Germany bringing peace with honour. I believe it is peace in our time."

Esther was overjoyed. 'There,' she said, 'I told you there wouldn't be another war. It was just a lot of old talk. And Hitler isn't nearly as bad as he's been painted.'

Harry smiled to himself at her gullibility. 'If you believe any of that,' he said, 'you'll believe anything. Chamberlain has only managed to get what he went for because he has sold the Czechs up the river. I don't understand much about politics but I do know that Hitler has pulled the wool over our Prime Minister's eyes and we're all going to suffer for it in the end.'

'Oh, shut up Harry,' Esther said.

Across the road at number nine, Jack and Phyllis talked about their plans for the future. 'If you could only find it in your heart to forgive me,' Jack said, 'there'd be no need for us to think about divorce. None of it makes sense to me, and I'm not going to take up with someone else just to give you the evidence you need.'

'You did it to suit yourself before,' Phyllis said bitterly.

'Yes, I did and I've never been allowed to forget it, have I?'

'Would you have forgiven me if it had been the other way round?' she asked.

'If *you* had been unfaithful to *me*, it wouldn't have been because you were married to an iceberg, as I was.'

'Well, perhaps if you'd not given me *four* children when I only wanted two, none of it would have happened.'

Jack leapt from his chair. 'My God,' he shouted, 'it's a good job Robert's out and didn't hear what you just said. And I've just about had enough.' He marched across the room and opened the door. 'All right,' he said, 'I'll give you your damned evidence, and I hope it makes you happy. But for now, I'm off out and don't wait up for me in case I decide not to come back.' He grabbed his hat and jacket then wrenched the front door open, slamming it behind him as he went out.

With no idea where he was going, and shaking with anger, he stumbled blindly down the road, his head swimming. He reached the corner and, without looking either way, stepped off the kerb straight into the path of a horse and cart. Before he could scramble out of the way, the startled horse reared with fright, Jack stumbled, fell under the cart, and as the terrified animal bolted, felt the weight of the cartwheels grinding over his right leg, then a crack as his head hit the kerb. The last recollection he had was of hearing the horse and cart rattling down the road, and seeing the blurred face of someone who'd run to help him. Then a searing pain made him cry out and the world turned dark as he lost consciousness.

Phyllis was preparing Sarah's supper when, about twenty minutes' after Jack had flung out of the house, a man hammered at the front door and told her he'd seen her husband being run over by a horse and cart. 'I work at the dairy,' he said, 'so I know your Jack. It 'appened right outside my 'ouse. Someone called for an amb'lance an' they've taken him off to 'ospital.'

She didn't stop for anything except to run across to see Esther and ask her to keep and eye on Sarah. 'The boys are still out,' she said, 'and she's on her own but I have to go.' She ran all the way to the bus stop and when, some twenty minutes' later, she arrived at St. Mary's Hospital, the Doctors were still examining Jack. She had to wait for what seemed an eternity to find out how badly he'd been hurt.

'His injuries are more serious than we had first thought,' one of them told her, when she was finally allowed in to see him. 'He's had a nasty blow to the head and is unconscious. He's also broken his right leg, and I think it might be a good idea if you could stay the night, *just in case.*'

Phyllis went cold. This was all her fault. If she hadn't made him so angry, he wouldn't have gone out in a temper and it wouldn't have happened. She sat, wide-awake by his bedside all night, hoping and praying she wasn't going to lose him, but towards morning, tiredness overcame her and she fell asleep in the chair.

Over the next few days, she spent as much time as she could with him but it was a week before he came out of the coma, and when he did, she was the first person he saw. She was holding his hand and her eyes were red with crying. When she saw his eyelids move, she was on her feet and running for the nurse. 'He's come round,' she bawled through the open door of the Sister's office. 'Jack's come round.'

'Poor old Jack,' Harry said, when Phyllis told him and Esther what the Doctors had told her. He'd had an operation on his injured leg but the severity of the break would mean he would always have a limp. The head injury had affected his balance but that might, or might not improve in time.

'This means,' Phyllis said, 'that he won't be able to take that job in the Dockyard. I asked the Doctor and he said it would too dangerous for Jack to work with machinery, as you have to Harry.'

'What I can't understand,' Harry said, 'is why he stepped into the road in front of that horse and cart. He must have been far away in some other world to do a thing like that. He wasn't drunk or anything was he?'

So far, Phyllis hadn't said anything about the row that had set the chain of events in motion. She'd felt too ashamed, but now she sprang to Jack's defence. 'No, he was not', she said. 'In fact, if it hadn't been for me, none of it would have happened.' She went on to tell Harry and Esther about the row that led to Jack storming out of the house in a rage. 'I'll never be able to forgive myself,' she said. 'His plan to leave the dairy is in ruins, and he'll be stuck in that job forever.'

'Well,' Esther said, 'at least he hadn't started work in the Dockyard. If he had, he would have lost his job there, and then what would you have done?'

'I don't know,' Phyllis said. 'In fact, I don't know anything any more.'

It was another week before the doctors would allow Jack to go home. The General Manager of the dairy, who owned a car, collected him from the hospital. 'Don't you worry about a thing Jack,' he said as he drove along Milton Road. 'Your job's there for when you're well enough to come back and in the meantime, I'll see to the running of the office. All you need to do is get well, and Phyllis will make sure of that. She hardly left your side the first few days you were in hospital.'

Jack smiled ruefully to himself. He doubted whether Phyllis had really changed, but she would have to face the fact that the money they'd saved for their plan to divorce would now be needed to keep their heads above water. There wouldn't be any wages coming in, and the sixpence a week sickness club Jack belonged to only paid out for the barest essentials. Life was going to be tough for a while, and yet, deep down inside, he had this feeling that his accident might have been a sent as a blessing in disguise, even if it *had* left him with a limp and ruined his chances of a job in the Dockyard.

'Let's have a really good Christmas,' Harry said at the end of November. 'All those extra hours I've been working means we're not short of a bob or two, so I reckon we should spend it on having a good time. What d'you think, Esther?'

Esther was too surprised to say what she thought. It wasn't like Harry to throw money away on frivolous things like Christmas but she'd be happy to go along with it if it meant cheering things up a bit. What with Jack's accident and, despite the Prime Minister's peace announcement, more talk of another war, a bit of fun was what everyone needed. 'What shall we do?' she asked. 'Have a party?'

'Why not?' Harry said. 'Jack and Phyllis would come, and we could invite the people next door, and perhaps Barbara and her mother.'

'We don't know Mr and Mrs Cheswick', Esther said. 'The only time I see *her* is when we're both hanging out the washing, and then she only passes the time of day.'

'No harm in asking though', Harry said. He'd been saving hard for several months, with the idea in his head of taking Esther and the children on a decent holiday next year to somewhere like Bournemouth but, in his heart, he knew, the same as nearly everyone else did, that the prospect of another war was a reality. By next summer, they could all be dead, so there was little point in making plans so far ahead.

The following Friday he gave Esther some extra money. 'Buy the children a decent present each', he said, 'and order whatever food you'll need for Boxing Day. That's when we'll have a Bit of a Do.'

Alex was doing some training with the Royal Navy and didn't know if he'd be able to get away but he said he would try to wheedle a couple of hours on Boxing Day, and Frances wrote, in reply to Esther's invitation, that she, Albert and David would love to come down for the party. Barbara said she would come but didn't know about her mother as she was still suffering from the shock of losing her husband so suddenly and couldn't face meeting people. 'Load of old rubbish,' Esther said, unsympathetically. 'She just doesn't want to mix with us *common* people, that's all it is.'

But it was the reaction from next door that surprised her. Mrs Cheswick said that, yes, they would love to come but would Esther mind if the two children came along too. 'They're four and five,' she said.

'Of course they can,' Esther said, a bit puzzled. Why would anyone think they'd have to leave their children alone on Boxing Day of all days? She'd never seen a sign of any children in the garden and had assumed they were grown up.

The man serving behind the counter at the Co-op ran his eyes over Esther's grocery order. 'Blimey, Mrs Cartarett,' he said, 'you feedin' the five-thousand for Christmas?'

Esther laughed. 'No, Mr. Simms, we're having a party on Boxing Day, and I hope you've got everything on that list, else I shall have to go down the road to Pinks.'

'Better get the boy to deliver this, hadn't I?' Mr. Simms said. 'You'd need an Army to carry this lot home.'

Phyllis offered to help get the food ready. She seemed much happier now although there were still some things she had to help Jack with, like putting his socks and shoes on as, if he bent over, it made him feel dizzy. They had put all thoughts of divorce to one side for the time being, and, as she said to Esther, the money Jack had been saving was helping to keep their heads above water, so they would have to wait and see. On Boxing Day morning, she went across to Esther's and the two of them started getting everything ready for the party.

Esther was on tenterhooks. If Alex could get a couple of hours off, it would mean all the family being together for the first time in years. Her excitement was clouded a little by the thought that no one knew what would be happening this time next year, but for now they must make the most of the present and try not to dwell on what might be ahead. At ten o'clock, Albert and Frances arrived with David, and a box full of Frances's home made pork pies, some shortbread biscuits, and presents for the children. By dinnertime when there was still no sign of Alex, Esther began to feel downhearted. She had so hoped that everyone would be together for this party but he was in the Navy now and she knew he couldn't just come and go as he pleased.

The party was due to start at five o'clock and at a quarter to, Esther answered the front door to find Mrs Cheswick standing on the step with her husband and two children. Esther did her best not to let her face register the shock of seeing that the youngest child was

Mongoloid but Mrs Cheswick was quick to notice. 'You did say we could bring them along,' she said.

Esther invited them in. 'You're all very welcome,' she said, wishing the ground would open and swallow her up. 'Come in and meet everyone else.' If only she had known about the child, she could have told the others and prevented the awful silence that followed when she opened the sitting room door and ushered her neighbours in. As it was, Frances saved the day by drawing them into the crowd and doing the introductions.

Betsy had the typical round face and almond shaped eyes of a Mongoloid, and was the elder of the two children; her brother Eric a normal four year old boy, who was the image of his father. Once the shock of seeing the child had worn off, the party went with a swing. Jack had brought along his gramophone and records, and he kept the children entertained with musical games until they fell about exhausted.

By the time the food was served, Barbara and her mother still hadn't turned up. 'I suppose,' Esther said to Phyllis, 'that woman has preyed on Barbara's sympathy and stopped her from coming on her own.' While she was handing round plates of food, she kept looking towards the door, still hoping Alex would make it. She didn't have long to wait, and had just taken some plates into the kitchen when the back door opened and there he was, all dressed up in his ratings uniform, and sporting a beard. 'Oh my God,' she said, 'what's that thing growing on your chin?'

Alex laughed as he stroked the mass of black, curly hair it had taken him weeks to grow. 'Lots of blokes have 'em,' Alex said. 'Saves gettin' up early to shave. An' the girls like 'em too.'

'*Alex,* you're supposed to be engaged to be married.'

He grinned. 'Yes Mum, but I'm not married *yet.*' He gave her a hug then went through to the sitting room. 'Is Barbara not here?' he said.

'No. she's not,' Frances said, 'and, judging by what I've just heard you say to your Mum, it's just as well she isn't.'

David had bought himself a camera. He took some photographs, and Esther noticed that Mrs Cheswick tried to hide Betsy behind her skirt, so she took the little girl's hand and pulled her to the front with the other children. Mr Cheswick offered to take one of the Cartarett family all together and Esther was pleased to see David and Alex posing with their arms around each other's shoulders.

'I'm just going to nip up the road and see if I can drag Barbara away,' Alex said presently but he was back within ten minutes with a glum face. 'Can't leave the old lady,' he said, 'and *she* won't come.'

The party began to break up when Albert said it was time to go, and Alex, who'd only managed to get a short pass out from the barracks, announced that he had to get back by ten o'clock or he'd be in hot water. It seemed to Esther that, one minute the house was bursting at the seams and the next it was almost empty. The Cheswicks left soon after Alex, and thanked Harry and Esther for inviting them.

'Do you know,' Esther said to Phyllis, who'd stayed behind to help clear up, 'we don't even know their Christian names. What an odd couple. And Mrs Cheswick seemed almost ashamed of that poor little girl. Did you see the way she tried to hide her when the photographs were being taken?'

Phyllis said she did, but it was understandable in a way. 'Lots of people are embarrassed when they see Mongoloids,' she said.

'I don't know why,' Esther replied. 'They're just little children who are a bit different, that's all.' She asked how Jack was getting on.

'His leg plays him up a bit sometimes but otherwise, he's doing all right,' Phyllis said. 'He should be able to go back to work in the New year.'

'That's good. And what about the divorce plans?'

'I don't think it'll come to that now,' Phyllis said. 'It's a pity that Jack had to have an accident to make us see sense, but we've both realised that we can't do without each other and must have been off our heads to even think about it.'

'I'm really glad Phyllis. And what do *you* think about the rumours going round about another war?'

'I think they are more than rumours,' Phyllis said, 'and it's *when*, not *if* any more. It frightens me to death when I think about it. Luke was talking the other day about enlisting in the Air Force and Terry says he'd like to join the Army.'

'Well, if it happens,' Esther said, 'they'll have to go anyway so they might as well volunteer now, and do what they want. I don't know about David. He's not mentioned it.'

'All we can hope for,' Phyllis said, 'is that it won't last long. Some of the Big Wigs up in the Government reckon just a couple of months but I don't believe that.'

'I do.' Esther said, optimistically.

The evening after the party, Barbara called in and apologised for not coming. 'It's very difficult,' she said, 'with mother the way she is, and I couldn't leave her alone on Boxing Day, could I?'

Esther felt like telling her that spending ten minutes with Alex would not have done her mother any harm, but held her tongue. She didn't want to be responsible for causing any trouble, and Alex wouldn't thank her for speaking her mind. 'Your mother needs an interest,' she said. 'She needs something to occupy her mind.'

Barbara agreed. 'If this war comes,' she said, 'she'll have to live on her own anyway because I've decided to join the Women's Auxilliary Air Force.'

And that, thought Esther, will see the end of Alex's little romance.

CHAPTER TWENTY

David couldn't get Sally out of his mind, and the more he thought about her, the more determined he was to see her again. For the first time in his life he felt as normal as the next man. All that talk of him being a Nancy Boy had been just the men at work, egged on by Totter, having what they thought was a laugh. It hadn't been very funny at the time, but it was all in the past and David just wanted to forget it. He'd almost made an ass of himself over Adrian but wouldn't do that again in a hurry. Bronwen was sweet, and he'd taken her out a few times, but she was just a friend, and in any case, she had decided to go back to Swansea to live. 'Mam's on her own and misses me,' she told him, 'and me brother's gone and joined the Air Force so she'd like me back home, especially now there's going to be a war.'

At the beginning of February, Esther was surprised to get a letter from David asking if he could come and stay for a few days. He didn't say why, and she wondered if there was anything amiss down in the New Forest.

'For God's sake,' Harry said when she told him, 'why do you always have to see things that aren't there? He probably wants to have a holiday before the smallholding gets busy, that's all.'

He arrived in the middle of a Monday afternoon, just as Esther was going to pick the children up from school. 'I won't be long,' she said, 'help yourself to whatever you want from the larder.'

David checked his pocket watch. Sally finished work at five o'clock and he wanted to be there for when she left the office. 'It's all right Mum,' he said. 'I'm off out, and I'll have something when I get back.'

As he strolled along Highland Road towards Southsea, where Sally worked, he wondered if he was doing the right thing by trying to steal someone else's fiancée away from them. After all, the man, whoever he was, had bought a ring, and Sally must have promised to marry him. Still, he reasoned, being engaged wasn't the same as being married to someone, and it was up to Sally to make her own mind up whose wife she wanted to be. People broke engagements off all the time, although there was always the risk of being sued for Breach of Promise.

The Accountants Sally worked for had its offices within one of the large houses in Tennyson Square, just a stone's throw from the seafront at Old Portsmouth. A heavy, sea fog had rolled in covering the name plates of the businesses that were carried on there, and David couldn't be sure whether or not he'd found the right address. He stood outside, underneath a lamppost and waited, and thought he'd had his patience rewarded when, about ten minutes' later, the front door of the house opened and several people came out. But there was no sign of Sally.

'What are *you* doing here?' He nearly jumped out of his skin as a hand tapped him on the shoulder and he swung round to see her standing behind him. 'Lucky I saw you, else you'd have been here all night. This is the wrong house.' She pointed to one three doors' down. 'That's it, over there.'

'I wanted to see you,' David said.

'What for?'

'I don't know, really.' He was beginning to feel a bit of a fool. How did he put into words that he'd come all the way from the New Forest to ask her to break off her engagement to a man that, for all he knew, she was in love with.

'Will you marry me Sally Totter?' he said. He couldn't believe he'd said it but there, it was out, and if she laughed at him, he'd be mortified. She didn't.

'You know I'm engaged, David,' she said, holding up her left hand to remind him. 'He's a nice man and I can't let him down.'

'Who is he?' David wanted to know. She'd said nothing about her feelings for this man, only that he was *nice*.

'His name's Howard, and I think you know him. He works at Dangerfield's.'

'Not Howard Drayfus?'

'Yes.'

'But he's *years'* older than you.'

'I know.'

It didn't make any sense to David. Sally must be about twenty now but this Howard Drayfus was at least thirty-five, and a widower with two children. Whatever was a girl like Sally doing promising to marry an old man like that?

'Look,' David said, as they reached the corner of the road where she lived, 'let me take you out tomorrow night; anywhere you like, and we can talk about this. I'm not going to stand by and see you marry someone nearly old enough to be your Dad.'

He went to kiss her, and she flung her arms around him. 'I do love you David,' she said, 'and always have, but I don't know if I can face telling Howard I don't want to marry him after all. He'll be so hurt.'

'Better to do that,' David said, 'than go through with it and spend your life being unhappy.'

They agreed to meet the following evening and David went back to Kestrel Road walking on air. He couldn't take it in that he'd proposed to Sally, and it looked as if she would accept him. His conscience bothered him a bit but Howard Drayfus would soon get over it and find someone else, nearer his own age.

'Where've you been?' Esther asked when he strolled in through the back door, sniffed the air and announced that the smell of steak and kidney pie was making him feel hungry.

'I've been asking a girl I know to marry me,' he said.

Esther stopped in her tracks. 'You've been doing *what*?'

'I've just proposed to Sally Totter. You know, the girl I used to take to the pictures on Saturday nights.'

Esther, her suspicions aroused about the motive behind this sudden announcement, went cold. She'd always wondered if there might be some truth in the names David had been called at Dangerfield's, and could only think that he'd decided to rid himself of the label by getting married. He'd only been out with this girl about half a dozen times, and hadn't, as far as she knew, seen her since his move to the New Forest. 'You can't marry someone you hardly know,' she said.

'I'm nearly twenty-two Mum, and can marry whoever I like.' The tone of his voice stopped Esther from saying anything more against what she thought was a ridiculous idea. She'd already alienated him once before and didn't want that to happen again.

'All right', she said, 'so when's the Happy Day?'

'As soon as possible', he said as he went through to the sitting room and switched on the wireless, 'before this war starts.'

They met at the corner of Sally's road the following evening and David told her about the plans he had. 'I'm quite rich now', he said, 'and I thought I'd buy a small cottage in the New Forest, close enough to Albert's so that I could still work for him, and we'd live there after we get married. You'd love it.'

'What about my mother?' Sally asked. 'She'll be left all on her own.'

'She can come too, if she wants,' David said, not caring what he was letting himself in for as long as Sally would be his wife. 'I'll buy one with three bedrooms so's there'll be plenty of room.'

'How about giving the bride to be a kiss then?'

Howard Drayfus was more than a little upset when the following evening Sally asked if he'd release her from their engagement. 'Is it someone else?' he asked.

'Yes. D'you remember David Cartarett who used to work at Dangerfield's?'

'Oh my God, not *him*. You must be off your head. D'you know what they used to call him at work? Nancy Boy, that's what.'

Sally already knew that from listening to her brother Sam and their father. She thought David was a bit well, *different* from most of the boys she'd been out with but didn't believe any of the stories that went around about him being unnatural. She knew him better than that.

'I'm really sorry, Howard,' she said, handing back his ring. 'It wouldn't work out, you and me. You need someone … well, *older*.'

In the end, he wished her well and she went home to tell her mother. Mrs Totter, who didn't want to lose her daughter to anyone, was relieved about the broken engagement until Sally told her about David and their plans. 'What about me?' she said. 'Am I to be left here all alone?'

'Oh, Mum, do stop feeling sorry for yourself. Of *course* you won't be left behind. David is going to buy a cottage big enough for all of us. Now isn't that kind of him?'

Harry, who had also had doubts about certain aspects of his eldest son, was pleased when Esther told him. 'If they're going to tie the knot,' he said, 'it had better be soon because, like it or not, we're going to be plunged into another war before very long.'

On 14th March, German troops marched into Austria, and the British people knew that all hopes of peace were lost. David and Sally brought the wedding, planned for June, forward to April, and on a day of unbroken, brilliant sunshine, they were married at Portsmouth Registry Office. This was to the relief of his parents, and the scepticism of his Uncle Albert and Auntie Frances who shared the view that any girl daft enough to wed their moody, unpredictable nephew, needed to have her head examined.

Sally, looking beautiful in a cream suit with matching hat and shoes, carried a posy of spring flowers, and Catherine acted as Bridesmaid. After a buffet tea, the newlyweds caught a train to Brighton for a two-day honeymoon and as the family waved them off, doubts Esther had about the marriage, and the reason for it, gave her the shivers.

'Cold?' Harry said.

'No, just someone walking over my grave,' she replied.

'Will you be sending Edwin and Catherine away?' Phyllis asked Esther, when news of plans for the evacuation of the big cities became widespread. They were sitting in Bransbury Park watching a gang of men fill sandbags, and then pile them up them against a newly built air-raid shelter.

'No', Esther said. 'The war, when it comes, will only last a couple of months, and besides, I don't want my children going off to God knows where, to live with strangers. Are you going to let Sarah go?'

'I don't think so, although Jack reckons there will be air raids, and maybe gas attacks, so he says we should think about it.'

'He's talking rubbish,' Esther said, determined not to believe the truth when it was staring her in the face.

It was July, and all over the city, preparations for war were underway. Brick air raid shelters seemed to have sprung up everywhere overnight, in parks, on corners of streets, and even in churchyards. The issue of gas masks had begun, and there was talk of conscription for men and boys over a certain age.

'Have you heard say that food is going to be rationed?' Esther said.

Phyllis laughed. 'That's another rumour going around. Like the one that says we've got to bury ourselves underground in some tin shed when the air raids come.'

'Anderson shelters you mean.'

'Is it true then?'

'All I know,' Esther said, 'is that everyone with a garden will get one, and in London, some people have been given theirs already. Harry says that you have to dig down at least four feet to put it up, and only very old and infirm people will get someone to do it for them. The rest of us will have to do it ourselves.'

'Jack won't be able to do that,' Phyllis said. 'He's still having problems with his leg.'

'Don't worry. We'll ask David to come down and give a hand.'

'How are the newly-weds getting on?' Phyllis asked. 'Have you heard?'

'They're all right as far as I know. David has bought a cottage, close to Albert and Frances, and he and Sally and her mother moved in last week, after all the legal bits had been settled. The trouble is, he's likely to be called up soon and how it'll all turn out I don't know.'

'You're not happy about it, are you?' Phyllis said. 'Them getting married I mean.'

Esther didn't answer right away. She'd had her doubts about the marriage from the start, *and* the reasons for David suddenly deciding to get married. She knew she shouldn't think ill of her own son, but not only was David difficult to live with, there was still the question of his preferences. How a sweet girl like Sally would be able to cope with his moods, Esther couldn't imagine. And there was the business of Sally's mother living with them too. 'I suppose,' she said to Phyllis, 'I'm worrying about nothing, as usual, but I do wonder if it'll all work out.'

'I've signed on for the R.A.F., Mum,' Luke announced. 'And Terry has joined the Army.'

Phyllis dropped into a chair, her head in a whirl. She'd just arrived back from her walk with Esther, to find both her sons home early from work, and waiting to break the news she had been dreading to hear for some time.

'Does your father know anything about this?' she asked.

'Of course not,' Luke, said. 'We only decided yesterday, didn't we Terry.'

Terry nodded. He hadn't been too sure about going ahead without telling their parents but Luke had said that their mother would have tried to put a stop to it had she known.

'In any case Mum,' Luke said, 'we'll have to go sooner or later and at least we've been able to choose what we want to do.'

'When?' Phyllis said.

Luke put his arm around his mother. 'In about a week or two, when our papers come through. Everyone's doing it Mum. Alex is already in the Navy, and David will have to do something soon. We've all got to go and do our bit.'

'I know son, but there are rumours that the Grammar School is going to be evacuated, and that means we'll lose Robert as well. Oh, my God, what *is* this world coming to.' She jumped to her feet, and in a rage, stormed off into the kitchen to get tea ready. 'And all because of some tin pot little German Dictator who wants to rule the world.'

Over the road at number twelve, Esther was reading a letter that had come by second post from David.

"Dear Mum and Dad,

Just to let you know that we have settled in our new home and everything's fine. I thought I ought to tell you that I've volunteered for the Royal Air Force and am waiting for my papers to come through. That's why I agreed for Sally's mother to come and live with us, so that Sally wouldn't be left down here on her own.
Will come and see you before I go.

Love David"

Esther stared at the scribbled sheet of paper, everything she'd been dreading now a reality. Alex would be joining his ship soon and although he wasn't allowed to say where he was going, she knew that wherever it was, he'd be in danger. Later that afternoon, Barbara called in to say that she'd signed on in the WAAF, and her mother would be giving up her nursing job and moving to Petersfield to stay with an old friend. 'It's the best thing for her,' Barbara said. 'It'll be safer out there than in Portsmouth, and I can go away without having to worry about her.'

Suddenly, Esther found herself thinking how selfish all the youngsters were. Never mind about their Mums and Dads, as long as they could do whatever it was *they* wanted. It was all very well being patriotic, but they didn't have a single thought in their heads for those who would be left behind at home to worry. She knew this was unreasonable but, what with children being sent away to strangers, and sons and daughters hardly out of nappies going off to fight a war no one wanted, there'd be hardly anyone under thirty left in Portsmouth before long.

Harry came home from work to find Esther banging about in the kitchen, her anger vented on whatever she could lay her hands on. 'What's up?' he said, as she flung an empty saucepan across the room and it landed with a crash in the sink.

She burst into tears and gabbled something about them losing all their children. 'Alex, David. Nearly half of our family gone, and who knows when, if ever, any of them will be back.'

She picked up a teapot but he took it from her in case she decided to throw that as well, drew her into the sitting room and pressed her down into a chair. 'Come on,' he said, holding both her hands in his, 'we've got to keep our chins up through all of this. Ours isn't the only family to be waving their children off to God knows where. And at least our boys are willing to go and do their bit, unlike some. There's a bloke at work who's having to put up with other blokes taunting him because they've found out his son is a Conchie, and is refusing to enlist in anything.'

'What's a Conchie?' Esther asked, sniffing into a handkerchief.

'It's a bloke who says he doesn't believe in killing. And that's all very well, but if every man thought like that, we'd soon be overrun by the likes of Hitler and his henchmen.'

'I suppose you're right,' Esther said.

'That's more like it. And now for some good news,' Harry said. 'I've some holiday to come and I thought I'd take it at the beginning of August when the schools break up. How would you like a day out to the Isle of Wight? And we could go down to the New Forest and see Albert and Frances, and David's new cottage. What d'you think?'

'That would be lovely,' Esther said.

'And to make it even better,' Harry went on, 'Jack is going to ask for the same week off so that he and Phyllis and their crew can come with us to the Isle of Wight.' A shadow crossed his face. 'It will probably be the last chance we'll have to enjoy ourselves for some time.'

At the end of July, Luke went off to Blackpool to do his RAF training and soon afterwards, Terry joined his Royal Artillery regiment in Yorkshire. It had already been decided that the Southern Grammar School should be evacuated to Winchester, and as Phyllis prepared to let Robert go, she thanked her lucky stars for Sarah, otherwise, there'd have been no one left at home bar her and Jack. Both Phyllis and Esther were looking forward to the holiday, which Harry had planned for the second week in August, and luck was with them, as it turned out to be the sunniest week of the month.

On the first day, loaded up with bags of food and buckets and spades, they caught the tram to Portsmouth Harbour where they boarded the paddle steamer Whippingham for their day trip to the Isle of Wight. Harry had already issued orders that there was to be no mention of the war while they were out, and as they sat on the crowded beach at Ryde, they tried to push all thoughts of what they knew was to come, to the back of their minds. The children paddled in the sea, played ball and built sandcastles while the grown ups relaxed in the sunshine, keeping their thoughts to themselves, although the war was never very far from any of their minds.

It was only when they were boarding the Whippingham to go home that they were reminded of the dark clouds hanging over Great Britain. Three men sitting together in one corner, their voices loud enough for everyone to hear, were discussing the reasons why they'd cut short their holiday and were on the way back to Portsmouth. They were all members of the ARP and each had decided to leave their families to finish the holiday on the island, and return home to where they knew they were needed.

'Looks like it's any minute now,' Jack whispered to Harry as they disembarked and made for the tram.

The following day, Harry, Esther and the children went by train to Southampton where Frances picked them up in the car. She had suggested they stay the night so that there'd be plenty of time to see David and Sally. 'It's a lovely little cottage he's bought,' Frances said, 'and they seem happy enough, except that David is going away soon.'

'How will Albert manage the small holding on his own?' Harry asked.

'David has been very generous and is paying for a man from the village to come in three days' a week to help out,' Frances said, 'although it won't be quite the same.' She began laying the table. 'Now, how about some dinner?' she said.

David's cottage was only a few hundred yards down the lane, and he was putting a coat of whitewash on the outside when they arrived. He climbed down the ladder and gave Esther a hug. 'I'm glad you could get down today', he said, 'because I'm off to Blackpool tomorrow. The papers came through last week and they don't give you much time to get going.'

Esther felt the familiar tightening of the knot in her stomach but she tried not to let her fear show. 'All these handsome young men in uniform,' she said, 'and two of them belong to me.'

'Us', Harry said from behind. He shook David's hand. 'All the best, son', he said, past differences forgotten now that his eldest was about to help fight a war, and might be one of its victims.

'Thanks Dad. Come inside and see Sally's Mum. Sally's found a job in the village and she'll be home at three.'

The cottage, which Sally had named Penny-Farthings, was spacious, with sloping ceilings and tiny, latticed windows. Esther felt almost claustrophobic but had to admit that Sally had turned it into a comfortable home, with its chintz furnishings and brass knick-knacks. Everywhere, there were vases of flowers, and pictures of country scenes covered the walls. Of course, Esther thought, David has plenty of money to spend on luxuries like that but all the same, Sally had spent his money wisely.

Her mother was a small, wizened woman, with what Phyllis would have called, a "disapproving slant" to her mouth. Esther tried unsuccessfully to steer the conversation away from the older woman's monologue about her aches and pains, and was relieved when Sally came home from work and changed the subject. She was working part-time for Adrian's father who was still the village Doctor. She typed his letters, answered his telephone, and made appointments for him to see his patients. 'I'm really enjoying it Mrs Cartarett,' she said. 'It'll keep me occupied when David goes away.' Her eyes filled with tears. 'I shall miss him so much,' she said.

When Harry, Esther and the children arrived back in Portsmouth, it was to find that the Corporation had delivered Anderson air raid shelters to every house in the road. Esther went across to see Phyllis. 'I'm sorry,' she said, 'but David is going away tomorrow so I don't know who we can get to help dig those contraptions in.'

'It's all right,' Phyllis said. 'Mrs Mc Andrew's boys are willing to give a hand ... for a price, of course. I spoke to her yesterday and she thought it would keep them out of mischief.'

On the 24th August, all Military Reservists were called up, and the following week, Royal Navy Warships were ordered to their War

Stations. Preparations went ahead for the evacuation of the City's children but Esther was adamant that Edwin, Catherine and April were staying put, although Phyllis said she'd have to let Robert go with the Grammar School. Most people thought the war wouldn't last more than a couple of months anyway, so what was the point of it all?

Esther and Phyllis had already managed to buy some blackout material from the Landport Drapery Bazaar and spent one whole day on Phyllis's ancient sewing machine, making curtains for the windows, and on September 1st, the new blackout regulations came into force, with severe penalties for anyone breaking them. 'You can even go to prison for it,' Esther said.

'Before long,' Phyllis said, 'you won't be able to cough in the street without being fined.'

Sunday 3rd September dawned sunny and warm and, just before eleven o'clock, Phyllis and Jack, who didn't have a wireless of their own, went across to number twelve to listen to the Prime Minister make the speech everyone had been waiting for.

"I am speaking to you from the Cabinet Room at 10, Downing Street. This morning the British Ambassador in Berlin communicated to the German Government that unless we heard from them by 11 o'clock that they were prepared at once to withdraw their troops from Poland, a state of war would exist between us.

I have to tell you that no such undertaking has been received and that consequently this country is at war with Germany. You can imagine what a bitter blow it is to me that my long struggle to win peace has ended."

None of them listened to the end of Neville Chamberlain's speech. They'd heard enough. Esther and Phyllis cried, Harry and Jack sat just looking at each other then Harry stood up and switched the wireless off and they all went out into the garden where the wail of the first air raid siren of the war was filling the air with its chilling warning of things to come. Harry reassured the two anxious women that it was just a practice run. 'Nothing to worry about,' he said.

They stood among the sprout plants and cabbages in Harry's vegetable patch and looked up at the clear blue sky of an autumn just beginning, and each had the same thoughts. Their lives and those of millions of other people were about to change forever and there was absolutely nothing any of them could do about it.

PART TWO

The misfortunes of War

1940-1945

Chapter Twenty-One

'I don't know why there was all this fuss about air-raid shelters,' Esther said to Harry. 'It's been over six months' since war was declared and we've not had a sign of a raid yet.' It was a Sunday morning in March 1940, and they were standing in the front garden, admiring the daffodils that Harry had planted around the edges of the Anderson shelter to brighten it up a bit. Now in full bloom, their bright yellow flowers lifted the gloom of the early months of a war that looked as if it was going nowhere.

The streets of the City were unnaturally quiet, with so many children having gone away to the safety of the country. Just in case the raiders came, their mothers said. David had finished his training as an Armourer while Alex, having passed his exams as a signalman in the Navy, had spent his twenty-first birthday "somewhere at sea." His fiancée, Barbara Tracey had joined the WAAF, and, having deposited her widowed mother with a friend at Petersfield, was in the Midlands, learning how to plot aircraft.

Across the road, Harry and Esther's friends, Jack and Phyllis had also waved "goodbye" to their three sons, Luke to the RAF and Terry to the Royal Artillery. Their other son Robert was in Winchester with the Grammar School.

'I think,' Harry said, snapping off the heads of a few flowers that had gone over, 'that we shall be glad of these shelters before long. Things are hotting up across the water.'

'Oh, Harry, why is it that you always have to look on the black side?'

'I'm only facing up to the truth, and I wish you'd do the same Esther.'

'I can't.' she said.

After one of the harshest winters in living memory, the early spring sunshine was a welcome break from weeks of bitterly cold weather. It was because of the ice and snow that the German bombers had not yet started their bombing raids over England, Harry told her. Now that weather conditions had improved, things would be different, she would see. It wasn't that he wanted to frighten her half to death but she just wouldn't face up to the fact that there could be more to this war than she was prepared for.

The daily papers had reported on the number of parents who were bringing their children home from the country, where they'd been evacuated for reasons of safety. The "Phoney War", as it was called, had fostered an attitude of complacency among the General Public, and there was wide concern within the Government.

Harry and Esther went indoors to find Edwin sitting at the table writing. Some of his stories had been on show at an exhibition of children's work, and one of them, about a boy and his magic umbrella had won first prize. Even Harry admitted that the boy was clever with words, and gifted but still warned Esther against harbouring any false hopes. As he'd said once before, story telling's fine as a hobby but not as a means of keeping a roof over your head. Esther listened and kept her own thoughts to herself.

That afternoon, Frances turned up without warning, and Esther's stomach turned over when she opened the front door to find her sister-in-law standing on the step. 'It's all right', Frances said, seeing the look on Esther's face, 'nothing wrong. Well, not really. I decided to come down by train for a couple of hours as I needed someone to talk to, and the natives where I live are still unfriendly. Not that I could discuss this with any of *them*.'

'Where's the car?' Esther asked as she poured tea, and Harry took his out into the garden to leave the two women to talk.

'No petrol I'm afraid.'

'Oh dear, something else in short supply I suppose. Now what did you want to talk about?'

'It's Sally,' Frances said. 'I don't know what's wrong, and it's not my place to ask, but she seems very unhappy. David has only managed one week-end's leave since he went away, so it may be that, although I doubt it. I wondered if you'd heard from her.'

'As a matter of fact, I have,' Esther replied, 'and reading between the lines, she sounded down in the dumps. Like you though, I thought it might be to do with David being away. What else could it be do you think?'

Frances looked blank. 'Goodness knows.'

'Why don't you ask her?' Esther said. 'I can't. I'm David's mother, but you're not as close to her as I am, and she might be able to talk to you.'

'Yes, maybe I will.'

Esther asked her if she'd like to stay to tea. 'I've made one my of famous fruit cakes', she said, 'although with butter and sugar on ration, it's getting difficult, and I had to make everyone take saccharin in their tea for a couple of days, so I could find enough sugar. You should have seen the long faces and heard the moans and groans.'

Frances said she would love to stay but not for too long as she had to catch the train back. 'I miss the car,' she said. 'And talking about shortages, meat's just gone on ration too. I don't know how we're supposed to feed our hard working men on what they've allowed us.'

'Nor I,' Esther agreed.

They were all at the tea table when Harry asked how Albert was managing with the smallholding.

'He misses David, of course,' Frances said, 'but there's a man comes in three times a week and he's very good. With food getting scarcer by the day, Albert hopes he'll be able to make a profit this year from his veg.'

225

'And what about you?' Harry asked. 'What do you find to do all day?'

'Oh, I make jam, bake my own bread, clean the house, do the washing and ironing, cook the dinner, and in between, stand on my head and sing "Rule Britannia". You know. All those interesting things we women love to do.'

Esther was surprised at the bitterness in Frances's voice.

'Why don't you join something?' Harry said.

'Because I don't want to become one of the Hats, Handbags and "have you heard?" … Brigade, that's why.'

Harry and Esther laughed at the quaint expression, and then dropped the subject. Frances left just after tea, and after she'd gone, Esther thought about the visit and wondered what was going on. Sally was unhappy, and Frances herself sounded despondent. Whatever was it about the New Forest that had this effect? Or was it simply the uncertainty about the war that was getting everyone down? Probably the latter, she decided, trying to push to the back of her mind all previous thoughts of David having married Sally in order to prove to himself, and others, that he was the same as other men.

On the 9th April, news came in that Germany had invaded Norway and Denmark. Esther was worried about Alex, whose well-censored letters told her nothing. He wrote as often as he could but, by the time half the contents had been blue-pencilled out, there was nothing much left to read. She had no idea where he was and just prayed he would come back home in one piece. David wrote occasionally from his airbase in Cambridgeshire, and all she knew about him was that he might be due for an overseas posting soon. The news, on the 10th May, was grim. Germany had invaded Belgium, Holland and Luxembourg, and Neville Chamberlain resigned.

'Who will we have as Prime Minister now?' Esther asked, not really understanding politics at all but trying to show an interest.

'Winston Churchill,' Harry said.

Esther had never heard of the man. She went back to reading her magazine, which was far more interesting.

The following morning, she went across to see Phyllis. It had become a habit for the two women to see each other at least once a day, in order to ask after their absent children. She told her what little news she had of David and Alex, leaving out the reason for Frances's visit, and then asked after Luke and Terry. 'Have you heard from them?' she said, as she and Phyllis settled down for their cup of tea.

'Both, in fact,' Phyllis said. 'Luke is doing well and loves the life. He's been made up to Leading Aircraftsman and is working in the Station Stores in Hereford. Terry is somewhere in France but it's ages since we had a letter, and the news doesn't look good from there.'

'How is Robert getting on?'

'He seems to be happy enough,' she said, 'but there's a lot of homesickness among the boys, and some talk of bringing them all back to Portsmouth, although I doubt if that'll happen, especially now that things in Germany are getting so much worse.'

Esther admitted that, at last she'd come to realise just how serious it all was. 'I suppose,' she said, 'I've been burying my head in the sand, and hoping it would be a nine-day wonder. Harry seems to think that the air raids will start soon.'

'He's probably right,' Phyllis said.

Five days' later, on the 15th May, German troops went into the Dutch capital, and a fortnight later, Belgium surrendered. Phyllis was out of her mind with worry. 'I've heard,' she said to Esther, 'that thousands of our troops are trapped, with no way of escape, and Terry is out there somewhere.'

'He'll come through, you'll see,' Esther said. 'And you don't want to believe everything you hear on the news.'

'Did you know that Mrs Mc Andrew's eldest boy has been called up for the Army?' Phyllis said. 'The other one is too young but the way things are going, they'll be after him next. Some of them are no more than babies.'

'No, I didn't know. I try my best to avoid her if I can,' Esther said.

That same evening, Harry mentioned evacuation for Patrick and Catherine but Esther was adamant that she didn't want them to go. 'Who knows where they'll end up,' she said. 'I've heard some terrible stories about how some of those poor little devils are being mistreated, and I'd rather keep our own children here with us.' She told him about Terry. 'They don't know where he is,' she said. 'Only that he's in France somewhere.'

'That's not good news,' Harry said. 'But don't go saying anything to Phyllis. Rumour has it that thousands of our troops are in retreat and heading for the beaches in Northern France, and that the Jerries are all set to blow them into eternity as soon as they get there.'

'My God,' Esther said, 'whatever is this world coming to?'

Private Terry Martindale lay on his belly in the sand dunes at Dunkirk, his hands over his ears in an effort to drown the noise of the guns and the screams of his comrades as they died at the hands of the Luftwaffe. 'Bastards,' he shouted to his friend Peter Jonas, who was sitting up with his head in his hands, crying like a child, and whose nerves had splintered into a thousand pieces. 'Get down Pete, for Christ's sake get down!'

Peter Jonas, as if he couldn't hear the warning, didn't move, whilst all around him bullets from the enemy machine guns skittered through the sand, missing him and Terry by inches. Terry raised himself on one elbow and, leaning over, gave his friend a shove, but he was too late to stop a hail of bullets from landing a direct hit in the other man's chest. For a moment, Peter's face registered shock as he rolled over on his back, arms and legs twitching like a half-dead fly, before sheer terror took him. He screamed, cried out for his mother, and then, his head rolling to one side, sank into oblivion. Terry watched, horrified as the jacket his friend was wearing turned bright red, and knew that it was too late for anyone to do anything for him. He leaned across and closed the dead man's eyes, then made the sign of the cross over him. Although he'd seen it done in films, he had no idea what it meant, except that it was some sort of mark of respect. Then he dug further into the sand in an effort to save himself from a similar fate.

All around was pandemonium and chaos. There were bodies everywhere; some dead, others badly wounded, with grown men, many with limbs hanging off or missing, crying out for their mothers and sweethearts. Relentlessly, the Luftwaffe kept up its attacks on the soldiers, who, with only the sea in front of them, had no way of escape. Terry had managed to crawl to the shelter of a sand dune and he, along with several others, sat and prayed that somehow they'd be rescued from this Hell.

Unknown to them, help was on its way in the shape of hundreds of boats that were trying to cross the English Channel without detection by the Germans. Under cover of darkness, craft of every shape and size were creeping across the water to rescue as many of the stricken men of the British Expeditionary Force as they could. Anything that could float had joined in the operation. There were river launches, old sailing boats, pleasure steamers, rowing boats, fishing boats and barges, many without even a compass to guide them. Most of the larger vessels were manned by Naval crews, the smaller boats being used to negotiate the shallower waters. Once the Germans realised what was going on, they intensified their attacks and dozens of the little boats, many full of soldiers who thought they were safe, were blasted, along with everyone on board, into eternity.

Terry crawled through the sand dunes until he reached the shore, where he kept his head down and waited. Suddenly, a small rowing boat loomed up out of the darkness. Jumping to his feet, he waded out to where he could reach it and, with the help of the skipper, climbed aboard. There was only room for about six men, and the little boat almost capsized when a fight broke out among those desperate for a chance to get away. In the end, eight managed to squeeze in, and as Terry watched the faces of those left behind; desperate men standing waist high in freezing water, he leaned over the side and was sick.

Dawn was breaking when the little boat crept silently away from the shore, somehow managing to dodge the worst of the enemy action. The Germans were strafing everything they could find, and Terry and the other men flung themselves to the deck as the sailing boat next to them received a direct hit from a bomb and exploded in a ball of fire, the remains of all its occupants tossed into the red-stained sea. The swell almost capsized the rowing boat Terry was in, but the skill of the skipper and his mate kept it afloat, and they battled on as if nothing had happened. Everywhere, there were bodies and bits of bodies floating in the sea. Bodies of men who, less than half an hour ago, had been celebrating their escape from Hell, but were now part of the flotsam drifting on the sea off some alien French coast, far from home. Terry thought briefly about his friend Peter Jonas, who was married with a two-year old son.

Once out of the shallow waters, the small boat transferred its passengers to a pleasure steamer, anchored about a mile offshore, and manned by the Royal Navy. The ship, having already taken parties of soldiers off the smaller boats, was already full, and there was barely room for more, but Terry managed to squeeze into a tiny space on deck, and the hazardous journey to Dover began. He dozed for most of the time, only waking when one of the other men in the boat went off his head and with a scream, jumped overboard into the sea. 'Poor Bugger', one of the sailors said. 'Come all this way, and then lost his mind.'

Terry couldn't be certain how long the journey had taken but when dawn broke and he woke up, the coastline of England was clearly visible. Soon, he'd be back in Pompey for a spell of leave, and after that? Who knew?

For three days after the news came out about the evacuation of Dunkirk, Esther spent as much time as she could with Phyllis while everyone waited to hear what had happened to Terry. They all dreaded the arrival at the door of the Telegram Boy and when, after the third day, nothing had happened, Phyllis was convinced her son had been killed.

'Don't give up,' Esther said. 'The soldiers are still arriving back in England and until everyone has been checked out, no-one knows what has happened.' She knew there was a possibility that Terry could be one of the casualties but Phyllis was in such a state that it didn't do to speculate about what had become of him.

It was on the 1st June that Esther, on her way to the shops, saw a frantic Mrs Mc Andrew waddling down her garden path, waving a newspaper in the air. 'Look at this Mrs Cartarett,' she said, stabbing a finger at a photograph on the front page. 'If that aint young Terry Martindale, I'll eat my 'at.'

Esther almost snatched the copy of the Daily Mirror from Mrs Mc Andrew's hand. The photograph of some of the survivors of Dunkirk, showed a group of haggard, dishevelled, soldiers having a meal inside a tent, and there, right in the front, was Terry. Without even asking if she might borrow the paper, she ran back up the road with it in her hand and hammered on Phyllis's front door.

'Look at this,' she yelled at the top of her voice. 'It's Terry. He's all right.' She showed the photograph to Phyllis, threw her arms around her and the two of them stood on the path crying their eyes out like a couple of children.

'I must go and tell Jack,' Phyllis said, running indoors to get her coat.

Esther said she'd look after Sarah, and Phyllis flew off to the dairy as fast as her legs would carry her. Once there, she ran past the astonished faces of the Milkies who were loading their carts for their second delivery, and into Jack's office.

He jumped out of his chair in alarm. 'What is it?' he said, snatching the paper from her outstretched hand. 'Is it Terry?'

'He's alive', was all she managed to say before keeling over in a dead faint.

Terry arrived home a few days' later for a week's leave. 'Is that all they've given you?' Phyllis said, 'after what you've been through.'

'Mum, there's still a war on,' he replied.

When Jack asked him what had happened on the beaches of Dunkirk, he refused to talk about it. He would never be able to forget the sight of his friend Peter lying dead beside him, or those poor devils blown apart in the steamship, and he didn't want to tell anyone what it was like. 'It was Hell on earth, Dad', he said, 'and that's all I want to say about it.'

'Where to now son?' Jack asked.

'I don't know, but there's some talk of us being posted to the Med.'

'Another trouble spot,' Jack said.

On the 10th June, Italy declared war on the allies, and when Terry went back to his station, he discovered that his Regiment would be leaving for the Mediterranean within two weeks.

'They haven't given the poor lads time to get over Dunkirk,' Phyllis complained, when she read the letter from Terry telling them about his posting.

'There's a war on, and they have to go where they're needed,' Jack said.

France surrendered to the Germans on the 21st June, and on the 1st July, they invaded the Channel Islands, the news prompting Harry, the following weekend, to do something about making things as comfortable as he could in the Anderson shelter. 'It's only a matter of time', he said to Esther, 'before we'll need to use it, and God knows how many hours we'll have to spend down there'. He found an old piece of linoleum for the floor, and made two bunk beds so that at least the children had somewhere to sleep. From a couple of old wooden crates, he made a bench, and Esther found some cushions to make it comfortable. A supply of matches and candles, some board games and a pack of playing cards, plus a chamber pot and they were all set up for the inevitable air raids that would start within weeks.

David called in to see his mother one afternoon, on his way through to Southampton. He was on his way home for seven days' embarkation leave, and decided to break his journey before travelling on from Portsmouth to Southampton. Esther, who was pleased to see him, thought he looked tired and a bit under the weather, and she asked if there was anything wrong.

'Not really,' he said, the look on his face stopping her from asking any more questions.

'Do you know where you're being posted to?' she asked.

'They don't tell us anything', he said. 'But I wouldn't mind betting it'll be Malta.'

She told him about Terry's ordeal at Dunkirk. 'He's off to the Med quite soon,' she said, 'and Luke, who's at Hereford, is being posted to Tangmere. It's not far from here, so he'll be able to come home quite often, which pleases his mother.'

'Some people have all the luck,' David said. He'd never liked either Luke or Terry much, and had not made a friend of either of them, so could not have cared less if they were going to the moon.

Esther felt her temper rising. 'I'd hardly call what Terry has been through luck', she said. 'It was hell on earth for the poor devils caught up in it.'

David couldn't stay long enough to see his father, who was still at work. He was anxious, he said, to get home to the New Forest to see Sally. What he didn't say was that, before he went overseas, he wanted to sort out the problems they were having.

Early in July, there was a letter from Alex to say that he was well, and hoped to be home in the near future, although he couldn't say any more than that. He asked if Esther had heard from Barbara, as he'd not had a letter from her for weeks. *"I expect she's been busy with her training and that,"* he wrote, but Esther had a suspicion that there was a bit more to it than that.

CHAPTER TWENTY-TWO

On the evening of the 11th July, the first air raid over Portsmouth took everyone by surprise. Harry had just come in from work, and Esther was getting the dinner ready when the wail of the siren spread across the city. There had been several practices but this was the real thing, and there was no time to lose. Esther, remembering to turn the gas off under the pan of stew, grabbed hold of April with one hand and Catherine with the other while Harry raced out into the back garden to fetch Edwin, collecting all the brown boxes containing their gas masks as he went. They ran to the shelter and scrambled down inside, Catherine crying because she'd hurt her knee, and within minutes, the air was filled with the drone of German aeroplanes coming in over the Solent. The noise was deafening and as the first salvo of bombs screamed towards earth, the ground rumbled and shook, and the shelter rattled as they hit their targets with a series of ear-shattering explosions. Catherine, her bad knee forgotten, screamed in terror and wet herself, and Edwin, his face as white as a sheet, sat on one of the bunk beds, his hands over his ears.

'My God,' Esther said, 'is this what it's going to be like?'

'Probably,' Harry replied, having a good idea that this was nothing compared with what was to come. The raid didn't last long and when the All Clear sounded, he climbed from the shelter and helped everyone out.

Most of the bombs had fallen in the Kingston area, and first reports the next day suggested that around eighteen people had died in the raid with more than seventy injured. The damage was mostly to business premises, although several houses, and a school used as a First Aid post also received a direct hit. Esther and Phyllis went for a walk to see for themselves the havoc caused by the air raid. They passed some badly damaged houses, whose roofs were full of gaping holes, and farther along the same street, a crater where a pile of rubble was all that remained of a row of terraced homes.

'Poor devils must have lost everything they owned,' Esther said, as they made their way back to Kestrel Road. 'And the next time, it could be us.' That night she wrote to Frances and told her about the raid, also asking if she'd found out what was wrong with Sally. The reply, when it came, didn't surprise her and only confirmed her own worst suspicions. Sally had confided in Frances that her marriage to David hadn't been properly consummated.

"Sally was glad of someone to talk to," Frances had written. "David can't ... you know ... finish what he starts, and aftermore than a year, Sally is still as pure as the day they married, if you understand my meaning. I didn't know what to say to the poor girl. Maybe you were right about him after all, but whatever the problem, he's going to need help to get it sorted out."

Esther didn't know whether to tell Harry or not. He'd always despised men who, according to him, weren't "normal," and he wouldn't make an exception for his own son, she knew that. In the end, she decided not to say anything for the time being. David was now on his way to Malta as far as she knew, so there was nothing to be gained by bringing it out into the open. In any case, it was something private between him and his wife and they would have to sort it out for themselves when he came home again.

On the 12th August, there was another air raid, lasting for over twenty-five minutes. Centred on the Portsea and Old Portsmouth areas, a public shelter received a direct hit, and a church destroyed. Although there was only one casualty from the shelter, the air raid resulted in a total death toll of thirteen people killed, with over one-hundred injured.

The evening after the raid, when the papers had confirmed the casualty figures, Harry brought up the subject of evacuation. 'We should think about sending Edwin and Catherine away,' he said, showing Esther the headlines in the Evening News. 'It's far too dangerous for them here, and even people who've brought their children back have started sending them away again.'

'Catherine's too young,' Esther said.

'She's nearly nine, and there've been others younger than that who've gone.'

'But where would they go?'

Harry laid his paper down. 'Anywhere it's safe,' he said. 'But it wouldn't be too far away. Think about it Esther, for goodness sake.'

She thought about it and knew it made sense, and she talked about it to Phyllis. 'Catherine will break her heart,' Esther said, 'but Harry's right. He says there's worse to come and that we won't always be as lucky at Eastbrook, living as we do near the Royal Marine Barracks. Sooner or later, the Jerries will be after that.'

Phyllis agreed, and at the end of August, Edwin and Catherine joined the crowds of other children who were destined for a place of safety somewhere in Surrey. Esther had to take them to the school first thing one morning, and the sight that met her brought tears to her eyes. Dozens of bewildered boys and girls, labels pinned to their clothes, were standing in lines in the playground. Clutching an assortment of carrier bags or battered suitcases containing their bits and pieces, and with a gas mask apiece in its familiar brown box, some were crying, others screaming, and Esther almost turned tail with Edwin and Catherine and took them back home.

'Poor little buggers,' a woman standing next to her said. 'But it'd be worse if they ended up under a pile of rubble, wouldn't it missus?'

'Yes,' Esther had to agree.

'Bloody Germans an' their bombs. My sister's just bin killed in the last air raid down at Portsea.'

Esther said she was sorry to hear that, and walked away, not wanting to hear the gruesome details. She hugged her children, and told Edwin to look after Catherine. 'Don't let them separate you,' she said. 'Keep together all the time. And don't forget to write and tell me where you are. Both of you.'

'Yes Mum,' Edwin said, fighting back the tears.

Catherine nodded. Esther was relieved that she seemed less upset than her brother did over the parting. They went to join one of the lines and the last she saw of them was as some officious looking woman in a Trilby hat herded them onto a Corporation bus, waiting to take them to the station to catch the train. She waved, hoping they could see her, and then went, with April, back to an almost empty house.

Within a matter of days, there were two letters. One was from Catherine who was staying with a family at Haslemere and seemed happy enough, although she was a bit homesick, and another from Edwin in which he said that he and several other boys were at a large house in Hindhead. *'I'm going to run away and come home,' he said. 'It's horrible here.'* The following afternoon, an official from the Evacuation Committee called at number twelve to say that Edwin was missing from his billet and had he turned up at home?

'No, he has *not*,' Esther said. 'And what are the authorities doing to allow a small boy to run away like that?' She told the woman to leave and that she, herself, would deal with it. Then she panicked. He might be eleven but he'd never been farther than the seafront in his life and would never find his way to Portsmouth from Hindhead. She didn't know what to do for the best, and in the end, went across to the Police Station in Milton Road, where she knew Harry's nephew would be.

'I shouldn't worry if I were you Auntie,' Walter Cartarett said, in his usual superior manner. 'All the road signs have been taken down so he won't get very far, and someone will find him. I'll give the Surrey Police a ring and tell them to look out for him.' He called in that evening to tell Harry and Esther that all the Police stations from Hindhead to Portsmouth had been alerted, and were on the look out for a small boy wandering around on his own. He said he had also had a telephone call from the house where Edwin had been staying, to say that he was missing. 'He'll be all right,' he said, giving Esther a peck on the cheek. 'You'll see.'

'Your nephew seems to have mellowed,' Esther said, after he'd gone, and she and Harry sat watching the clock and listening for the front door.

'Yes, well he's married now,' Harry said, 'and there's nothing like having a wife for making a man change his ways.'

Esther laughed for the first time that day. 'Funny we didn't get invited to his wedding though, isn't it?' she said.

Harry was about to answer that when there was a knock at the front door. Esther flew out of her chair and tore the door open to find a Police Constable on the step. She invited him in. 'Nothing to report yet,' he said. 'But he'll be found, never fear. He won't get far, not in the blackout.'

Harry thanked him for calling and showed him out. 'Now,' he said to Esther, 'you get off to bed and I'll stay up in case anything happens.'

Esther refused. 'No, Harry,' she said. 'I'll sit up with you.'

Edwin was lost. Darkness had fallen and there wasn't a chink of light to be seen anywhere. He'd forgotten about the blackout, and that there were no street lights, and heavy penalties for anyone showing even the tiniest sliver of light from the window of a house. He'd also forgotten that, for security reasons, every road sign had been removed.

Earlier that evening, just after tea, he'd slipped back to the room he shared with nine other boys, collected his case and gas mask and crept away from the house. It was still daylight, and he'd not realised that, once the sun went down, the whole of Great Britain would be plunged into darkness. Now, even if he'd wanted to go back to the Big House, which he didn't, he wouldn't know in which direction it lay. He'd hated it so much, with its dark, narrow dormitories and terrible food; especially the watery cabbage, and some disgusting pudding called Tapioca that reminded him of frog spawn. He always gave his to the boy sitting next to him, who would eat anything. Most of the time Edwin went hungry, and longed for his mother's neck of lamb stew or her steak and kidney pie and thick, golden, crispy chips. His mouth watered at the thought.

He groped his way along the road, holding on to anything he could find in the way of a gatepost or fence, and nearly died of fright when, through the gloom, he saw a pair of green eyes watching him. It was only a cat sitting on a wall, and when Edwin spoke to it, it jumped down and wound itself round his legs, purring loudly as he felt in the dark and tickled it under its chin. He was just beginning to despair when suddenly, the wind blew the clouds apart and a full moon bathed everything in light. He looked around and saw that he had been walking down a tree-lined avenue, on what looked like a main road. On either side, tall, imposing houses stood silhouetted against the night sky, and he noticed that across the road, there was a bus shelter. He made for that, the cat trotting along behind, and settled down on a bench for the night. Tomorrow, he would be able to find out where he was and how he could get from here to Portsmouth.

The following morning, a Police Constable from Haslemere found him, still asleep, with the cat curled up in a ball at his feet. The Policeman gave Edwin a gentle shake. 'Up you get Sonny Jim,' he said. 'The adventure's over.'

Edwin awoke with a start, unable to remember, for a few minutes, where he was. He looked up into the kindly face of the Policeman. 'I'm not going back to the Big House,' he said, as memories of his escape came flooding back to him. 'Not ever.'

'Well Sonny, that's a matter for your Dad when he gets here. Meantime, you'd best come back to the station with me, and we'll send a message to him to come and fetch you.'

'Where's the cat?' Edwin asked, looking round to see what had become of his night's companion.

'Skipped off back to the comfort of its own home, I shouldn't wonder,' the Policeman said. 'Now, let's get going.'

Harry and Esther arrived at the Police Station together, having had a visit from Walter with the news that Edwin was safe and well, and a Policeman had found him asleep in a bus shelter just outside Haslemere. Edwin burst into tears as Esther put her arms around him, and he begged her not to send him back to the Big House. Esther looked at Harry who nodded. 'It's all right,' she said, 'you can come home with us.'

Another air raid, on the 24th August, in broad daylight, killed more than a hundred people and left a large part of the city in ruins. It was a Saturday and the city was full of shoppers when the Germans launched their terrifying attack. Harry was at work, and Edwin, who wasn't supposed to go farther than the end of the road, had disappeared with some of his friends. When the siren went off, Esther grabbed April and ran to the shelter, hoping he would have the sense to find somewhere safe to hide out until it was over.

The bombing was far worse than in the two previous raids, and as Esther sang nursery rhymes to April, she prayed for the safety of her family, and wondered whether anyone of them would live to see the end of this war. When the All Clear sounded, she clambered out into the sunshine, thankful to be still in one piece. The bombs had fallen closer than before and she looked around to see if there had been any damage to the house.

'That was awful, wasn't it?' a voice from over the fence said. It was Mrs Cheswick, with her two children. 'I've been under the stairs, and the house shook as if it were going to fall down and bury us alive.'

Esther hadn't seen her neighbour in weeks, and couldn't understand why they didn't have an Anderson shelter like everyone else. 'You'd have been better off with one of those', she said, pointing to theirs.

Mrs Cheswick gave Betsy a look. '*She'd* scream the place down if we tried to get her to go down into such a small space. As it is, she'll only go under the stairs if we leave the cupboard door open, and she can sit in front of it.'

'I haven't seen you for ages,' Esther said, with one eye still on the front gate looking for Edwin. 'Are you all right?'

With another look at the unfortunate Betsy, Mrs Cheswick said that yes, she was perfectly all right, but couldn't take *her* anywhere without everyone staring at them.

Esther went indoors, her sympathies with poor Betsy, who seemed to be such a burden to her mother.

When, after half-an-hour, there was still no sign of Edwin, she began to worry. Surely, he wouldn't have gone far, and should be back home by now, unless something had happened to him. Her imagination began to run riot. He was lying injured beneath the ruins of someone's house, and the rescuers couldn't reach him. He was crying, asking for her, but no one could hear him, and she saw his face, all the colour gone, just as Daniel's had on that terrible Sunday morning when he'd died in her arms. By the time she heard the footsteps running down the side of the house, he was dead and they were taking him to the cemetery to bury him alongside his brothers.

'Where the hell have you been?' she screamed at him as, covered in black dust and shaking like a leaf, he tore through the open back door and into the kitchen. 'Get those filthy things off and go to your bedroom. *At once.*'

He opened his mouth to say something but she silenced him. 'Don't you ever do anything like this again. D'you hear me?'

He nodded, not sure which was worse, the air raid he'd been caught up in or his mother's temper.

After he'd dropped his clothes on the floor of the kitchen, and gone upstairs, Esther sat in a chair and cried her eyes out. Instead of showing him how pleased she was that he hadn't come to any harm, she'd gone off at him like some madwoman; a natural reaction Phyllis was to say later, when relief turns itself into anger.

That air raid had devastating consequences. Eight of the fatal casualties were in the Princes Theatre, which had a direct hit and was not far from Wimple Street. Esther wondered about The Shambles and if any of it was still standing. She put the kettle on a low gas then crept upstairs to see what Edwin was doing. He was sitting on his bed staring at the wall, his face still as white as a sheet, his eyes filled with tears and terror.

She sat beside him and put her arm around his shoulder. 'I was worried about you,' she said. 'That's why I lost my temper.'

Edwin couldn't understand that. If you were worried about someone, why did you go mad when you knew that they were all right? Grown ups just didn't make sense to him.

Esther asked him where he'd been during the raid. At the far end of Kestrel Road, an old dump was an open invitation to boys, and sometimes girls, who could play at almost anything there without the risk of a telling off by some miserable adult. Edwin and two of his friends had decided to go and see if anyone had dumped anything worth having when the siren sounded. 'We didn't think we'd get home in time,' he told Esther, tearfully. 'So we found this old tin shed and went in there 'til it was all over.'

'You frightened the life out of me,' Esther said, giving him a hug. 'And don't ever do anything like that again, will you?'

'No Mum, I won't.'

Esther pulled him to his feet. 'Now come down and have some tea. And not a word to your father about this. Promise?'

Edwin was happy to keep his escapade a secret.

Esther knew she shouldn't encourage the children to deceive their father but if Harry found out about the afternoon's events, he'd insist on sending Edwin away again, and she didn't want that. As it was, Catherine was now pleading to come home. She was with good people but felt homesick, she said in her letters, and, as Edwin had been allowed home, why wasn't she?

When Harry arrived home, he took Esther to one side to tell her that most of The Shambles was in ruins. 'Wimple Street's gone', he said, 'and most of the other streets, and there's nothing left of Old Joe Rigby's shop. The poor devils didn't have Anderson shelters, and there were plenty killed, so I heard from a bloke at work who lives there. He didn't know what had happened to his family and was sent home to help search for them.'

Esther was choked. 'I want to bring Catherine home,' she said. 'If we're going to die, I want us all to go together.'

'All right love, if that's what you want,' Harry said. 'We'll write to the people she's with and arrange to go and pick her up.'

At the end of August, Barbara, looking very smart in her WAAF uniform, came home on leave and called in to see Harry and Esther. She was only passing, she said, and would be going to Petersfield to stay, once she'd checked the house in Kestrel Road to make sure everything was all right. Esther noticed that she wasn't wearing Alex's engagement ring and couldn't resist asking where it was.

Barbara looked uncomfortable. 'I took it off,' she said, 'because it was getting tight, what with all the weight I've put on since joining up. I've put it away somewhere safe.'

They talked mainly about Alex, and Esther asked Barbara whether he still wrote to her. 'Yes, he does,' she replied, 'but not very often. He's not allowed to say what he's doing, or where he is, but I think it's something to do with escorting our troopships to wherever it is they're going.'

'I don't suppose you know when he'll be home for a spot of leave,' Harry put in. He was more than a bit worried about the number of British ships being sunk by German submarines, although he'd not said anything to Esther.

'In his last letter he said that he was hoping to be home sometime during the next couple of months,' Barbara said. 'The trouble is, I doubt if I'll be able to get home to see him as I'm shortly being posted to Scotland, and what with travel restrictions and that, it won't be easy.'

'I suppose not,' Esther said.

It was a tense visit, and Esther was glad when Barbara said she'd have to go to catch her train to Petersfield. 'Mother's expecting me,' she said, 'and you know what she's like.'

After she'd gone, Esther asked Harry what he'd thought.

'The same as you, I daresay,' he said. 'I think our Alex's going to be in for a shock when he comes home.'

Chapter Twenty-Three

April started school in September, and there was good news from Alex who wrote to say that he'd be coming home for a week at the beginning of October. He couldn't say where he'd been or what the ship had been doing, but the tone of his letter suggested he was tired. Harry and Esther had been to Haslemere to collect Catherine, the air raids seemed to have eased off a bit for the time being, and Esther, still convinced the war would soon be over, felt happier than she had for ages. She went across to Phyllis for their daily bulletin on the family.

'I thought,' she said, 'that Luke would come home more often than he does. After all, Tangmere's only just the other side of Chichester, and that's not far.'

'Oh, he's met some girl over there,' Phyllis said, 'and spends all his week-ends at her place. Kestrel Road's not good enough any more.'

'I'm sure that's not true,' Esther said. 'Anyway, why don't you ask him to bring her over here to meet you and Jack?'

'I have, and I'm still waiting for him to answer my letter.'

They exchanged news, and Esther told her that Alex was coming home. 'It'll be lovely having him home for a while. He sounded a bit down in his letter and I'm wondering if it's anything to do with

Barbara. She's not written to me since she was here in August, and that's unusual.'

'Perhaps she's met someone else,' Phyllis said. 'After all, it was a bit of a whirlwind romance. And people change when they leave home.'

Esther knew something was wrong the minute she set eyes on Alex when he arrived home. He looked older than his twenty-two years, and had lost much of the old sparkle he'd had when on the Merchant Ships.

'It's been terrible,' he said, when Esther asked what he'd been doing. He told her that the ship he was on had been helping escort convoys trying to get to Russia. 'The sea was swarming with German U-Boats and for weeks we were lucky if we could snatch a couple of hours' sleep at night, what with the fear of being hit ourselves, and the sights we saw when other ships were torpedoed.' He stared into his teacup. 'Then we were diverted to help with the rescue of the City of Benares but by the time we reached it, it was all over. All those children on their way to Canada and safety, as they thought, and so many of them drowned, Mum,' he said.

Esther remembered hearing about the evacuee ship torpedoed and sunk by a German Submarine in the Atlantic. There was so much loss of life, with more than eighty children lost, including five from one family. Now, she couldn't think of a thing to say that would ease the pain of remembering the tragedy for Alex. To change the subject, she asked after Barbara, thinking that might cheer him up. 'I haven't had a letter from her recently,' she said.

'That's because she's met someone else,' Alex said. 'Didn't take her long after she joined the WAAF did it?' He sounded bitter. 'It was my own fault really. I was daft enough to tell her not to tie herself down to me if she didn't want to be a grass widow. Still, with things as they are, maybe it's all for the best.'

Esther went over to the sideboard. 'I know it's more than a year late,' she said, 'but here's your twenty-first birthday present from your Dad and me.' She handed him a small package containing a pocket watch, just like the one they'd bought for David.

'Thanks Mum.'

Alex's leave went all too quickly and it seemed no time at all before she was waving him off from the garden gate, her heart as heavy as lead as she wondered whether or not she'd ever see him again. He couldn't tell her where he was heading for but promised to write as often as he could, and as he turned the corner of Kestrel Road, waved and disappeared from her sight, she said a silent prayer that he'd come safely back home again. There had been one letter from David, who was now in Malta, but most of it had been censored, so she'd no idea what was happening to him. She tried hard not to think about the problems he was having in his marriage. After all, it wasn't her business but she couldn't help feeling sorry for Sally, who must be wondering what she'd let herself in for.

One afternoon, a few days' later, Esther was shopping in Charlotte Street Market when a familiar voice caught her attention. She turned round and saw Molly Garnett, who was in the middle of an argument with one of the stallholders over the price of his Brussels Sprouts. 'It's disgusting,' she was saying. 'Everyone's trying to make money out of this bloody war, and it's fools like us that have to pay through the nose for everything.'

Esther watched with amusement as the stallholder cheerfully reduced his price and a triumphant Molly snatched her bag of sprouts and started to walk away, but not before she'd spotted Esther.

'*Esther.*'

'Hello, Molly. How are you?'

Molly, it seemed, was doing very nicely. She'd moved in with her mother at Southsea, along with the children, and was looking forward to getting married again.

'Divorced?' Esther asked.

'Widowed,' Molly said. 'Chad went down with his ship about six months' ago.'

Esther was shocked, and for a fleeting minute, pictured Chad Garnett giving her the eye which, she had to admit, had made her feel good despite her dislike of him. He may have been a rogue, but all the same, she was saddened to hear he was dead.

'Would you like to come to the wedding?' Molly asked. 'It's only Registry Office but my mother is giving a party afterwards. It's on the 10th December.'

A wedding, Esther thought, is just what I need to cheer me up. 'Yes,' she said, 'We'd love to.' Harry wouldn't be too pleased, she knew, but he needn't go if he didn't want to. They parted, with Molly promising to send a formal invitation, and Esther forgetting to ask about the husband-to-be. As she made her way home, she wondered what sort of a man would be willing to take on a ready-made family of five children. Someone rather special, she thought.

As she turned the corner into Kestrel Road, she turned cold as she saw a telegram boy coming out of Mrs Mc Andrew's front gate. She hesitated for a minute, wondering whether to knock on the door to see if anything was wrong, and had just decided it would be best not to intrude when Mrs Mc Andrew herself appeared. She was in a terrible state, and Esther knew, before the poor woman said anything, that it was bad news. She took the telegram from her trembling hand and read it. The War Office regretted to inform the parents of Private Peter Mc Andrew of the Royal Artillery that he was missing presumed dead while on active service in North Africa. Esther helped the older woman indoors and asked how she could get in touch with Mr Mc Andrew.

'Gawd knows,' Mrs Mc Andrew said. 'He's a traveller an' could be anywhere, though you could tell them at the office, which is over the top of the International Stores in Highland Road. They might be able to find 'im.'

Esther promised to do that. It wasn't far and in less than and hour, she'd left a message there and Ted Mc Andrew was on his way home from his sales area in Chichester.

'God, Peter was only eighteen', Esther said to Harry that evening.

'Sorry love,' he replied, 'but age has nothing to do with it if your time's up.'

The one thing Esther had noticed since the beginning of the war was that people began to speak to one another, and among the residents of Kestrel Road there was an air of goodwill that had never been there before. It was the same, of course, everywhere, in every town and village, and somehow, knowing that everyone else was in the same boat as you, helped make things easier to bear. Nowhere was this more evident than when Peter Mc Andrew lost his life. Almost the entire road paid their respects to his parents, either by writing to them or by calling to see if there was anything they could do, and Mrs Mc Andrew was overwhelmed by the kindness shown to her from those who previously wouldn't have even bothered to pass the time of day. But she was never the same afterwards. She no longer hovered over her garden gate, waiting to have gossip with whoever was willing to stop for a few minutes. Instead, she shut herself away inside the house, refusing to see anyone, and when Peter's younger brother Jimmy reached his eighteenth birthday and received his call-up papers, she completely lost her mind.

'This war's doing terrible things to people,' Esther said, when she heard that Mrs Mc Andrew had been admitted to the local hospital for mentally ill patients. 'And not only to the men in the front line, either.'

Harry had to agree with that. His job in the Dockyard now included two nights' a week fire-watching duty which was compulsory for any man working there, and he knew that, although air raids had been few and far between since the last one in August, there was much worse to come. After what he'd seen during the last war, he wasn't sure how he'd be able to deal with the aftermath of bombing.

The invitation to Molly's wedding arrived at the end of October and Esther was pleased that Phyllis and Jack had also been invited. Much to her surprise, Harry said he would go, and even gave her some extra money to buy a wedding present, if she could find anything in the shops. This was just the thing she needed to put some cheer back into her life, and she set off one morning with Phyllis for the Co-op in Fratton Road, now rebuilt after the fire. Everything was in short supply, she learned from the girl behind the counter, and in the end, she had to settle for a wooden pastry board and rolling pin. 'At least Molly will be able to give her husband his just desserts when he rolls home drunk late at night,' she said to Phyllis, who had managed to find a pair of linen pillowcases to give to the happy couple.

'I wonder what her fiance's like,' Esther said, as they hurried along Goldsmith Avenue under dark skies threatening rain.

'We'll soon find out,' Phyllis said. 'It's only a few weeks to the wedding. And I don't know about you but I'm looking forward to it, after all the doom and gloom there's been in this road lately.'

'Poor Mrs Mc Andrew,' Esther said. 'I wonder if she'll ever be well enough to come out of that hospital.'

'Goodness knows,' Phyllis said.

Molly looked beautiful in a pale blue short dress of Guipure lace, and tiny, pillbox hat in the same material. Instead of flowers, she carried a prayer book, which, she said, made her feel as if she'd been married in church instead of a soulless Registry Office. Her new husband, Arthur, a large, jolly man with hair greying at the temples, scarcely left her side as the pair circulated among the guests. Molly's wealthy mother had bought an enormous house overlooking the sea at Southsea, and Esther and Phyllis stared in amazement at the opulence of the room in which they found themselves after the ceremony. Rich, velvet drapes at the windows, a thick Indian carpet on the parquet floor, solid oak bookcases filled with books, and a china cabinet in which was displayed a complete Wedgewood dinner service. There were deep armchairs, upholstered in uncut moquet, several coffee tables dotted about, and a magnificent Adam fireplace that almost dominated the room. Everywhere they looked, they could see flowers. On the windows sills, in the hearth, on top of the bookcase and the china cabinet and in niches set into the walls. Molly's mother, a pleasant, attractive woman bustled about introducing herself, and took no notice at all of the children who were running amok through her beautiful home. Harry and Jack stood on the sidelines watching, both looking uneasy and a bit out of place among the unaccustomed luxury, and the well-to-do guests who were Molly's relations.

Esther had quite forgotten that other people's children, as well as her own, had grown up, and was surprised to hear that Molly's twin sons were both in the R.A.F. 'They're only just eighteen,' she said. 'Not much more than babies really, but I'm very proud of them and have to live in hope that they come out of it alive.' And she was very much in love with Arthur, who was quite a lot older than her, had never been married before, and treated her children as if they were his own. 'He's going to make a good husband and father, and I'm very lucky,' she told them with confidence.

At five o'clock, Molly and Arthur left for a weekend honeymoon. They were only going as far as Eastbourne, and the children were being cared for by their Grandmother. As everyone waved goodbye, Esther thought sadly of Chad. He'd been a bit of a devil but hadn't deserved to die, any more than Mrs Mc Andrew's boy, or any of the thousands of other young men cut down in their prime. Or, for that matter, the civilians who'd died in the recent air raids. As they were walking back to Eastbrook, she clung to Harry's arm, thankful that she still had him and, so far, all their children.

Phyllis invited Harry, Esther and the children in for a cup of tea when they arrived home. It had been ages since the two families had spent some time together. What with the two men working long hours, and Esther and Phyllis preoccupied with the younger children, there never seemed to be enough hours in the day to sit down together and have a good yarn.

They talked about Molly's wedding and how lovely it was to do something enjoyable for a change. 'I hope she has better luck with her husband this time,' Phyllis said. 'That Chad she was married to was a wife-beater and she's better off without him.'

For some reason, Esther felt upset at Phyllis's comments, and found herself defending the man. 'We don't know that for sure,' she said, 'and the poor bloke's dead now and can't answer back.'

Phyllis gave her a funny look and changed the subject. 'You're resigned to staying at the dairy now, aren't you?' she said, turning to Jack.

Jack pointed to his gammy leg. 'I don't have much choice,' he said. 'This damned thing stops me from doing a lot of things. And I still get giddy if I'm not careful. Still, it could have been worse, and what with the air raids and that, I'm probably safer at the dairy than if I were in the Dockyard.'

Harry looked at Esther, whose thoughts had already gone off in that direction more than once. She hated it when he had to do Firewatch duties, although, up to now, there hadn't been much enemy activity after dark, and she was still convinced there wouldn't be any more air raids. Apart from a serious raid on 5th December, and a few hit and runs, things had been quiet of late, and the war was ending soon, wasn't it?

Just before she and Harry went to bed that night, she mentioned Christmas, and the fact that there was very little to be found in the shops. 'And you have to *queue* for every blessed thing,' she said. It was only a fortnight away, and she hadn't even been able to make a pudding or a cake this year.

'It doesn't matter,' Harry told her. 'We aren't exactly going to starve. And I've been making things for the little ones, while I've been on Firewatch. There's nothing to do bar sit and play cards or read a book, and I'm not bothered about either, so I found some bits of wood, and there's something for each of them for their stockings.'

The "something for each of them" turned out to be a parrot that could be perched on a finger and swung back and forth for Catherine, the same only in different colours for April, and a box with enough room in which to keep pencils and pens, for Edwin.

'Oh, Harry,' Esther said, when, a few days' later he brought his handiwork home, 'they're lovely. I didn't know you were so clever at woodwork. It must be where David gets his talent from.'

'Yes. And I've never understood why he gave up that job with Jim Dangerfield.'

'Nor I,' Esther agreed.

Christmas passed quietly enough. Albert and Frances couldn't make it as Albert had been a bit under the weather and didn't feel up to the train journey. There was a letter from Alex and another from David, but Harry and Esther learned nothing very much from the little bits that remained after the censor had been at them with his blue pencil. It was, as Esther said to Phyllis, the first Christmas without one or other of the older boys being there, and she missed that but otherwise it wasn't too bad at all.

'It *will* all be over soon, won't it Harry?' she said on New Year's Eve as they sat and waited for the clock to strike twelve.

'I wouldn't put any money on it love,' he said. 'There's too much going on in too many places at the moment, so I have me doubts.'

'Always the pessimist,' she said, laughing.

A few days' into the New Year, Phyllis came running over one morning, waving a letter in her hand. 'It's from Luke,' she said, wild eyed, and with her hair practically standing on end. 'You'll never guess what he's done.'

'No. What?' Esther had not seen her friend in such a state since the business of the abortion.

'Only gone and put this girl he's been seeing in the family way. That's all.'

Esther dropped into a chair. 'Oh, Phyllis,' she said, 'how on earth did he do that?'

Phyllis started to laugh hysterically. 'What a bloody silly question to ask,' she said, seeing the funny side of it. 'The same way as we all did, unless of course you know of any other way of getting up the duff.'

They looked at each other, Esther remembering all those years' ago when she'd broken the news to her own parents about her condition. The shame of it and the disownment of her as if she'd committed some heinous crime. The hatred her mother-in-law had always shown towards her for, as she'd put it, "trapping her son". She caught hold of Phyllis's hand. 'Don't be angry with them,' she said. 'He'll marry her of course … *won't he?*'

'I don't know. He's far too young to get married.'

'Does Jack know?'

'No, I've only just had the letter. Oh, my God, whatever will he say?'

'I doubt if he'll make as much fuss as you are.' Esther said. 'And who knows? He might be quite pleased at the thought of becoming a Grandfather.'

'He won't be very pleased when he finds out what Luke is asking us to do.'

'Oh. What's that?'

'He wants us to give this girl a home. Her parents don't want anything more to do with her and she's nowhere else to go.'

It's all so much like what happened to me all those years' ago, Esther thought to herself. Except that Phyllis isn't Lydia, and would show only kindness to Luke's girl.

'Would that be so bad?' she said.

'No. I suppose not. But I'll have to talk it over with Jack and see what he thinks.'

They fell silent for a few minutes then Esther smiled. 'Fancy you being a Grandma,' she said, and they both laughed at such a preposterous idea.

CHAPTER TWENTY-FOUR

Frances was worried about Albert. Just lately, he seemed to be losing interest in the smallholding, although it had been making a small profit ever since food had become scarce in the shops. Ed Kershaw, the man whose wages David was paying, only came in twice a week now, and, due to an old war injury, wasn't able to do any of the heavy work, which meant that Albert had to cope with it on his own.

'We'll have to get someone a bit younger than Ed,' Frances said one day when she found Albert fighting for breath after he'd been humping bags of fertilizer from his shed to the vegetable plot, in readiness for the new season. His face was an unhealthy shade of pink and he was sweating profusely. 'And you'll have to go and see Adrian's Dad for a check up.'

The next day, she caught the train to Southampton, and put an advertisement in the local paper for a man, fit and capable of hard work, and preferably experienced on the land. Her thoughts, as she was on her way home, were not only of Albert and his health but also of Sally and her problems. Frances had made a friend of her brother's daughter-in-law and the girl looked upon the older woman as someone on whom she could unload all her troubles. Sally knew that, if she confided in her own mother, who had joined almost every club there was in the village, David's problems would be all over the place in no time at all and he'd become a laughing stock.

When Frances arrived back at Riverside Cottage, she walked down the lane to see Sally. She wanted to know if Doctor Addison could see Albert. 'I'm really worried about him,' she said. 'He's doing too much and poor old Ed is past it I'm afraid.'

'I'll check the appointment book in the morning,' Sally said. 'But I'm sure the doctor will be able to fit him in. He's not all that busy at the moment.'

'Is there any news from David?' Frances asked.

'Not much,' Sally replied. 'He doesn't like Malta. Says it's too "white", whatever that means. I know from what I've read in the papers that it's being bombed, but of course, David's not allowed to say much about it.' Her eyes filled with tears. 'What am I going to do when he comes home, Frances?' she said. 'I love David so much but I can't go on the way we were before he went away.'

Frances was at a loss for words. Her own love life had finished some years' ago now but she was middle-aged and it didn't bother her in the least that Albert was no longer able to make love. She'd have liked children, but Albert hadn't been very keen so it was probably just as well that she'd never been able to have any. But Sally was a different matter altogether. She was young and pretty and of course, she needed to be loved properly by a man, and to have his children.

'I wish I knew,' was all she could think of to say.

Oliver Twee was a tall, well-built young man in his twenties, and when he shook hands in a vice like grip, Albert knew he was right for the job. Albert didn't have the nerve to ask why a strapping young man like him wasn't out fighting the war. There must be a reason and it wasn't any of his business, but all the same, he did wonder whether he might be one of those "Conchies" who were refusing to join any of the services on account of their beliefs. He told Albert that he was living in an old caravan in a field owned by one of the local farmers, until he could find somewhere permanent. It all seemed above board and both Albert and Frances concluded that, even though his name was a bit odd, it would best not to ask too many questions. All they wanted was for someone to take on the heavy work, and it was none of their business after all. Ed cut his hours down to one day a week, just to do odd jobs, like pricking out seedlings and tidying up a bit, and Oliver came in for two days. He was a bit of a mystery man but a willing worker and by the end of his first week, had made a big difference to Albert, who was able to take things a bit easier.

Frances still insisted he went to see Doctor Addison, who, after giving him a good going over, told him his blood pressure was too high, and if he didn't ease up a bit, he'd be in trouble. After asking about David, he said that Adrian was doing well and hoped to get married shortly to Isobel. 'I think they should wait until this damned war is over,' he said, 'but you know what young people are like.'

Albert agreed. 'The trouble is,' he said, 'the war looks like going on for some time yet. What do *you* think, Doctor?'

'Who the devil knows?' Doctor Addison replied. 'You could be right. Now, come and see me again in a month to have your blood pressure checked.'

On the way home, Albert remembered the time David had talked about the problem of his feelings for Adrian. Poor David, who probably was as normal as the next man, but according to what Frances had said, couldn't consummate his own marriage with Sally. Albert wished he could help, but it was a private thing between husband and wife and not up to him to offer advice, even if there was any he could give.

New Year 1941 began quietly enough. There was a letter for Harry and Esther from Frances telling her that Albert had seen the doctor, and taken on a young man to help around the smallholding and another from Alex to say that he'd no idea when he would be home on leave but was hoping to be back in Blighty soon. On the morning of the 10th, Esther went shopping with Phyllis. It was a cold but pleasant day for January and as they strolled back through Bransbury Park, Esther made a remark that she would never forget as long as she lived. 'It looks like we've finished with air raids, doesn't it?' she said. 'And thank goodness for that.'

'I wouldn't be so sure if I were you,' Phyllis said. 'You've only to look at what's been going on in places like Coventry and Southampton to know what the Jerries are up to, and I don't think Pompey's seen the last of them yet.'

'Oh, *you*. You sound just like Harry.'

It was late that evening when the wail of the siren filled the air. Harry was on Firewatch Duty in the Dockyard, and Esther was in two minds whether to rouse the children and take them to the shelter or leave them sleeping in their warm beds. Had it not been for Edwin waking up and insisting they should go to the shelter, she would have remained in the house and left them undisturbed. She bundled the girls into warm clothing and they all ran down the path to the Anderson, aware of the now familiar monotonous drone of hundreds of German bombers, already overhead and thundering across the city. Esther had a feeling they were in for a long night. She tucked the girls up together on one bunk, made Edwin lie down on the other, and sat on Harry's homemade seat and waited. The raid went on all through the night, and as she sat on the little bench listening to wave after wave of German aircraft pounding the city, she wept into her hands at the thought that, somewhere out there, in the thick of it, was Harry, who might not ever come home again.

She pulled the wooden door of the shelter to one side and peered out into the night. The sky was just one sheet of orange, and the air filled with the stench of cordite and burning. Edwin, who hadn't been able to sleep, asked if his Dad would be all right.

'I don't know, son,' Esther replied. 'I just don't know.'

When, at last, the All Clear sounded, they all climbed from the shelter, stiff and shivering with the cold, and went indoors; only for Esther to discover that there was no electricity. The Power Station must have been hit she thought, rummaging in the dark for some matches and candles. She lit the gas under the grill and made some toast, but when she went to fill the kettle, there was a horrible gurgling sound from the taps, but no water. If only she had listened when Harry had told her to keep some empty milk bottles filled, "in case of emergencies", he'd said.

All that morning, she was backwards and forwards to the front gate looking for Harry and when, by twelve o'clock, there was still no sign of him, Edwin volunteered to go over to the Police Station to see if he could find out anything.

'All right,' Esther said, 'but don't hang about in case those German barbarians decide to come back.'

Edwin hoped his cousin Walter would be on duty but he wasn't there and the Policeman behind the desk asked what he could do for the young lad. Edwin explained about his Dad being at work in the Dockyard and that his Mum was worried because he hadn't come home.

'There's lots of Dads didn't get home last night, Sonny, but I'll give the Dockyard Police a ring and see if I can find out anything.' He went through to a room at the back but returned almost immediately with the news that all the telephone wires were down and he'd no idea when they'd be working again. 'I tell you what,' he said, 'give me your address and as soon as I have anything to report, I'll send someone round.' Edwin thanked him and went home.

By nine o'clock that night, not only was there no sign of Harry, but no news from the Police either. Jack came across and told her that he'd heard that all available men in the Dockyard had been needed to help in a massive rescue operation. 'I'm sure that's what he's doing,' he said, 'so try not to worry.' He didn't tell her that he'd also heard about the high number of dead and wounded, and that the City of Portsmouth was in ruins, with many people still buried under tons of rubble. Or that the area around the Dockyard had been hit badly, the Guildhall had gone up in flames, and there were hardly any shops left standing.

As it grew dark, Esther stopped looking over the front gate for Harry. There was no point any more.

How she managed to get through the next day, she had no idea. She walked around like someone in a trance, mechanically cooking dinner for the children, and going through the motions of washing the dishes and doing the weeks' ironing. Anything to keep herself occupied. Jack and Phyllis took it in turns to pop back and fore to see if there was any news, and although she was grateful, all Esther really wanted was to be left alone with her thoughts. Edwin, who was now nearly twelve and old enough to understand what might have happened to his father, sat at the table with his pencils and paper and when Esther looked over his shoulder, she saw that he'd been sketching a man, leaning on a spade surveying his garden. At the bottom of the page, he'd written "My Dad".

Just after tea, she answered a knock at the door and opened it to find Walter standing there, twisting his helmet round and round in his hands. She invited him in, terrified of what she might be about to hear.

'It's all right Auntie Esther,' he said. 'Uncle Harry's alive and well. He's been helping with the rescue operation, and will be home in about an hour, when he's had some refreshments. It's been a grim two days, I can tell you.'

Esther sank into her chair. 'Oh, my God, Walter,' she said, tears of relief streaming down her face, '*Thank* you. You have no idea what I've been through these past hours. I thought he must be dead.' She offered him a cup of tea.

'No thanks Auntie,' he said. 'There's a lot still to be done and it's "all hands on deck", as it were, so I must get back to the station. And I'm glad I was able to bring you some good news.'

Esther stood on tiptoe and kissed this nephew of Harry's, who until now had been so unpopular with both of them. Now, as far as she was concerned, he was top of the class. 'God Bless you Walter,' she said.

It was seven o'clock before she heard the back door open. She jumped out of her chair and ran to the kitchen to see Harry standing in the doorway, his face and clothes covered in red dust, his eyes fixed with that haunted look she'd seen so often but had never dared ask questions about. He stared at her as if he'd never seen her before, then dropped into a chair, rested his elbows on the table, and, with his head in his hands burst into such a paroxism of weeping that it frightened her to death. She had never before seen a man cry and was at a loss as to know what to do. She put the kettle on and made a pot of strong tea, then filled the copper and lit the gas beneath it so that Harry could have a bath, all the while saying nothing. Then she took a chair next to his and sat holding his hand. She had no idea how long they sat like that but it was some time before the sobbing subsided and he was able to speak to her.

'Tell me about it,' Esther said, determined that he wouldn't bottle *this* up inside, as he had with his experiences in France.

'In its own way,' he said, stumbling over the words, 'it was worse than being in the trenches. Then, at least you knew that the men killed or wounded were soldiers fighting a war, but this ... this was something different Esther. Innocent people crushed to death or burnt alive under what was left of their own homes, once those bastards had finished dropping their bloody firebombs on them. Women, children, and do you know Esther, there was one old couple we found, both dead, who were still sitting on their sofa, in the middle of what was left of their little home, holding hands. Darby and Joan we called them.' He buried his head in his hands again.

'Oh, Harry. What can I say?' Esther put her arms around him, so relieved that he was alive but so saddened by what he'd been through. 'It must have been terrible. And I was afraid that you had been killed.'

She baled the hot water from the copper into the bath then sprinkled some soap flakes on the top to soften the water for him. Even though it was a modern house with a proper bathroom off the kitchen, there was no running hot water and they usually made do with a weekly "top to toe wash down" rather than go to all that trouble. Today was different though, Harry needed to unwind, and what better way other than to have a good soak.

Once he had bathed and changed into some clean clothes, he felt more able to talk about the horror of the air raid. He told Esther that both the city centre and Southsea were in ruins with hardly any of the shops left standing. The Eye and Ear Hospital had gone, the Royal Hospital severely damaged, and so many homes destroyed that thousands of people were now homeless. Portsmouth's pride and joy, the Guildhall was still burning after dozens of incendiary bombs had fallen on it and set it alight. 'There's not much left of Portsmouth,' he said, 'but at least, thank God, they didn't touch this end of the city. All the time I was helping to dig people out from the ruins, I was wondering what had happened to you and the children.'

Esther persuaded him go to bed, and shortly afterwards, when she crept in beside him, he was sound asleep and snoring gently. Unable to sleep herself, she lay staring into the darkness until she heard the clock downstairs strike three. She slipped out of bed and went down to the lavatory, then picked up a magazine, sat by the dying embers of the fire and tried to read, but the words were just a blur and all she could see was Harry's distressed face, as he'd recounted the horror of the things he'd seen on that terrible night. Her head drooped and she dozed off, waking with a start a few minutes' later to see him standing in the doorway, his face full of concern. He walked towards her. 'Come back to bed Esther,' he said, his trembling hand taking hers. 'I *need* you.'

At the end of January, Harry met the Prime Minister Winston Churchill who was visiting Portsmouth, to see for himself the devastation caused by the 10th of January air raid. Harry was in the front of a crowd of Dockyard workers who had lined up alongside the wharf in the hope of catching sight of the man, and he felt a sense of pride when he found himself within touching distance, and Churchill shook his hand and made a comment. A lifelong supporter of the Labour Party, Harry had to admit that Conservative Winston Churchill was one of the greatest leaders of all time. 'Although he's just like any ordinary bloke,' he told Esther when, full of the day's events he related his meeting with the Prime Minister, exaggerating a little about the length of time Winston Churchill had spent talking to him.

Frances, having heard about the terrible raids over Portsmouth, wrote and offered to have the children for a few weeks. In her letter, she said that, although there had been raids on Southampton, and the oil works at Fawley were only a few miles' away, it was still a safer place to be. There was a small school in the village, with plenty of room to take all three children, so their education wouldn't suffer.

Harry thought it was a good idea, but Esther wondered what she'd find to do with herself with no family to look after.

'They're looking for volunteers for the canteen down in the Guildhall Square,' Harry said. 'You'd only have to work to suit yourself,' he added, 'and it would give you something to do.'

On Wednesday, she went down to the Guildhall to meet a woman from the W.V.S., who said she'd be delighted if Esther could spare one or two days' a week to help out. 'We're desperate for help,' she said, introducing herself simply as Joan. She consulted a rota of helpers. 'Could you manage Tuesdays and Fridays?' she asked. 'We seem to be a bit thin on the ground on those two days.' Esther said she could do that, and would be able start this coming Friday if that was all right.

The next day, Frances came down by train to collect the children, and there were a few tears from April but otherwise they all went off happily enough. When, after seeing them off, Esther went back into an empty house, she was surprised to find that, rather than the sense of desolation she'd expected to feel, she was actually looking forward to some time to call her own. 'I must be the world's worst mother,' she said to Phyllis, who had come across, fully expecting to have to offer a shoulder to cry on. 'I never thought I'd be glad to see the back of any of my children.'

'I expect,' Phyllis said, 'that you're glad to see them off to a place of safety, and it's nothing more than that. You'll soon be missing them, you'll see.'

It was hard work, making dozens of mugs of tea, and handing out what little food there was to the hungry soldiers and sailors who'd been seconded to help with the clearing up following the big raid, and by the end of the first day, Esther was exhausted. She began to wonder what she'd taken on, but Joan, and her band of helpers, were good company. Despite her tiredness, Esther enjoyed herself and it did her morale good when some of the men, who were young enough to be her sons, laughed and joked with her, calling her names like "sweetheart" and "good-looking". What Harry would say if he knew, she'd no idea.

That night, as she sat at the dressing table Harry had recently bought, she pulled a face at her reflection in the mirror, and decided it was time she did something to improve herself. Now in her early forties, the ravages of time were beginning to show. Her hair was still as thick and luxurious as ever, with not a grey one in sight, and the blue of her eyes as intense as it always had been, but the dark shadows beneath them made her look tired and old. She'd never before worn make-up because Harry didn't like it, but tomorrow, she'd see if the Chemist in Cormorant Road had any Ponds face cream on their shelves, and maybe some powder to take the shine off her skin. She might even buy a lipstick, if they had any. And as for Harry, well he could say whatever he liked. If she wanted to use a bit of make-up she would, and too bad. She grinned at herself in the mirror. Yesterday, she had been just another housewife, pandering to her husband and children, but today, she was someone special with an important job to do. She felt almost as if she'd been set free after a long prison sentence. It was an amazing feeling and one that led to her determination to teach her own two girls that, just because they were female, didn't mean they were second-class citizens. She'd teach them to have minds and opinions of their own, and to stand up for their rights. Teach them that they didn't have to ask *any* man's permission to do whatever it was they wanted to do, be it put powder on their noses or have a laugh and a joke with other men. She went to bed feeling happier than she had for a long time, and when Harry joined her and demanded his "needs" be met, she smiled up at him sweetly and said, 'Not tonight love, I've had a busy day and I'm tired.'

CHAPTER TWENTY-FIVE

'Esther, this is Luke's young lady, Louisa.'

Esther was in the front garden when Phyllis suddenly appeared with a young girl in tow. She was pretty, with long, dark brown hair tied back with a ribbon, a flawless skin, and eyes the colour of jade, and she was very young. Esther shook her hand, said she was pleased to meet her and asked if she would she like a cup of tea.

'No, thank you Mrs Cartarett,' Louisa replied. 'I haven't been able to touch tea since …' her voice trailed off and she rubbed a hand over the tiny swelling that was just beginning to show beneath her dress.

'Would you like some Barley water?'

Louisa shook her head. 'A glass of plain water would be lovely please,' she said.

Esther invited them in and learned that Louisa would be moving in with Jack and Phyllis until the baby was born. At first, there was no mention of a wedding and Esther thought it best not to ask too many questions. Seeing Louisa, young, unmarried, and expecting, brought back memories of the past she would rather forget. She'd always loved Harry but often felt that if she'd had a bit more sense, she would not have tied herself down to marriage and children at the age of seventeen. Louisa couldn't be any older than that, and what if Luke didn't intend to marry her? Esther felt a sudden rush of sympathy for the girl. At least Harry made an honest woman of me, she thought to herself, despite his venomous mother trying to put a stop to it.

Louisa's baby was due to be born in June and, as long as there were no complications, the confinement would be at Kestrel Road, with Midwife Mary Williams in attendance. Luke hoped to stay at Tangmere so that he could get home at weekends to see Louisa and the baby, and, once the war was over, he and Louisa would decide whether to marry or not. It all seemed very cold and calculated to Esther, who saw no reason why they couldn't marry right away. As if reading her thoughts, Louisa said that she wasn't sure about tying herself down at so young an age, as there were things she wanted to do with her life first.

Esther bit back the desire to say that it was a pity Louisa hadn't thought of that before getting herself in the family way. No one, not even Phyllis, seemed to have any thought for the child who would be born without a proper father.

Esther missed her children but Edwin sent letters to say that they were all happy staying with their Auntie Frances, and didn't mind being away from home. This hurt a bit but she was enjoying her job helping at the canteen, and volunteered to do extra hours if needed. It didn't seem to matter that she didn't get paid; the mere fact that she was meeting people and having a laugh with the soldiers and sailors, was enough. She had managed to find some Ponds Vanishing cream, a box of Outdoor Girl face powder, and a lipstick, but so far, despite her bravado, she hadn't had the courage to put her "face" on until Harry had left for work, removing the offending makeup before he came home in the evening. What she hadn't bargained for was Harry deciding one day to spend his dinner break walking along Queen Street to the Guildhall Square to see for himself what she was doing.

At the precise moment he arrived, she was sharing a joke with an Army Sergeant, and Harry couldn't believe his eyes when he saw her, with her face all made up, larking about with another man. He barged to the front of a queue of soldiers and sailors who were waiting to be served. 'Get your coat,' he shouted to Esther, 'and get off home. *Now!*'

Eileen D. Frost

The Sergeant swung round. 'Now just a minute, don't you dare talk to this lady like that,' he said. 'Who the hell do you think you are?'

Harry's face was scarlet with rage. 'I happen to be her husband, that's who I am, as if it's any business of yours. And I don't expect to come here and find her getting off with the likes of you.' He poked a finger in the other man's chest. 'So get back to doing what you're being paid for.'

Esther screamed for Harry to get out of the way, but it was too late. The Sergeant's fist caught him on the chin; he lost his footing and fell to the ground, blood spurting from the side of his mouth. The queue of soldiers and sailors stood watching with amusement. There was nothing to beat a good scrap to liven up the day.

'Oh my God.' Esther ran from behind the counter, dropped to her knees and cradled Harry's head in her lap. 'See what you've done,' she bawled at the Sergeant.

'Too bad,' he said, as he turned and walked away. 'He shouldn't have opened his big mouth to me.'

Harry struggled to his feet, rubbing his chin. 'It's all right Esther,' he said. 'I've bitten my tongue, that's all.' He looked up at the Guildhall clock. 'I'd best be getting back to work,' he said, 'and in the meantime, you're to go home, wash that stuff off your face, and we'll talk about it later.'

Her response both frightened and surprised her, and astounded Harry. 'I'll do no such thing, Harry,' she said, returning to her work behind the counter. 'The days when you can get away with treating me like some chattel are over, and if I want to do this job, then I'll do it, and you won't stop me.' She paused to catch her breath. 'And if I want to put a little something on my face to make it look better, I'll do it, whether you like it or not.' She addressed the queue, which had doubled in length, all eyes watching with interest for the next instalment in this domestic squabble. 'Next please', she said, with a fixed smile on her face.

After Harry had stormed off, she couldn't stop shaking and spilled tea all over the counter.

'Blimey Missus,' the man at the front said. 'You're in for a good 'iding tonight, when *he* gets 'ome, I'll be bound.'

266

Esther mopped up the mess. 'Don't you believe it,' she said. 'There's no man on this earth is going to tell *me* what to do.'

'That's the spirit Gel,' he said, as Esther served him with a cup of tea and a bun.

Harry, with a large purple bruise on his chin, and a sore tongue, said nothing until he and Esther had eaten their dinner and she had cleared up. She had not bothered to remove her make up; there was no point, and it was the first thing he mentioned.

'You know I don't like that stuff you've put on your face,' he said. 'It makes you look cheap and common.'

'Thank you Harry, for those few kind words,' Esther replied, getting ready to do battle.

'Get rid of it then.'

'No.'

He looked at her askance. 'What the devil's got into you lately, Esther?' he said. 'Since you've been helping out at that canteen, you've changed.'

'Well, fancy that.'

'No need to be like that. And I don't want you to go there again. Is that clear?'

Esther left her chair and walked over to the window. It would be so much easier to give in to Harry's demands, but she must make a stand now that she had gone this far. She turned to face him. 'I am not,' she said, speaking slowly and clearly, 'going to stop putting a little makeup on, for you or anyone else. As for it making me look common, I will treat that as an insult. What is more Harry, I'm not giving up my work at the canteen. It was you suggested I do it in the first place, and I enjoy it.' She gave him an icy stare. 'Or is that the real reason you want me to stop going there?'

'Oh, I can see why you enjoy it,' he said. 'All those men giving you the eye and making you laugh. *I* saw the way you were looking at that Sergeant this morning. The next thing we know, you'll be bringing him home to bed while I'm at work.'

Esther could hardly believe what she was hearing and was close to tears. 'How *dare* you say a thing like that,' she said, deeply hurt that he could even think such a thing, let alone throw that kind of accusation at her. She went over and stood in front of him. 'For two pins,' she said, 'I'd walk out of this house, here and now, and never come back, you selfish, self-centred pig.' Snatching up the magazine she'd bought that day, she said, 'I'm going up to bed to read this in peace, and *you* can sleep in the spare room. *Goodnight.*'

For some time afterwards Harry sat with his head in his hands, wondering what was going wrong with his marriage. He knew he shouldn't have said those things, but Esther had changed so much over the past year or so; ever since, in fact, this war had begun, and sometimes, she had to be put in her place. He'd seen some of the results of the woman being allowed to wear the trousers in the home, and it wasn't going to happen in *his,* so she could please herself. He went quietly up the stairs, hesitated for a minute outside of the door of their bedroom, and then went silently into the room once shared by David and Alex.

There were more air raids in March. On the ninth, the Germans returned to inflict terrrible damage on Portsmouth, and on the tenth, a further raid lasting for most of the night, destroyed the Royal Sailors Home Club, a Synagogue and a Hotel in Southsea. There was no let up and, the next night, another raid sent the death toll in the city soaring.

During the worst of these raids, Harry was on duty in the Dockyard, and Phyllis invited Esther to share their shelter rather than be on her own.

'I don't know how much more of this we can take,' Esther said, as they all settled down to spending another night underground. 'There can't be much left of Portsmouth to bomb.'

'As long as they don't turn their attention to this end of the city,' Jack said.

In the days' following the air raids, there was much work at the canteen to do for Esther and the other women. With the Sailors Club gone, and almost every other eating-house destroyed, it was in great demand, and they found themselves run off their feet. Esther was careful not to lark about too much with the customers, just in case Harry decided to come along and start another scuffle with any of them. She still made her face up each morning but as a concession to Harry's feelings on the matter, removed it before he came home at night. That much, she was prepared to do, but no more. He was back in his own bed with her, although there was no loving between them, but that was more to do with them both feeling exhausted rather than their quarrel.

Frances wrote to say that the children could stay with her for as long as Esther wanted them to. They were happy and doing well at the local school, and although there had been some heavy raids over Southampton, the New Forest was still a safer place to be than Portsmouth. When Esther read the letter, she was horrified to realise that she'd become so used to being without her children that, just lately, she'd barely given them a thought. She wrote back and asked if she and Harry could visit for April's birthday on the 27th April.

Harry said he wouldn't be able to go as he had Firewatch duty over that weekend but he didn't mind if Esther went on her own, and was a bit taken aback when she said, without argument, that she would. A few months' ago, she'd have refused to go without him, but things had changed, and as far as he was concerned, not for the better.

Esther travelled down on the 26th and was amazed at how well the children looked. All that fresh, country air, and not having to spend hours below ground in a damp air raid shelter, had done them good. And they seemed happy too. April clung to her a bit but Catherine and Edwin, after a swift "Hello Mummy", soon disappeared and weren't seen again until teatime.

'I can't believe that April will be six tomorrow,' Esther said later that evening when she, and Frances were having supper, and Albert had nipped down to the Horse and Groom to see if there was any beer to be had. 'Time flies when you're getting old.'

Frances threw back her head and laughed. 'For goodness sake Esther,' she said. 'You're forty-two, and here you are talking about getting old. What's the matter?'

Suddenly, Esther burst into tears. 'It's Harry and me,' she said. 'We're growing so far apart that we seem like a strangers.' She went on to tell Frances all about the business of the make-up, and the bit of bother with Harry at the canteen. 'He still thinks we live in the Victorian age,' she said, her voice rising in anger,' and I'm not going to be dictated to by any man.'

Frances didn't say anything for a minute. Out of loyalty to her brother, she would rather have kept her opinion to herself, although Esther had a point. Harry *was* one of the old school who thought a woman's place was either in the bedroom or in the kitchen, she knew that. But she could see *his* side of things, although that didn't help Esther, who had now recovered, and was quietly sipping her cocoa, waiting for her to say something by way of support.

'You'll not change him now Esther,' she said. 'He's middle aged and set in his ways.'

'Well that's too bad,' Esther replied, 'because, he's going to have to put up with a few more changes whether he likes it or not.'

After dinner on Sunday, April's birthday, they took the children to see Sally who was sitting in the garden knitting baby booties when they arrived. Esther's face lit up and Sally laughed. 'Not for me, Mrs Cartarett,' she said. 'They're for Adrian and his wife. She's expecting.'

Esther turned to Frances. 'You didn't tell me they were married,' she said.

'It was all very hush hush. A shotgun affair I think.'

'Well I never. I always wondered about Adrian.'

Frances threw her a warning look. 'He's always been a bit of a devil for the girls,' she said, and changed the subject to ask Sally where her mother had gone.

'To one of her club meetings,' Sally replied. 'She's always off somewhere or other.'

They sat in the garden until teatime, Esther savouring the peace and quiet after the recent bombardment of Portsmouth. All through April, the raids had continued, and there was still no sign of any let up. If it hadn't been for Harry having to go to work, she would have suggested they all move in with Frances until things quietened down a bit. As it was, she'd have to go back home either tomorrow or Tuesday, leaving the children with Frances again until it was safe for them to return to Portsmouth.

The following day, she took April down to the village shop to choose something for her birthday. April loved anything to do with reading, and came away happily clutching a book by Enid Blyton, one of her favourite storytellers. As they strolled up the lane and approached Riverside Cottage, Esther noticed that Frances was hanging over the gate waiting for them. She seemed agitated and Esther asked what was wrong.

'Albert thinks you should go back home today,' she said. 'We've just been listening to the news on the wireless and Portsmouth was hit badly again last night.' She grabbed Esther's hand. 'If Harry's been in the thick of it again, he'll need you there,' she said.

Esther needed no second bidding, and an hour later, after a quick goodbye to the children, she found herself sitting on the bus on the way to Southampton to catch the train home. The journey to Portsmouth seemed to take forever, with the train stopping at every halt and station en route, and by the time it drew into Fratton, she was exhausted, and full of foreboding. She caught a bus to Eastbrook and almost ran all the way to Kestrel Road, where she found the house empty, with no sign that Harry had been home since she'd left the house two days' ago. She went straight across the road to see Phyllis.

'My God', Phyllis said, when she opened the door to find a fraught, wild-eyed Esther standing on the step. 'You look as if you've seen twenty ghosts.'

Esther practically fell inside. 'Have you seen or heard anything from Harry?' she said. 'I've been indoors but it looks as if he's not been there since I went away.'

Phyllis hadn't seen Harry but suggested he might have slept in the Dockyard over the weekend. 'If he was on Firewatch duty,' she said, 'he wouldn't have been able to get home anyway. Now calm down before you burst a blood vessel or something. I'll make us a cup of tea.'

'It's been a bad weekend for raids, hasn't it?' Esther said presently.

Phyllis looked everywhere except at the bag of nerves sitting opposite. Jack had told her about the heavy casualties, and that rescue parties were still searching for more bodies among the debris. He knew that Harry would have been on duty in the Dockyard and couldn't help wondering what had happened to him.

'Yes, it was dreadful,' Phyllis said. 'But I'm sure Harry is all right. You know how it is when these things happen. Anyone who's

271

available is expected to work non-stop until everyone is accounted for.'

Esther went home shortly afterwards and, to give herself something to do, she set about cleaning the house. As she swept and dusted, her thoughts drifted to the problems she and Harry had been going through lately. They still loved one another, of that she was certain, but this war had put a strain on everyone. What with the family gone, food shortages, hours spent in a damp, smelly air raid shelter, interrupted sleep, and the knowledge that there was no end in sight to all of that, it wasn't surprising that relationships were suffering. She threw things into cupboards, tossed a pile of old newspapers of Harry's into the dustbin then vented what was left of her anger on the kitchen table, scrubbing at the wooden top furiously until her arms ached. She went upstairs to their bedroom and found Harry's gardening jumper on the floor where he'd left it. She picked it up and put it to her face, breathing in the smell of Woodbines, and the Jeyes Fluid he used in the garden. She sat on the bed, buried her nose in the softness of the woollen garment, and cried.

'Is there anyone at home?'

Harry's voice echoing up the stairs brought her to her feet, and she hurriedly dried her eyes and went out onto the landing to see him standing, grinning from ear to ear, in the hall below. Still clutching his jumper to her chest, she flew down the stairs like a ten year old and leapt into his arms, almost knocking him over in her eagerness to satisfy herself that it really *was* him and not a figment of her imagination.

They clung together without a word until, presently, Esther moved away and held him at arms length. 'I shall *never*,' she whispered, her eyes searching his face, 'leave you alone again.' She laughed. 'You can't be trusted.'

Oliver proved to be an excellent worker. He came in twice a week, on Tuesdays and Fridays, always punctual, always clean, and Albert would never have been able to manage the smallholding without him. It was Ed who raised the question of why such a strong young man should have been excused serving in one of the armed forces.

'There's nothin' wrong with 'im as I can see,' he said to Albert one morning. 'An' the funny thing is, 'e never goes anywhere. Not even to the 'orse and Groom for a pint of beer when there's any to be 'ad.'

'How do you know all this Ed?' Albert said. Maybe the old green-eyed monster was rearing its ugly head and Ed was just jealous of the younger man.

'Well, 'e rents that old caravan from farmer Hatcher, don't 'e, and 'e reckons that , except for when 'e wants a bit of shopping, or comes down yere to 'elp you, young Oliver stays indoors all the time. *And* 'e never opens 'is curtains either.'

'This is all idle gossip Ed,' Albert said, 'and it's best ignored if you ask me. What Oliver does in his spare time is none of our business.'

'Please yerself.' Disgruntled, Ed shuffled away to attend to some cuttings in the greenhouse. If Albert and his wife couldn't see that something was amiss, that was up to them. He had tried, in a roundabout way, to warn them.

Albert wasn't going to tell Ed that he and Frances had also, for some time, been worried about their handyman. Oliver never talked about having a family or friends, or whether he was married or single, and it seemed strange that the only job he had was with Albert, which didn't pay much. How he managed was anyone's guess. Albert told Frances about his conversation with Ed, and she agreed that it would have been better if they had found out a bit more about their general help before taking him on.

It wasn't until the end of May that all their questions were answered. Frances had been down to the village for a paper. As she turned into the lane, Sally's mother was at the gate of Pennyfarthings, and she asked if Frances was expecting any visitors because there was a strange vehicle parked outside Riverside Cottage. Frances hurried on and had the shock of her life when she saw Police Constable Gordon Hacker standing in the drive talking to Albert. The strange vehicle was an armoured car, with two Military policmen sitting in the front.'

'What's going on?' Frances said as she drew level. Albert's face was as white as chalk and he seemed to be having difficulty in standing still.

'We're looking for a young man,' P.C Hacker said. 'And we understand that you recently took on some hired help in the shape of a young man who calls himself Oliver Twee.'

'That's right,' Frances replied. 'What exactly has he done?'

'He's a deserter from the Army Madam, and you and your husband could find yourselves in a lot of trouble for helping him to avoid capture.'

'Don't be ridiculous,' Frances said. 'We know nothing about him.'

'Then you should not have employed him without making checks, should you. I find it hard to believe that you didn't think there was something funny about a fit young man living on the proceeds of two days' work a week. And that's not all. Twee isn't even his real name.'

Frances glanced at Albert, who looked as if he was about to faint. 'My husband isn't well,' she said. 'Perhaps we could all go inside and talk about this.'

P.C Hacker told them that when Oliver, who was one of thousands of soldiers rescued from the beaches at Dunkirk, heard that his regiment was going overseas to the front, he panicked and went absent without leave. He'd made his way from his station in Sussex to the New Forest where he thought he would not be traced, changed his surname to Twee, but hadn't reckoned with the suspicions of someone from the village, who'd tipped off the local Police. Albert thought it must be Ed, and who could blame him when his own son had died at Dunkirk.

The following Friday, the Military Police hid their vehicle in the trees and lay in wait for Oliver. Frances didn't like the methods they were using and no amount of persuasion from P.C. Hacker could convince her that what they were doing was right.

'You're laying a trap for him,' she said, 'as if he's an animal. And why can't you arrest him at his caravan instead of here?'

'Because,' the police constable explained, 'the caravan is in an open field and he'd see us coming a mile off. Now, Madam, would you kindly let us get on with our work and if you don't want to watch, I suggest you go indoors until it's all over.'

Frances went round the back to find Albert, who was sitting on an upturned box in the greenhouse. 'What will they do to him?' she asked. 'They won't shoot him like they did some of the deserters in the last war, will they?'

'Of course they won't,' Albert said, 'but the punishment for desertion is severe, and so it should be. He'll probably spend years in jail.'

'Poor little devil. What a waste of a life.'

Albert gave his wife a puzzled look. 'And what about the waste of life for all those other "poor little devils" as you put it, who've been killed doing their duty? *They* didn't run away and hide, did they?' He stood up and walked out into the morning sunshine to play his pre-planned part in the arrest.

As Oliver turned into the front gate, Albert stopped him to pass the time of day. Frances, who was watching from the living room window, put her hand to her mouth when she saw the look of terror on the young man's face as the two Military Policemen stepped out from under the shadows of the trees to arrest him. He didn't put up a fight, and as he was led away in handcuffs, he turned once to look at Albert as if to say, "Why did you do this?" Frances slumped onto the settee and wept.

'Well that's that then,' Albert said when it was all over.' What do we do now?'

Jack and Phyllis became grandparents on the 6th June, when Louisa gave birth to a son. Midwife Mary Williams, unable to hide her disapproval at the unmarried status of the mother, delivered the child at four o'clock in the morning, after a long and difficult labour. The new mother, under the contemptuous gaze of the midwife, cuddled her baby, and announced that his name would be John William.

'You'll be putting him up for adoption I imagine?' Mary Williams said, reaching out to take the baby from Louisa to put him in his Moses basket.

'I will *not,*' Louisa said, handing over her new son. 'He stays here with me ... and his Grandparents.' She turned pleading eyes to Phyllis. 'Isn't that right Mrs Martindale?'

Phyllis perched on the edge of the bed and looked at her first grandchild. 'Of course it is dear,' she said. 'You'll have him adopted over my dead body.'

Mary Williams, who was looking more like a witch than ever these days, sniffed. 'The child needs a father,' she said.

'He has one,' Louisa replied.

'Ah, yes. Conspicuous by his absence, is he not?'

Phyllis decided to intervene. 'My son,' she said, 'is, as you well know, the child's father, and his absence is due to him serving his country in the Royal Air Force.' She looked at John William who was now sleeping peacefully in his basket. 'We are very grateful for all you have done, Nurse Williams,' she said, 'but if you have finished, I think my future daughter-in-law needs to rest, don't you?'

Jack, who despite the circumstances of the birth, was thrilled to bits at finding himself a Grandfather, slipped out of the dairy to the Post Office at nine o'clock, to send Luke a telegram. He hoped and prayed that his son would do the honourable thing and marry the girl, who was not much more than a child herself. As he stood at the end of a long queue, his thoughts drifted to his other sons. Terry, as far as he and Phyllis knew, was still in the Middle East. There had been a couple of censored letters but nothing for over a month now and Phyllis was beginning to wonder what had happened to him. Robert was still with the Grammar School in Winchester but he was nearly sixteen and would soon be old enough to go to the Technical College. Jack glanced along the queue at the grim faces of his companions. There were several wearing black armbands on the sleeves of their coats and they all looked worn out and beaten down by the events of the past few months. All, that was, except for one little old lady who, fed up with the long wait, decided to "entertain the Troops", as she put it. Her rendition of a rude song to the tune of Colonol Bogey had everyone in stitches and when she lifted up her grey flannel skirt to show a large expanse of pink bloomer, the Manager of the Post Office had to come out into the street to restore order.

'Miserable Bugger,' she said as the queue, now silent again, began to move forward and eventually, Jack reached the front and sent off his telegram. As he stepped out into the street, he glanced to left and right but, of the little old lady, there was no sign and he wondered if he'd imagined the whole thing. He limped back to the dairy, with the unmistakeable feeling that he was getting old.

CHAPTER TWENTY-SIX

On the 7th December 1941, the Japanese bombed Pearl Harbour, and the following day America entered the war. After listening to the news on the wireless, Harry turned to Esther. 'If you thought this war was coming to an end,' he said, 'you'd better think again. The Americans are in, and they, and this country, have declared war on Japan.'

At the beginning of the following February, in a quiet, Registry Office ceremony, Luke married Louisa. Jack and Phyllis were there, but apart from an Air Force friend of Lukes, and Louisa's sister, no one else was invited, not even Harry and Esther, and the couple, with their baby son, stayed at home for their honeymoon. Luke was about to be posted overseas, and had persuaded Louisa that, even if she wasn't quite ready for marriage, for financial reasons it was the most sensible thing to do.

'Not a very good start,' Esther said to Harry, remembering yet again, the similarity to *their* shotgun wedding. 'Still, at least he did the decent thing in the end.'

That same month, Japan invaded Singapore, Alex came home on shore leave, and Esther thought it safe to bring the children back from the New Forest. She gave up her canteen job, and was glad to have her family around her once more, even though Alex would be off again within a week. It was just like old times and she made the most of it by keeping the children away from school for a few days so that she could spend time with them and they could get used to being home again.

Alex went down the town to do some shopping one day and was shocked when he saw the damage inflicted on Portsmouth. 'I couldn't believe it,' he said to Esther. 'There's hardly anything left, except around here. I couldn't even find anywhere to buy a shirt.'

'I know,' Esther said, 'we've been lucky at Eastbrook. A row of houses in the road behind us got a direct hit, but otherwise, we've escaped the worst of it.'

'And how's Albert and Frances?' he said, feeling that the use of "Uncle" and "Aunt" was unnecessary now that he was getting on for twenty-three.

Esther told him about the young man who'd been such a help to Albert but was now incarcerated in prison. No action had been taken against Albert for harbouring the man, as it was accepted that if he'd known that Oliver was a deserter, he'd have handed him in. 'The trouble is,' Esther said, 'they haven't been able to find anyone to take his place and Albert hasn't been too good lately. I don't know what they're going to do if this war doesn't come to an end soon so that David can come home.'

'And what's my big brother up to these days?' Alex said, with still the same old hint of sarcasm in his voice when he spoke of David.

'He's still in Malta,' Esther said. 'It's a long time since we had a letter from him, and Sally says he doesn't write to her much either. Mind you, according to the news on the wireless, the bombing over there is worse than we've had here, so perhaps the mail can't get through.'

'Maybe,' Alex said without interest. He didn't mention Barbara until the last day of his leave when he asked Esther if she'd heard from her.

'Not a thing,' Esther said. 'In fact, I don't think she's been down to check the house since last August when she called in to see us.'

'Probably married to this other bloke by now,' he said.

Esther would have liked to ask if he'd found another girl but thought better of it. He would have told her if he had. She was sorry to see him go back. This war, and his short romance with Barbara, seemed to have done something to him; taken away his sparkle. As she waved to him from the front gate, she prayed with all her heart that it would soon end and they could get back to being a family again.

The telegram came at the end of February. When Esther saw the familiar figure of the boy on his bicycle turn the corner into Kestrel Road, her heart missed a beat, and when he stopped at her gate and handed over an orange envelope, she almost fainted.

'Any reply Missus?' he said, as he watched Esther read it. He was only a young lad, but had delivered bad news so often in recent months that watching someone turn deathly white, or pass out at his feet, was commonplace and no longer affected him.

She shook her head. 'No son', she said, trying not to cry in front of him, 'there's no reply.'

Once indoors, she read it again. It was from Sally and said that David had suffered injuries in a bombing raid, and was on his way home to England for treatment. It didn't say how bad he was, or where he would be going but that he would be back in this country within the next week or so. Esther scribbled a hasty note to Frances asking her to find out more if she could, and let her know.

A few days' later, Frances's reply came to say that David had arrived and was in Queen Alexandra Hospital at Cosham.

"It's just a bus ride away for you," she wrote, "and Sally can get a train from Southampton to Cosham, or maybe she could stay with you for a while?"

Harry agreed that it would be best if Sally stayed with them for a couple of days. 'It'll be company for you,' he said to Esther, 'and she'll be able to see David, and talk to the Doctors without worrying about having to traipse back and forth to Southampton.'

Esther sent her a telegram to say that she was welcome to use the boys' room for as long as she liked, and within a couple of days, she had settled into Kestrel Road, and was waiting anxiously to see David. When she walked into the ward, he was sitting in a chair by the bed, his right arm and leg in plaster, his face covered in cuts and bruises, and the initial shock of seeing him like that must have shown in Sally's expression.

'I don't look *that* bad, do I?' he said, reaching for her hands.

She laughed and leaned forward to kiss him lightly on the mouth. 'Of course you don't,' she said. 'But I didn't expect to see you looking as if you'd done ten rounds with Joe Louis.'

'I was one of the lucky ones,' David said. 'You should have seen some of the others. Legs and arms blown off, faces burned so badly that, even if they pull through, they'll never see again. At least I can walk, and I can still look at my beautiful wife and wonder what the hell she sees in me.'

'Oh David, *please* don't talk like that.'

'Well, it's true, isn't it? I haven't been much use to you as a husband so far, have I?'

Tears welled up in Sally's eyes. 'All that matters,' she said, 'is that you get fit and well again. After that, we'll see about the other problem and what can be done about it.' She moved her hand gently across his face. 'I love you David,' she said, 'and always will, no matter what.' She told him that his mother and father would be visiting on the coming Sunday, and that she, herself, would be staying with them for a few days. 'They've been so good to me,' she said, adding with a giggle, 'and it's lovely sleeping the bed you used to have. It makes me feel all warm and happy inside.'

David smiled at the girl sitting beside him, who had been his wife, in name only, for almost three years now, and who had never once complained about his inability to make love to her. He made up his mind there and then that, when he'd recovered from his injuries, he'd seek help for his problem so that he could give her the love she deserved.

The arrival of a nursing sister, who asked if Sally would like to speak to the Consultant dealing with David, ended their conversation, and she followed the tall figure down the corridor to a room at the end where Hugh Stallybrass sat at a large desk. He invited Sally to take a seat, and then consulted, for some minutes, a large folder containing David's case notes.

'Ah,' he said at last, 'you'll want to know about your husband's injuries, Mrs Cartarett, and my prognosis.'

Sally nodded. 'Yes, I would, Mr Stallybrass,' she said, feeling slightly overawed in the presence of this man, who was well known for his work with injured servicemen and women. Doctor Addison had spoken of him many times, and Sally knew that David couldn't be in better hands.

'Well, I'm please to tell you that his injuries are not life-threatening, although they *will* leave him with some problems,' Hugh Stallybrass said. 'Not least, that he may have to be discharged from the Royal Air Force.' He leaned forward in a conspirital manner, and Sally wondered what was coming next. 'You see,' he went on, 'he has broken his right leg and his right arm. Not in themselves serious, but the leg injury does give me some cause for concern. The bone is shattered in several places and he'll need an operation before I can tell how bad it is. And of course,' he went on, 'there is the problem of him being right-handed, and the injuries being on that side.'

'Does he know?' Sally asked. 'About having to leave the Air Force I mean?'

'Not yet,' Hugh Stallybrass said, 'but I shall be having a long talk with him sometime during the next few days.' He glanced at his watch, then stood up and offered his hand across the desk. 'Tempus Fugit Mrs Cartarett', he said, adding, as he noticed the perplexed look on her face, 'Time Flies, and I'm a busy man with many patients to see, so forgive me if I leave you in the capable hands of Sister O'Reilly.' And with that, he walked smartly to the door and was gone.

The Sister allowed Sally back into the ward just to say goodbye to David, who was having the wounds on his face attended to by a nurse. She blew him a kiss, said she'd be in to see him again the next day, then with a wave, went through the double doors and down the stairs. The lump in her throat felt like the size of a golf ball, and as she crossed the road to catch her bus, she had to stuff her fist into her mouth to stop herself from crying and making a fool of herself. Poor David, she thought. If the injury to his leg meant that he would have to leave the Air Force, what would he do? Although money wouldn't be a problem, as he still had a considerable amount of his inheritance invested, he wouldn't be able to go back to the job with Albert that he loved. And as for the other business, once he was better, he would have to get help with solving *that* problem. Until now, she had been too embarrassed to complain about his impotence and had simply accepted it as something that would cure itself. Now, she thought differently. Not only did she want children, David's children but, although she loved him wholeheartedly, she couldn't face a life of celibacy with him. As she turned into Kestrel Road, she made up her mind that, whether David liked it or not, when she went home to the New Forest, she'd speak to Doctor Addison about it.

Doctor Addison was sympathetic but not able to offer much help. He told Sally that impotence was a problem many men experienced, although it was unusual in someone of David's age. He cast his mind back to when his son Adrian had been a friend of David's and remembered that, at the time, he himself had had some misgivings about the friendship. It had seemed that David wanted to spend every minute of his spare time with Adrian, and was forever finding some excuse or other to either touch him or get uncomfortably close. Not in an unpleasant way, but as a young man would with a girl he'd fallen in love with.

'Get David to come in and see me,' Doctor Addison said. 'Perhaps the only thing he needs is to talk his problem over with another man.'

Sally thanked him and went back to her desk, and as the consulting room door closed behind her, Dr Addison wondered why an attractive girl like Sally couldn't arouse the man she was married to. He knew hardly anything about homosexuality and was not convinced that David's problem was due to that, but all the same, later that day, he went to his library of medical books and looked it up.

The Royal Air Force discharged David as "Unfit for Service due to Medical Grounds," in June. The operation on his leg had been successful, but left him with a marked weakness that would be permanent, and mean, Hugh Stallybrass said, that he would be unable to carry out any heavy work.

On a balmy June evening, David sat on the verandah of Pennyfarthings absorbing the smell of honeysuckle and mock orange, and contemplating his future. Not only was he of no use to his wife, but now, he was of no use to Albert either. He stared at Sally, who was sitting opposite, reading a book, and she, aware that he was watching her, set her book aside and looked at him.

She smiled. 'Is anything the matter, David?' she said.

'Yes', he said. 'I wish I were dead.'

CHAPTER TWENTY-SEVEN

Although there were a few lulls in the air raids, the Germans still chose Portsmouth as one of their main targets. Esther, fed up with dragging the children out of their beds and down into the shelter whenever the siren went off, decided she would let them sleep on, blissfully unaware of what was going on over their heads. After all, Eastbrook had so far escaped any damage and, apart from the Royal Marine Barracks, there was nothing of interest to the Germans around here. Harry, who seemed to be on permanent Firewatch duty in the Dockyard, knew nothing of this, and if he did happen to be at home when there was a raid, then down into the Anderson they all went.

It was on a warm evening in late June that Catherine asked if she could go to Bransbury Park to play on the swings with her friends from school. Esther didn't like the idea but said she could go as long as she went into the public shelter if she heard the siren. Her friend Annabel Bridger, with three other girls from their class, was already there when she arrived and they all made a dash for the swings. Annabel had the most beautiful long, blonde hair that fell naturally over her thin shoulders like a golden cape, while Catherine, had to endure having hers rolled up in rags every night, and then combed out into silly ringlets the following morning, and she hated it. She had always envied Annabel her hair but Esther liked to see ringlets on small girls, so ringlets it had to be.

The higher Annabel went on the swing, the more the wind took her hair, blowing it this way and that like a curtain of spun gold. Catherine, waiting for a swing to come free, stood transfixed, the picture of her friend with the beautiful hair imprinted on her mind forever. If only my Mummy would let me do my hair like that, she thought, as they swapped places and Annabel gave her a push to get her started. They stayed for about an hour then Annabel said she had to go home, and they parted company, promising to see each other in class in the morning.

In the middle of the night, the siren went and, as Harry was at home, Esther had to get the children up. They all ran for shelter and had just settled in when a massive explosion shook the ground beneath them, the force of it lifting the door out of its opening and tossing it into the hedge. 'God Almighty,' Harry said as he peered through the gap where the door had been, 'I don't know what *that* was, but it was too bloody close for comfort, and there won't be much left of whatever it landed on.'

There was pandemonium at the school when Esther and Phyllis arrived next day with their children. The Caretaker's house had lost its roof and windows, and the school most its windows. Broken glass, tiles and miscellaneous debris littered the playground, and all that remained of the houses in the vicinity was a huge crater of rubble, which was full of soldiers, sailors and A.R.P workers, who were frantically digging in the ruins to see if they could find anyone who was still alive.

Despite the damage to the school, and the layers of dust and shards of glass everywhere, Headmistress Jane Wetherspoon insisted the pupils pick their way carefully over the debris and assemble in the hall for prayers as usual. Because of the tragic circumstances, she invited anyone who had accompanied their children to join them.

Esther and Phyllis joined the assembly, and Miss Wetherspoon talked to an audience of shocked mothers and pupils about the dreadful results of a landmine meant, everyone thought, for the Royal Marine Barracks, which had missed its target and fallen instead on the roads immediately bordering the school. It was too early to say how many casualties there were, she told the shocked gathering, most of who were by now in floods of tears, but the place where the landmine had fallen would be unlikely to yield up any survivors. At least a dozen children, all from the school, had lived along that road, and the fact was that most, if not all of them would not have stood a chance. She promised to post a full list of casualties at the school gates as soon as their names were available. She bowed her head and asked that everyone should pray for the victims of this terrible disaster, and afterwards, the singing of the hymn, 'There's a place for Little Children, up in the Bright Blue Sky,' echoed eerily along the corridors of the school.

'I could not have borne one minute more in that place,' Esther said, as she and Phyllis made their way home. 'And I'd have thought that Miss Wetherspoon would have sent the children home, at least for the rest of the day.'

'Perhaps she thinks it best if they carry on as normal,' Phyllis said. 'As she explained to them, the business of having to move all their stuff from their classrooms to another part of the school will give them something else to think about.'

For several days afterwards, Catherine refused to eat or go out to play. All she wanted to do when she came in from school was lie on her bed and stare at the shadows on the ceiling. Esther began to worry about her, and when, on the following Saturday, she showed no interest in a trip to the park, Esther took her to one side, determined to find out what was wrong.

'What is it, pet?' she asked, lifting Catherine onto her lap. 'What's wrong?'

Catherine stared at the photograph of Daniel on the wall and pressed her lips firmly together.

'Is it the land mine?'

There was a short pause, and then Catherine let out the most horrible scream Esther had ever heard. She flung herself to the floor, writhing about like someone in a fit, and banged her clenched fists repeatedly on the linoleum, her legs going nineteen to the dozen, her face contorted with rage. Alarmed, Esther leapt from her chair and grabbed the child by her arms, forcing her to her feet. Then she slapped her hard across the face. Twice.

'That is enough!' she shouted. 'Now stop behaving like a demented dog and tell me what is wrong. If you don't, then you can go to bed for the rest of the day, because I have had quite enough of you and your sulks.'

Catherine, shaken out of her hysteria, burst into tears, and Esther, ashamed of herself for losing her temper, put her arms around the sobbing child. 'Now tell me what it is,' she said in a gentler tone of voice. 'Tell Mummy all about it.'

'My friend Annabel,' she said, in a small voice. 'She was killed Mummy. When that landmine fell, it was on her house and she was killed.'

Esther was speechless. She'd read the list of casualties Miss Wetherspoon had posted on the school gates but none of the names had meant anything to her. Whole families had been wiped out on that terrible night but Esther hadn't given it a thought that any of the child victims might be friends of Catherine's.

'Oh, Catherine, I'm so sorry,' she said, burying her face in the little girl's ringlets. 'I didn't know. You should have told me.'

Catherine, now partially recovered, told her mother about Annabel's lovely hair. 'It was really long,' she said, 'and all golden and shiny, like Veronica Lake, the film star.' She began to cry again. 'We were playing in the park the other day,' she said, 'and when she went home, she promised to meet me at school in the morning. And now she's *dead.'*

Esther had never felt at such a loss for words. She held Catherine tight. The poor child hadn't recovered from losing her small brother, and now this.

'Do you want to go to the park now?' Esther said presently. 'It's a lovely day and we could ask Auntie Phyllis if she wants to come, with Sarah.'

The forlorn little figure shook her head. 'No, Mummy. But could I go and stay with Auntie Frances please?'

Esther was shocked. She knew that Catherine had been happy when she'd stayed with Frances before, but it was difficult not to feel hurt that her little girl would rather be there than in her own home, with her own mother. 'Is that what you'd really like to do?' she said.

'Yes Mummy.'

After Esther had spoken to Harry about it, she wrote to Frances and the reply came back by return post. She'd love to have Catherine to stay, for however long it took for the child to get over the loss of her friend, or even longer than that if she wanted. Esther couldn't help feeling that yet another of her children was being lured away by the attraction of living in the New Forest and she wondered how long it would be before April started begging to be allowed to join her older sister at Riverside Cottage.

'We have had a letter from the Headmaster of Edwin's school,' Esther said, the minute Harry arrived home from work, one evening in July. 'He's asking if we could go and see him about Edwin.'

'I'll have to leave that to you Esther,' Harry said, wearily. 'In what little time I have off from work, I want to put my feet up, not go chit-chatting to some school master about nothing in particular.'

'I doubt if it's "nothing in particular," as you put it,' she said. 'He probably wants to talk about Edwin's future.'

'No need to go there to talk about *that*', Harry said. 'Edwin will leave school at the end of the month and get a job, same as his two older brothers did.'

'Oh *Harry*, he's clever enough to go to the Tech. You know that.'

Harry rubbed his hands over his face. Like everyone else, he was tired of the war and its ramifications, and had neither the energy nor the inclination to deal with arising family matters. Edwin might well be clever but he'd have to face the fact that children of Dockyard workers didn't go on to better themselves at fancy colleges; they went out to work at fourteen and contributed to the running of the home. 'I'm sorry Esther, he said, after a pause in the conversation, 'but that's the way it is and you'd be wasting your time going up to that school.'

Esther dropped into her armchair. 'Well I'm going,' she said, 'whether you like it or not.'

'Oh, please your bloody self,' Harry said. 'You usually do anyway.'

The Headmaster, Vernon Collair, spoke frankly to Esther. 'Edwin,' he said, 'has a rare talent for English. He has maintained his lead at the the top of his class in that subject, right through the year, and is worthy of being recommended for one of the few teaching scholarships that are available for the children of working class men.' He removed his glasses and dabbed with a handkerchief at a watery eye. 'I'm surprised,' he went on, 'that your husband isn't with you. Generally speaking, the fathers take more interest than the mothers.'

'My husband,' Esther replied, 'is a very tired and overworked man Mr. Collair, and would have been here with me had he been able to take time off from his job.'

'Quite so.' Vernon Collair said, unimpressed. 'Well perhaps you'd like to talk it over with Mr. Cartarett and let me know of your decision about Edwin. Only don't take too long about it as these scholarships are few and far between and soon snapped up.'

Esther thanked him and walked home with a heavy heart. She knew that Harry would stick to his guns over this, and insist on sending Edwin out to work in some lousy factory or shop where his talent would be totally wasted. She let herself into the house and sank into a chair, her mind working this way and that in an effort to come up with a way of persuading Harry to let Edwin's name go forward for a scholarship. After all, they were no longer so hard up that they needed the few miserly shillings he would earn if he went to work, and what was wrong with *her* getting a job to help pay for the books and things he would need?

By the time Harry came in from work that evening, she had her argument ready and word perfect.

As summer faded and turned to autumn that year, Esther thought how much all their lives were changing. She had to accept that Catherine did not want to return to Portsmouth ...*ever.* Frances said she was quite happy to keep her niece, and Esther began to wonder whether the whole thing had been some sort of plot on the part of her sister-in-law to wean Catherine away and treat her as the daughter she was never able to have.

'That's a bit unkind,' Harry said when Esther voiced her opinion on the matter. 'Frances has always loved our children as if they were her own, you know that. And if Catherine's happy there, why not let her stay?'

'Because she's *our* little girl, 'Esther said.

'No one's saying she's not,' Harry replied. 'But why not leave things as they are for now and see what comes of it?'

Esther wasn't happy with that but she didn't want to start another domestic war with him. They had already had endless rows about Edwin applying for a scholarship, and in the end, she'd had to go along with Harry's determination that their son should leave school, find a job and make his own way in the world. Headmaster Vernon Collair had been very understanding. He knew from experience that children of the working classes were, with few exceptions, expected to start work at fourteen, hand over their wages, and leave any highfalutin ideas about higher education to those who could afford it. It was wrong, but an unpleasant fact and he always did his best to help such children find a suitable job. He told Esther that there was a vacancy for an office boy at a local newspaper company. 'They are looking for someone with a high standard of English, and Edwin fits the bill perfectly,' he'd said, when Esther went to see him to tell him of Harry's decision. At the beginning of August, Edwin began working for The Portsmouth Argos in what was to be the first step towards his writing career.

At the end of September, Phyllis came across to number twelve one morning, waving an air letter in her hand. 'It's Terry,' she said. 'He's on his way home, and should be back in England next week.'

Esther invited her in. 'Sit down Phyllis,' she said, 'before you *fall* down.'

Phyllis collapsed into a chair. 'I can't believe it,' she said. 'It's ages since we've heard from him, and now *this*.'

'I'm so happy for you,' Esther said. 'What with Robert at home as well, you'll soon have a houseful to look after again.'

The two women stared at each other, the same thing dawning on both of them at once. 'My God,' Phyllis said, breaking the silence at last. 'Where am I going to put everyone?' Louisa and the baby were still living with them, and Sarah couldn't share a room with her brothers. 'Sarah will have to sleep in our room, that's all,' she said.

Esther laughed. 'Oh yes, I can just see Jack putting up with that,' she said. 'Your Sarah's nine don't forget, and she'll see and hear things she shouldn't.'

'There's not much *to* see and hear these days,' Phyllis said.

'It must be their ages,' Esther said, referring to Jack and Harry. 'Even Harry's gone off the boil. Not that I mind all that much, and to tell the truth, I'm so blessed tired lately that it's a relief to get into bed and go straight to sleep.'

'Have you heard from Alex?' Phyllis asked.

'Yes. He'll be home for Christmas, and might even be shore based at Portsmouth for a time, he says.'

Phyllis's eyes lit up. 'Perhaps we could have a Bit of a Do this year, on Boxing Day maybe. What d'you think?'

'That's a good idea, if we can find anything in the shops to eat,' Esther said. 'Everything's in short supply, and you can't get anything without queueing up for hours. Still, we need something to cheer us all up.'

After Phyllis had left, Esther fell to thinking about David. She would like to go and see him, especially since she'd had the letter from Sally to say how worried she was about his bouts of depression. Esther asked Harry if he'd mind if she went the following weekend.

'Of course not', he said, 'and I'll come with you if you like. Things have quietened down a bit in the yard and I can have Saturday and Sunday off if I want. We'll have to make our own way there as Albert can't afford to use up his petrol coupons to run around for us any more.'

'That's settled then,' Esther said, already making plans to try to woo Catherine back to where she belonged, in Portsmouth.

While Doctor Addison was waiting for David to turn up for his appointment, he thumbed through some papers on his desk. After he'd spoken to Sally about her husband's problems, he'd gone to a great deal of trouble to find out more about impotency. A friend of his from Medical School days had specialised in male sexual difficulties and it was to him that he turned in an effort to help the young couple.

He'd collected and studied as much material as he could, and was now hoping to put an end to the misery of David Cartarett and his pretty wife Sally. He had decided to see David on his own first, to give him the chance to overcome any embarrassment he might feel at discussing such a delicate subject.

David arrived on time and Sally, who was working for the Doctor that morning, showed him into the consulting room. Now that he was actually facing the father of his one time friend, he didn't know how to begin but Doctor Addison soon put him at ease and opened the conversation by explaining about the research he'd been doing into the case.

'As I see it, David,' he said,'there is no reason to suppose that you are homosexual. The name-calling that Sally told me about, happened when you were young and very impressionable, and probably sowed the seeds of doubt in your mind. It's easily done.' He unscrewed his fountain pen and sat with it poised over a note pad. 'What I want you to do is to start at the very beginning and tell me everything you can remember about when all this self-doubt began. No matter what you tell me it will be treated as confidential, so don't hold anything back, and do your best to forget that I am Adrian's father.'

David talked for almost an hour, about his dislike of girls, the tormenting by the men at work, and, to his own surprise, the feelings he once had for Adrian. Doctor Addison made notes, nodding his understanding now and again but without interrupting, and the consultation only ended when David finally said 'Well, that's about it Doctor.'

Doctor Addison finished writing his notes, then leaned back in his chair. 'What I intend to do, David,' he said, 'with your permission of course, is to talk to Sally and then see the two of you together. I'm quite convinced that we will be able to overcome this problem, although it may take some time, and a good deal of patience on all sides.'

David left his chair and shook the hand proffered across the desk. 'Thank you. I'm very grateful for all you've done,' he said, 'and would be happy for you to see Sally. After all, she's suffering as much as anyone isn't she?'

'Yes.'

Before he left, David asked after Adrian.

Doctor Addison smiled at the mention of his only son. 'He's doing well,' he said. 'Passed all his exams so far and he now has a beautiful little daughter, Chloe, which makes me a Grandfather at the grand old age of fifty-one. And his wife Isobel is a Gem.'

'I'm glad,' David said, truthfully. As he left the surgery, Sally gave him a broad smile then left her desk and went into the consulting room.

David walked back to Pennyfarthings, taking the path through the forest, and along the banks of the river. He was deep in thought. Was it only a week or two ago, that he could cheerfully have jumped into these fast moving waters and put an end to his life and all its problems? Night after night since then Sally had sat up into the small hours with him, listening, sympathising and persuading him that his life, at least to her, was precious and he was not to think about ending it, for whatever reason. Now, there was a spring in his step and as he let himself into the cottage and looked around at the home Sally had made for him, he realised just how much he loved her. The demons that had haunted him for so long, were at last being laid to rest, and he knew that, in time, he'd be able to love her in the way she deserved to be loved, and give her the children they both wanted.

His throat was dry after all that talking so he drank a glass of water, and then went out again, to see Albert about the future of the smallholding and what he, David, could do to help keep it going. He was fit enough for light work now, and had enough money to put a substantial sum into the business if Albert would agree with some of the ideas he had in mind.

On the following Saturday, Harry, Esther and the children arrived for the weekend and Esther couldn't help noticing the change in the atmosphere from when they were last here. 'It's almost as if they're celebrating something,' she said. 'Everyone seems so *happy.*'

'That makes a nice change,' Harry said, drily.

Catherine was quiet, and Esther noticed that there was something different about her hair. It hung down her back, straight as a ramrod, with not a ringlet in sight. 'What's happened to all your lovely curls?' she said.

Defiantly, Catherine looked her mother straight in the eye. 'I wanted it to be like Annabel's was before she was killed,' she said. 'And Auntie Frances said I could. *So there.*'

'Well,' Esther said, angry at the way Frances seemed to have taken over, '*I* think you should wear it in ringlets, and I shall tell Auntie Frances that when you come home with us on Monday, we will go back to putting it in rags every night.'

'I'm not coming back with you. I'm not. I'm not!' Catherine was stamping her feet and screeching at the top of her voice, and it brought Frances running to see what was going on. Catherine clung to her as if her life depended on it. 'Tell her Auntie Frances,' she said, 'that I want to stay with you. I don't want to go back to horrible Portsmouth.'

Frances calmed the child down and told her to go and find Edwin and April while she talked to Mummy.

'I'm really sorry Esther,' she said, when they were alone. 'I didn't mean this to happen but Catherine seems to have a *thing* about Portsmouth. She doesn't want to go back there ever again, she says. What are we going to do?'

'I'll talk to Harry,' Esther said, the weekend already spoilt.

David and Sally came to tea, and to make the most of the last days of the sunny weather, everyone sat on the verandah to eat. Esther thought that David looked well, and she hoped to be able to get Sally alone so that she could ask how things were going with him and his problems.

'He's much better since he saw Doctor Addison,' she told Esther when the opportunity arose, and, to Esther's annoyance, promptly changed the subject. Sally didn't know how much her mother-in-law knew, and didn't want to say anything more in case David found out. 'Is that right that Catherine is going to stay with Frances for good?' she said.

Esther pulled a face. 'To tell the truth,' she said, 'that's one of the reasons we came down this weekend. I want to take her back with us but David's father thinks we should let her stay, and I don't know what to do. I've already had an unpleasant little scene with Catherine about it.'

'She's very happy here,' Sally said. 'And Frances dotes on her.'

'Yes, but she is *our* little girl.'

Sally didn't feel it was her place to give advice but felt that it would be a big mistake to uproot the child, when she was so happy living with her Uncle and Auntie.

That was Harry's opinion too, and in the end, Esther, as usual, was the one who had to put her own feelings to one side to keep everyone else happy. As she said to Phyllis later that week, 'First it was Edwin and his scholarship, and now Catherine not wanting to come home. What *I* want doesn't seem to matter, as long as his Lordship gets his own way.'

'Never mind,' Phyllis said, 'have a nice cup of tea.'

CHAPTER TWENTY-EIGHT

Alex was home for Christmas and, much to Esther's delight, said he would be stationed at the Royal Naval Barracks in Portsmouth for the foreseeable future. 'I've met this girl,' he said, when Esther asked him what he'd been up to recently. 'She's in the W.R.N.S, and I think you'll like her. I wondered if she could come to the party.'

'Of course she can,' Esther said. 'The more the merrier.'

'Thanks Mum,' Alex said, dropping a kiss on the top of her head. 'Her name's Jenny and I call her Jenny Wren. She's from Carlisle.'

It was a lean Christmas, with nothing much in the shops, but Esther managed to find a pen and pencil case for Edwin, a rag doll for April and, for Catherine, a book by Angela Brazil, which she sent by post. No further mention had been made of Catherine coming back home and it was now accepted that she might be living with Albert and Frances for good.

They held the party on New Year's Eve instead of Boxing Day, so that they could all see 1943 in together. Esther and Phyllis did their best with the food that was available, putting everyone on saccharin for a week so that they'd have enough sugar for a cake, and pooling coupons for some tinned fruit. To go with the fruit, the man at the Co-op produced, from under the counter, a tin of Ideal milk, and for the sandwiches, a tin of corned beef. 'That'll use up most of your points for this week,' he said, 'but why worry. Tomorrow we may all be …'

Esther cut him short with one of her dark looks.

Alex's girl friend Jenny turned out to be the surprise of the evening. Knowing Alex, Esther had expected some sort of glamour girl, but she was nothing short of plain, with straight, mid-brown hair, and almost colourless blue eyes. She was also a stone or two overweight. All the same, her smile lit up the room and Esther could see why Alex was attracted to her. She greeted Esther warmly and, in her soft, Northern accent, said how glad she was to meet Alex's family. She was at the Royal Naval Barracks and would be able see more of Alex now that he too was shore based. Terry, who was stationed at Colchester, had managed to get leave and brought along his new girl friend, an A.T.S girl called Maggie, and Esther had invited the Cheswicks from next door. By the time everyone had arrived, the sitting room was bursting at the seams. Jack produced two bottles of wine, courtesy, he said, of the dairy management, and Harry had been able to get hold of half a bottle of whisky, while the children had to make do with some lemonade left over from the summer.

They all enjoyed the get together, and Esther was pleased to see that Mrs Cheswick let Betsy play with the other children, who hardly seemed to notice that she looked a bit "different" from any of the others. Harry surprised everyone by teaching them the words of "Knees up Mother Brown", and by the time they had learnt the song off by heart, he went on to show them how to dance to it. In the end, everyone else, except Mr. and Mrs Cheswick, joined in.

'He's a bit of a dark horse, isn't he?' an exhausted Phyllis said to Esther. 'I never expected to see Harry let himself go like that.'

'Nor I,' Esther said.

At five to twelve, Harry poured drinks for the grown-ups. Another year gone, he thought, and still no sign of an end to a war that seemed to be going on forever, and from bad to worse. He wondered how many more young men had to die before someone, somewhere pulled the plug on it.

As the clock struck twelve, they all raised their glasses to welcome in 1943. 'A Happy New Year,' they said in unison, as they had done so many times before, each time hoping the coming year would bring peace.

David and Sally spent New Years' Eve with Albert and Frances. Sally's mother had gone to stay with the sister of a man she'd met at one of her Social Clubs in the village. Henry Callow, a widower and man of considerable means, had taken a fancy to the woman who had brought cheer back into his humdrum life. Once he had crossed the hurdle of his sister, who didn't care over much for Mrs Totter, he had every intention of asking the lady to marry him.

A frost had already formed on the ground by the time David and Sally left Riverside Cottage at twelve-thirty in the morning on the first day of 1943. As they walked down the lane towards home, they held hands, and Sally stopped for a minute to look up at the sky. 'I love the winter,'she said. 'When else can you see a sky like this? Just look at that moon and those stars.' She turned her gaze to David and wished with all her heart that he wanted her as much as she wanted him, but his face was passive.

They had talked and listened to Doctor Addison, separately, and together, and now there was nothing more he could do and they just had to wait and see if his advice bore fruit. They reached home and turned in at the gate. David unlocked the front door, and they went into the warmth of Pennyfarthings, shedding their outdoor things in the hall. In the sitting room, the fire, banked up before they'd gone out, was still alight, and David lit the two oil lamps, setting one on the table, the other on top of the bureau. They sat for a while, talking about nothing in particular, and then Sally said she was off to bed.

'Don't go,' David said, reaching for her hand.

She laughed. 'It's gone one o'clock David.

'Come here.' He left his chair and pulled her to him, and when she looked into his eyes, she saw something that had never been there before. The dark blue pupils were almost black, and full of such longing that she was almost frightened and had to look away.

'What is it?' she asked, her heart racing.

He didn't answer, and then, like a film in slow motion, he began to undresss her, and she him, their clothes dropping silently, piece by piece to the floor until, completely naked, they lay down together in front of the fire. To begin with, David was gentle, but the frustration of the past three years took over, and Sally cried out in pain as she lost her virginity to his frenzied, almost brutal, lovemaking. She thought it would never end, and then suddenly he left her and rolled away and she could hear him crying. She sat up and put her arms around him.

'I hurt you, didn't I?' he said.

Sally, remembering someone telling her that the first time was always the worst, laid her head on his chest. 'It will be all right next time,' she said. 'I promise you it will.' And it was. David made love to her twice more that night, and each time it was better and less painful than the last. They finally went to bed at five o'clock, and as Sally, completely satisfied and unbelievably happy, began to drift off to sleep, she was unaware that a tiny seed inside her body had been fertilised, and was alrcady starting to multiply and grow into her and David's first child.

Sally told no one, not even Doctor Addison, about New Year's Day, until about six weeks' later when, after missing a period, she started being sick in the mornings. 'You kept that a secret,' he said when she asked if he thought she might be expecting. 'And you certainly have all the right symptoms but we'll give it another couple of weeks before I examine you, just to be sure.'

David knew, of course, that she might be having a baby, and could hardly believe that he'd been able to father a child. They made love at every opportunity and Sally couldn't remember a time when she'd felt so happy.

David had talked Albert into the two of them going into partnership, and had invested quite a sizeable lump of his inheritance in the business so that they were able to employ a man to do all the heavy work. It was David's job to take care of the lighter jobs and he began using his carpentry skills to make bird tables for sale. A sign above the entrance to the smallholding now read, "Albert Brettle and David Cartarett ... Growers of Fresh Fruit, Vegetables, and Flowers." and business was brisk, with customers coming in from all over the place to buy what they couldn't find in their local shops. David too, was happier than he'd ever been, and when, at the end of February, Sally's pregnancy was confirmed, his happiness was complete.

When in March, Esther read the letter telling her and Harry that they were going to be Grandparents she could hardly believe it was true. All her fears and suspicions about David had been groundless, and now, perhaps, he would be able to rid himself of the demons and devils that had dogged him for so long. It was, she knew, no use dwelling on the past but if, all those years' ago, Harry had only talked to David about his problem, then maybe things might have turned out differently and Sally not had to live in a loveless marriage for three years. Still, everything was rosy for them now, and Esther was looking forward to her first grandchild.

Emily Jane Cartarett was born on the 12th September, on what would have been Daniel's eleventh birthday, with Doctor Addison insisting on doing the delivery himself at home. It was an easy labour and when at last David was able to see and hold his daughter for the first time, he experienced a feeling of such deep love for Sally and their child that it frightened him. He sat with them for a while, and then deciding he needed to see Albert, kissed Sally, telling her he wouldn't be long. As he walked down the lane to Riverside Cottage, he wondered whether he would be able to cope with the responsibilities of being a husband and father.

He went down the side of Riverside Cottage and called out. There was no answer, and the unusual quiet, with not a sign of anyone about, worried him. The door to the greenhouse was open, and he went in and looked around. Albert was in the corner perched on his stool and slumped over the potting bench, his head resting in a tray of cuttings.

CHAPTER TWENTY-NINE

'Did you know Mrs Mc Andrew is out of hospital?' Phyllis said to Esther. They were standing in the queue at the butchers after hearing rumours that he'd managed to get hold of some offal and it would be on a first come, first served basis.

'No, I didn't,' Esther said. 'Things have been pretty hectic lately, what with Albert being ill and that. When did she come out?'

'Her next door neighbour told me she's been home for ages, but no one knew as her husband won't allow her to go out; not even as far as the front gate it seems.'

'Why?'

'Probably thinks there's some shame in her having been in a Lunatic Asylum I suppose.'

'Men!' Esther said.

They reached the end of the queue and bought liver, which was all the butcher had left. 'I was hoping for some hearts,' Esther said, as she gave him her money.

'Sorry love, you're lucky to get anything, the way things are.'

On the way home, Phyllis asked after Albert.

'He's on the mend, but it was a near thing,' Esther said. 'If David hadn't called in to see, him, goodness knows what would have happened, because Frances had gone out shopping with Catherine.

He's had a slight stroke but luckily, apart from a bit of weakness down his left hand side, he'll be back to normal soon, and out of hospital.'

'The trouble is', Phyllis said, 'we're all getting old.' She pointed to the front bedroom window of her house, where the curtains were still drawn. 'Looks like Lady Muck's still in bed,'she said. 'Honestly Esther, I don't know what I'm going to do about Louisa. She is *so* lazy. I can't get her to do a thing to help in the house, and Jack says he's going to look out for a place somewhere else for her. He is fed up with the mess she leaves everywhere, and wants her to leave.'

'I didn't know,' Esther said. 'What about John William? Won't you miss him?'

Phyllis made a face. 'In a way I suppose, but he's a spoilt little monkey and screams his flippin' head off if he can't have his own way.' She opened the front gate. 'Tell the truth, I'm past all that now, and just can't stand the noise and carryings on. And now that Robert's at the Technical College, he needs peace and quiet to study.'

'It's a pity Luke's abroad. He wouldn't put up with it.' Esther said.

'No, he wouldn't.'

'How is he?'

'Still in North Africa somewhere and all right, as far as we know,' Phyllis said. 'At least he didn't get caught up in that business in Sicily, but the war is spreading out there so goodness knows what'll happen next. I'm only glad that Terry is out of it. I couldn't bear it if they were both in the firing line. And I hope the war will be over before Robert is old enough to be called up.'

'Let's hope so,' Esther said. She looked up at the leaden sky of a late October afternoon and shivered before going indoors and banking up the fire.

The air raids had been less frequent recently, and the sudden wail of the siren, at ten minutes' to four of an afternoon, took her by surprise. April, who was still at school, would go with the other children to the basement shelter, so Esther saw no reason to take herself off to the Anderson. Since the lull in the air raids, it had fallen into disuse and was practically running with water, and she didn't like the idea of sitting down there on her own anyway. She picked up a magazine and settled into her armchair. If the raid turned out to be heavy, she could always get in the cupboard under the stairs.

Miss Wetherspoon, looked out of the assembly hall window at the thick, dark blanket of cloud that hung like a grey blanket over the city. Despite the air raid warning that had sounded just at the close of afternoon prayers, she would send her pupils home. There was no point in organising a mass evacuation to the shelter that ran beneath the school, when so many of them lived just a short distance away and could reach home quickly. Since the terrible landmine tragedy in which so many children had died, she'd had nightmares about the entire school being trapped in an inadequate, underground shelter, and felt they would be safer at home with their own families.

'You have plenty of time,' she told the assembly of girls. 'Run as fast as you can and don't stop for any reason *whatsoever*.' A mass exit followed as a swarm of frightened girls pushed and shoved one another on the stairs in an effort to be first through the double doors leading out of the building. Most would be home within minutes but April Cartarett had farther to go and as she fled through the network of small streets, the first spots of heavy rain turned into a downpour and in seconds, she was soaked to the skin.

The pain of a stitch in her side slowed her down and it seemed like forever before the corner of Kestrel Road came into view. A Corporation dustcart sat in the middle of the road, and a gang of dustmen were emptying grey, metal bins into its open jaws. Above all the clatter, she could hear the now familiar drone of enemy aircraft and, as she looked up, the clouds parted and one of them, its engines screaming, suddenly dived straight towards her. She cried out, and then felt herself scooped up in a pair of strong arms, and thrown under a nearby hedge, the sound of bullets tinkling along the pavement where she had been running only seconds' before. A man's voice told her not to move, and she lay very still, the weight of him on top of her squeezing all the breath from her lungs.

It was over in a few minutes, and the sound of the aeroplanes grew fainter as they flew out to sea. April's rescuer lifted her to her feet, and having made sure she was all right, told her to get along home as quickly as possible.

'You shouldn't 'av bin out in this, Miss,' he said kindly.

'Miss Wetherspoon sent us home,' she said, as if he would know exactly who Miss Wetherspoon was. She thanked him, wondering what her mother was going to say about her saturated coat. The All Clear sounded just as she reached the gate and she went to the shelter, but not finding her mother there, ran along the path and hammered on the front door of the house.

'What on earth are *you* doing home?' Esther said, as April, water dripping from her coat and her hair hanging in limp ringlets over her shoulders, scrambled over the step.

Tearfully, she related the story of the machine-gunning, and how the dustman had protected her with his own body. 'He said I shouldn't have been out,' she said.

'He was damned well right,' Esther said, 'and tomorrow I shall go and see this Miss Wetherspoon and tell her what I think. You could have been killed.' She changed April out of her wet clothes then sat her by the fire to get warm.

'You are to go and see that woman tomorrow, Esther,' Harry said, when she told him about the afternoon's events. 'She needs her head examined to let those girls out like that when there was a raid on.' He patted a now fully recoverd April on the head. 'And you can tell her from me, that if it happens again, she'll find herself out of a job.'

Miss Wetherspoon, who, when Esther went to see her the next day, had already been on the receiving end of other irate mothers, apologised and explained her reasons for taking the risk of sending the girls home. 'I can understand your anger Mrs Cartarett,' she said, 'but at the time, I thought it was for the best. There's usually plenty of time between the siren going off and the raid, but this time I was mistaken.'

Esther felt a bit sorry for the woman. It was no easy task to be responsible for so many children and their safety. 'I hope, Miss Wetherspoon,' she said, 'that it won't happen again. If it hadn't been for that dustman doing what he did, April might have been killed.'

The question of trying to find a place for Louisa to live resolved itself just after Christmas. Jack had asked his roundsmen to keep their ears open, and one of them, Tom Beattie, told him about a Mrs Lars-Hillier who lived alone in a large house at Southsea and was looking for a girl to live in, mainly for company, but also to do a bit of housework. Jack smiled to himself at the thought of bone idle Louisa doing any cleaning. He was tired of going home from work to find the place upside down. Toys and clothes scattered everywhere, and a fractious child, ignored by its mother who had the nerve to be sitting in *his* armchair, reading a magazine, while Phyllis sweated it out in the kitchen. He'd just about had enough of it, and so had Phyllis. He used the office telephone to ring the number Tom Beattie had given him, and asked to speak to Mrs Lars-Hillier.

'Daphne Lars-Hillier speaking.' The voice was refined and educated.

Jack introduced himself, then told her about Louisa; that his house was really too small for her to be able to live with him and his wife any longer; her husband, *his* son, was abroad, serving with the Air Force, and there was a small child.'

'Do send her along to see me, Mr Cartarett,' she said, much to his surprise. 'Shall we say tomorrow afternoon at two o'clock?'

Louisa was pleased when Jack told her. She was just as fed up with living with her in-laws as they were having her live with them. The bedroom she had was too small, and not only that, she knew that Phyllis disapproved because she didn't give a hand around the house. Overall, she was sorry she'd got herself into trouble and wished she'd never kept the baby, let alone married the child's father. And why should she be expected to clean someone else's house when she was always so tired trying to cope with a difficult child. At least if Mrs Lars-Hillier took her on, she'd be paid for what she did. She went off for the interview the following afternoon, and took great pleasure later, in telling Phyllis that Mrs Lars-Hellier had offered her the job, and wanted her to move in as soon as possible. She would have a large room of her own, a separate bedroom for John William, *and* the use of a telephone.

'Well dear,' Phyllis said, 'I hope it works out for you. And Luke's father and I would still like to see you and John William whenever you feel like paying us a visit.'

Louisa, who had no intention of ever returning to Kestrel Road, made no comment to that and, two day's later, a relieved Jack helped her move her few possessions to Southsea.

'I do hope she's written to Luke and told him where she is,' Phyllis said, as she and Jack relaxed in the peace and quiet of their living room. 'I hate to say this but he'll need to inform his C.O, in case anything happens to him.'

'Yes,' Jack said, not wanting to think about that possibility.

It was on a Sunday morning at the end of January that Phyllis answered a knock at the door to find Louisa, minus John William, standing on the step. Her eyes were red where she'd been crying, and Phyllis knew, before the girl said anything, that it was bad news. She invited her in and they went through to the kitchen where Jack was mending a pair of boots. He looked up, met Phyllis's eyes and, his face expressionless, put aside his hammer as Louisa pulled a yellow envelope from her handbag and handed it to Phyllis. With trembling hands and racing heart, she slumped into a chair and, the words becoming a blur as her eyes filled with tears, read it aloud to Jack. Luke, their son, was dead. Just like Peter Mc Andrew, and in the same place. "Killed while on active service in North Africa" was all the information the telegram gave them.

Phyllis squeezed Louisa's hand. 'What will you do now?' she said, already foreseeing the struggle her daughter-in-law faced to bring up a child on her own.

'Mrs Lars-Hillier says I can stay as long as I want,' Louisa said. 'She loves John William and I get on really well with her. She likes taking him out, and he's with her this morning.'

'You can come back here if you want to,' Esther said.

Jack's heart sank, and then rose again when Louisa said that it didn't work the first time and things were best left as they were. Thank you, but she'd be all right with Mrs Lars-Hillier. She didn't stay long and, after she'd gone, Phyllis was able to let go of the pent-up emotion inside her. She cried in Jack's arms until she thought her heart would burst, and then, mustering as much courage as she could, she rinsed her swollen face under the tap and insisting Jack went with her, crossed over the road to see Harry and Esther.

On the 18th March, Harry awoke to the realisation that today was his fiftieth birthday, and he felt every day of it. The war that was supposed to last just a couple of months, was nearly five years' old, with no sign of peace in sight. Morale had never been lower, with so many families bereaved, either through air raids or through having lost someone on the battlefront. His thoughts drifted to Jack and Phyllis, and to Luke who had lost his life in North Africa, and he counted his blessings that at least he and Esther still had *their* sons.

He raised himself up on one elbow and watched Esther as she slept beside him. Her coal black hair, which was spread across the pillow, was as profuse as when she was seventeen, except that he'd recently noticed the appearance of a few silver strands here and there. She was still beautiful, and he loved her so much. She stirred and turned over, her dark eyes meeting his, inviting him to love her in the way that only he knew how. She remembered then what day it was and wished him a happy birthday. 'Pretend you're sick,' she said, 'and take the day off.'

He laughed. 'You're still not awake, sweetheart,' he said. 'It's Saturday, and my turn for a day off, so I don't have to go in anyway.'

'So why don't we go out for a trip somewhere?'

His eyes rested on the creamy skin of her bare shoulders. 'Yes. Why not,' he said. 'But first, come here and give me my birthday present.' He pulled her up against him. 'I might be knocking on a bit but there's life in this old dog yet.'

They had breakfast and then caught a bus to the top of Portsdown Hill, taking April with them but allowing Edwin, who wanted to go out with his friends, to stay behind. When Esther protested, Harry pointed out that the boy *was* fifteen after all and at that age, would not want to go out on bus trips with his Mum and Dad.

The view from the hill was breathtaking. Against a background of the dark hills of the Isle of Wight, the city spread out before them as far as the eye could see, with Langstone Harbour to their left, and Porchester Creek to their right. From where they were, it was difficult to imagine that most of Portsmouth lay in ruins. It all seemed so peaceful, and the war a million miles' away. They strolled along the top of the hill, to where they were able to see Porchester Castle, and in the far distance, the chimneys of the Fawley oilworks. 'Fancy being able to see all that way,' Esther said. 'It's not far from where Albert and Frances live.'She slipped her arm through Harry's. 'We must try and get down to the New Forest to see everyone,' she said.

'Our grandaughter will be grown up by the time we get to see her, and Catherine must be quite the young lady by now.'

Over the next few weeks, the military activity that seemed to be going on along the South Coast, set tongues wagging that something important was in the offing. People coming from the villages on the other side of Portsdown hill into Portsmouth to work, reported huge complements of tanks, armoured cars and lorries, setting up camp along all the main roads leading into the city. Soldiers, British, Canadian and American were sleeping rough by the roadside while they waited for their orders, and the authorities were making it difficult for ordinary people to go about their day-to-day business. One man, who came into the Dockyard from Horndean, said he'd never seen anything like it in all his life. 'They're every bloody where,' he told Harry. 'Hundreds of 'em, and by the time you get home from work, you can't even get a drop of beer in the pub.'

'There must be something big coming up,' Harry said. 'There's been talk of a second front. Perhaps this is it.'

During the first few days of June, the military convoys started to pack up and move towards the coast. They came from left, right and centre, rumbling through the streets, the soldiers waving and calling out to bystanders, or, like Winston Churchill, holding up two fingers in the V for Victory sign. Women were crying, children cheering as one cavalcade after another drove through city and headed for the port. Then all of a sudden, an eerie silence as the last of them boarded one of the hundreds of ships waiting in the harbour. On their way, it turned out, to invade Normandy and take France back from the Germans.

On 6th June, Esther switched on the wireless to listen to the news. Despite appalling weather conditions, the troops had landed on the beaches at Normandy, and the fight to claim back France for the French had begun.

'It's the beginning of the end for Adolph Hitler,' Harry said. 'And it's my bet that the war will be over before Christmas.'

CHAPTER THIRTY

Harry had a week's holiday to come, and he took Esther, Edwin and April to the New Forest for a few days. It had been an age since their last visit and Esther was shocked to see how ill Albert looked, and how much Catherine had grown. She was almost thirteen now and came up to Esther's shoulder. Esther gave her a hug, and Catherine rewarded her with a big-toothed smile. 'I want to come home Mummy,' she said. 'Auntie Frances knows, and it's all right. *Honestly.*'

Esther was overjoyed. She'd missed having Catherine at home, and would be glad to have her back, as long as Frances didn't mind. She took Frances to one side as soon as there was an opportunity. First, she asked about Albert. 'He looks a bit under the weather,' she said.

'He's getting better all the time,' Frances said, 'but the doctors say it'll be quite a long job. David has been very good and he's paying for a man to work full time at the smallholding, although Albert and I have talked about giving it up. It's not making that much money and we could still get by without it, although we're not sure where that would leave David.' Her voice dropped to a whisper. 'Don't say anything, but I'm looking to get a job myself. There's a home for orphans and deprived children in the next village and they're looking for women to give a hand with them. I haven't said anything to Albert yet but it's something I'd love to do, especially if Catherine goes back with you.'

'Ah, yes,' Esther said, 'Catherine has already told me she'd like to come home, but you've had her for so long, it doesn't seem fair to you to take her away.'

Frances caught hold of Esther's hands. 'She's *your* daughter Esther', she said, 'and I always knew that one day she'd want to go back to Portsmouth. I think it was just that she was terrified of the air raids, and after that business of losing her friend, she wanted to be as far away from there as she could. If you want to take her home with you, it's all right by me, although I shall miss her.'

'You're a real gem, Frances,' Esther said, 'and always have been.'

'By the way,' Frances said, 'I've invited David and Sally to tea today. I thought it would save Sally all that work, as she's been looking a bit peaky and tired lately. They should be here any minute now.'

Emily was nine months' old, and Esther felt all fingers and thumbs when she tried to keep hold of the energetic baby. 'I'm not used to this any more,' she said, handing her back to Sally. 'I think you'd better take her before she lands on the floor.' She was a beautiful child, very much like David to look at, and bearing a close resemblance to Daniel.

David looked well, and happier than Esther had ever seen him, and after tea, she went for a stroll in the back garden with him. He showed her the bird tables he'd been making. 'I could sell more than I can make,' he said, 'but it's not easy to get hold of the wood.'

He seemed a bit edgy and she asked if his leg was giving him any trouble.

He laughed. 'It's not my leg that's the problem,' he said.

'What is it then?'

'It's Sally. She's having another baby.'

'What, so soon after Emily?'

'*Mum*, you're a fine one to talk.'

It was Esther's turn to laugh. 'Yes, I am. Does anyone else know?'

'Not yet', David said. 'We thought you should be the first.'

Esther stood on tiptoe and kissed him. 'I'm so glad David', she said, 'after all that you've been through, one way and another.' They went back into the house laughing together and Harry wanted to know what was going on.

David looked at Sally and she nodded. 'I have permission from the wife,' he said, grinning from ear to ear, 'to tell you all that there is another little Cartarett on the way. It's due around about Christmas time.'

Albert immediately went to the sideboard and produced a bottle of wine. 'Don't ask where it came from', he said, 'or I'll end up inside His Majesty's Prison.' He poured each of them a glass and they drank a toast to David and Sally, Emily Jane, and the new baby.

'Let's hope it's a boy this time,' Harry said, 'to carry on the family name.'

Esther asked Frances how Sally's mother was. 'She and her man friend, Henry Callow, gave everyone the slip,' Frances said, 'and went off to Southampton one day and got married. I thought Sally would have told you.'

'No, she didn't, but good luck to them,' Esther said, 'although I'm blowed if I'd get married again if anything happened to Harry.'

'You sound as if you're unhappy.'

'It's not that,' Esther said. 'But I think women get a raw deal. And I'm not the only one to think so. There was this meeting in Portsmouth a couple of weeks' back, to form what they called the National Married Women's Association, and I heard that the chairman said that the status of wives and mothers is that of serfs.'

'Did you go?'

'No. I couldn't get there, and there wouldn't have been much point anyway. I love Harry but he'll never change his Victorian attitude towards women, if he lives to be a hundred.' She smiled ruefully. 'But I'll make sure my own two girls grow up with a different outlook on marriage, and what it's meant to be.'

Frances smiled. 'By the way,' she said, 'I've heard that your little April is becoming something of a singer.'

'Yes. She's forever trilling away at some song or other, and she's been asked to join the school choir.'

'Will you let her have singing lessons?'

'It depends on Harry,' Esther said. 'You know what he's like.'

'Ah, yes, I *do* know what he's like. All the same, if she's a good singing voice, it would be a pity not to have it trained.'

'We'll have to wait and see.' Esther said.

It was lovely to have Catherine living at home again. Now that she was growing up, she was good company for Esther, especially since she no longer saw very much of Phyllis who, since Luke's death, had shut herself away from everyone. Esther, remembering the terrible time after Daniel, understood how her friend must be feeling and did nothing to force the issue. Phyllis would come round in time but meanwhile, it was best to leave her to her grief. The only person other than Jack she wanted to see was Terry who had managed to get a spell of compassionate leave, but had now gone back to his regiment at Colchester. There had been some talk of him and Maggie getting married, but they had decided to postpone it for a few months to give Phyllis time to come to terms with losing Luke.

August 25th saw the liberation of Paris, which was a major triumph for the Allied Forces but at a huge cost in human lives. 'It makes you wonder,' Esther said to Harry after they had listened to the news, 'what this war is all about.'

'It's about getting rid of a madman who, if he'd been given the chance, would have taken control of half the world, including this country, 'Harry said, wisely. 'Make no mistake, if that had happened, you and I wouldn't now have the freedom to be sitting here, in our comfortable home, talking to one another, even if we'd still been alive.'

'I suppose you're right,' Esther said, 'as usual.'

Now that Alex was stationed just a bus ride away, he often visited Kestrel Road, sometimes bringing Jenny with him, and it was just before Christmas that they announced their engagement. 'We won't get married until the war is over,' he told Harry and Esther, 'but with the Germans on the run now, that shouldn't be long.'

Sally gave birth to George Daniel on Christmas Day, following a long and difficult labour, after which Doctor Addison took David to one side and advised against her having any more children. 'It's usually the first baby that causes all the trouble,' he said, 'but this little blighter just didn't want to come out into the world. And who can blame him?'

As soon as the Post Office re-opened after Christmas, David sent a telegram to Harry and Esther to tell them the good news. He was worried about Sally, who, after three days, seemed to have lost all her strength, and showed little interest in her new son. 'The birth has taken everything out of the poor girl,' Frances said, when he asked her advice. 'All she needs is lots of rest and good food, and she'll soon be back to her old self. You'll see.'

David did see, but not what Frances saw. Sally became tearful and was forever crying until in the end, he lost his patience with her. 'For goodness sake snap out of it,' he shouted at her one day, when she'd been weeping for most of the morning, and no amount of gentle persuasion could make her stop. 'That's all you do these days, is cry, and I'm fed up with it.'

She looked at him as if he'd hit her in the face. 'You don't know what it's like,' she wailed. 'I can't stop myself. I only wish I could.'

David felt terrible and, full of remorse, he dropped down on the sofa beside her and took her in his arms. 'I'm sorry,' he said, kissing her tear stained face. 'I don't know what came over me.' He hugged her close to him. 'Why don't you go and see Doctor Addison?' he said. 'He may be able to help.'

Doctor Addison recommended a tonic. 'Parish's Chemical Food,' he said, 'will do you the world of good and bring back some of the colour to your cheeks. You can buy it at the chemist. It tastes a bit like old iron but persevere with it and I guarantee it will make all the difference.'

David bought two bottles of the rust-coloured liquid, and for two weeks, stood over Sally three times a day to make sure she took it. It gave her constipation and discoloured her teeth but after the first week, she began to feel better, although she still burst into tears at the slightest thing. Frances invited them over for Christmas dinner and after they had listened to the King's speech on the wireless, told everyone that she would be starting work at the home for orphans and deprived children after the New Year. Albert, who had never approved of married women going out to work, said nothing.

New Year's Eve in Portsmouth was the liveliest and most optimistic for six years. Blackout regulations forgotten, the lights went up in the city, and 1945 seen in by a blast of sirens, factory hooters, church bells, and almost anything else that made a noise. Crowds thronged the Guildhall Square and the mood of the people was confident for the first time in almost six years. The end of the war was at last in sight. Harry and Esther had invited Jack and Phyllis across to see in the New Year, and Esther was pleasantly surprised when they accepted. She had missed Phyllis's companionship and hoped that this would mean they could get back together again, and things would be almost like old times. She was glad in a way that Alex hadn't been able to join them as it would have made things more difficult for Jack and Phyllis if he'd been there. Edwin and Robert had gone to a party, and Catherine, April and Sarah, allowed to stay up late for the occasion, had disappeared into the front room to play board games. For most of the evening, the adults were in a reflective mood. The events of the past year had been a mixture of sadness and joy, with Jack and Phyllis losing their son and, in a way, their only grandchild, and Harry and Esther gaining a grandson to add to the grandaughter they already had.

'We've a bit of good news for a change,' Phyllis said, as they sat and waited to see in the New Year. 'Terry and Maggie are getting engaged.'

'Oh Phyllis, I'm so pleased,' Esther said. 'When's the happy day?'

'As soon as the war is over I believe.'

As the hands of the clock moved towards twelve, Jack suggested they go out into the street to see if anything was happening. They carried their glasses of wine outside to find most of the street had decided to do the same. Neighbours they barely knew had come out of their houses, and were patting each other on the back, and wishing everyone a Happy New Year as the sound of sirens and church bells filled the air. Someone started singing Roll out the Barrel, and soon the street echoed with the sound of the songs that had kept their spirits up over the past few years, when all had seemed lost. Jack had to take Phyllis, who was in floods of tears, home and when Harry and Esther finally went back indoors, Esther said she thought that they would never recover from their loss.

Easter came early that year and when Esther heard that some of the beaches had been cleared of barbed wire and were once more open to the public, she talked Phyllis into going for a walk. 'We haven't done this for a long time,' she said as they strolled along the sea front, and Sarah and April raced each other across the stony beach. Catherine, who thought she was much too grown up for such childish things as going for a walk with her mother, had gone to a friend's house for tea. 'It's almost like old times. The last time we walked along here, we were both pushing prams.' She asked Phyllis if she was feeling any better.

'I'll never feel any better,' Phyllis said. 'But life has to go on, doesn't it. There are the others to consider, and Jack has not been well, especially since it happened.' Her voice broke. 'I think the worse part is not knowing how Luke died, or where he is buried. I think it would be more bearable if we knew that.'

'That must be awful for you,' Esther said. 'But I'm sure the War Office will let you know as soon as they can. And do you ever see Louisa, and John William?'

'Oh, I've seen *her* all right,' Phyllis said. 'Arm in arm with a sailor she was, the last time I clapped eyes on the little madam. And no, she doesn't bring the little boy to see us but maybe that's for the best because he looked so much like Luke, I think my heart would break if I saw him now.'

Esther could not think of anything to say to that. At least she had a grave to visit if she wanted to, although it had been some time since she'd last gone to the cemetery. Somehow, the war had taken over to the exclusion of everything else, and she had put it off, but she made herself a promise that, just as soon as Easter was over she'd take some flowers to her lost children.

By the end of the week, temperatures had risen and there was a heatwave. The children were on holiday from school, and the beaches at Southsea packed. Esther couldn't stand the hot weather and spent most of the time indoors during the day, only venturing out in the evening as it cooled down. She kept her promise to go to the cemetery and felt guilty when she saw the state of the little grave. It was unkempt, and the flowerpot covered in green algae. Tearfully, she trimmed the grass as best she could with a pair of scissors, and then washed the pot under the tap and filled it with spring flowers.

'Do you still miss Daniel, Mum?' Catherine asked. 'Is that why you're crying?'

'Yes love, of course I still miss him.'

'So do I,' a small voice said.

As the month wore on and the Allied Troops marched towards Berlin, excitement mounted and everywhere there was talk of an end to the war. 'It'll be all over in a matter of days,' Harry said. 'By the end of the month, you'll see.'

Alex came home for a weekend and told Harry and Esther that he and Jenny had been making plans for their wedding, which was to be as soon after peace was declared as possible, and that she wanted to get married at her home in Carlisle.

Esther understood but explained that she and Harry wouldn't be able to travel all that way. 'Apart from the restrictions still in force,' she said, 'it would take too long to get there, but we could always have a party when you come back.'

'Good idea Mum,' Alex said, 'and thanks for that.'

On the 1st May, Esther and Phyllis, who had started going shopping together, just as they used to, were on their way home from the Co-op when they saw the familiar figure of Mrs Mc Andrew standing at her garden gate. 'My God, he's actually let the poor woman out,' Esther whispered as they drew near. They stopped to ask how she was.

'I'm better now,' she said, 'which is more than can be said of some.'

'Who?' Esther asked.

'I've just had me wireless on,' Mrs Mc Andrew said, 'an' Hitler's gone and committed suicide. *And* that woman friend of 'is, Eva Braun.'

'Are you sure?' Phyllis said.

'Sure as I'm standin' 'ere talkin' to you two.'

Esther and Phyllis exchanged glances. It seemed too far-fetched to be true. Poor Mrs Mc Andrew had been through so much and maybe she was imagining things. 'Well, if he *has*,' Esther said, 'that's the best bit of news we've had in a long time.'

Mrs Mc Andrew agreed, and turned to Phyllis. 'I was so sorry to 'ear about your boy,' she said. 'I know what it's like to lose one of yer own. I got took bad when my boy went, but you can't keep a good woman down, and I'm on the mend now.'

'It's lovely to see you out and about again,' Phyllis said. 'We've missed you.'

Mrs Mc Andrew's face broke into a smile. 'Thanks Mrs Martindale,' she said, jerking a thumb in the direction of the house, 'but if it were left to 'im in there, I'd still be lookin' through me bedroom winder to see what's going on, instead of over me garden gate.'

'Do you know,' Esther said, as she and Phyllis moved on, 'I really *did* miss her.'

'Me too,' Phyllis said.

The following day, the Allies marched into Berlin, and on the seventh, Germany unconditionally surrendered. That evening, Harry and Esther, with Jack, Phyllis and all the children, sat glued to the wireless, as first reports started coming in confirming that it was all over.

'I can't believe it,' Esther said, bursting into tears.

Phyllis did likewise. 'Nor me,' she said.

Harry and Jack patted each other on the back as if the end of the war was all their doing, Edwin leapt up in the air, waving a rolled-up newspaper, and the girls danced around the room shouting that they wouldn't have to go to school for two whole days. *'Miss* said that if the war ended tonight, our school would be closed until Thursday,' April said, and no one minded whether that was true or not. Later, after Jack and Phyllis had left and taken their children home, Harry and Esther sat up until the small hours and talked about the effects six years' of war had had on them.

'We're lucky,' Harry said. 'At least David and Alex came through it alive.'

'Yes. And Edwin's's just missed being called up.'

Harry squeezed her hand. 'You women have had a lot to put up with,' he said. 'I don't know how you've managed to keep going the way you have.'

'Sheer bloody willpower, and this war has proved that we're not the delicate little flowers that men seem to think we are.' Esther's voice rose as she warmed to her subject. 'One of these days, Harry,' she went on, 'women will be accepted as equal to men, in *every* way. It won't happen in my time perhaps, but within the next twenty years or so. You'll see.'

'Blimey Esther, all I said was, I didn't know how you'd put up with so much. I didn't ask for a flippin' lecture.'

'Sorry, but it's something I feel strongly about,' she said.

'So, what little schemes have you got up your sleeve?'

Esther smiled enigmatically. 'Now that would be telling, wouldn't it. All I know Harry, is that I'm thankful the war is over and that we have all survived.'

'It's not quite all over yet,' he said. 'There's still the Far East to be settled, and that could go on for some time.'

'Oh, *Harry,* will you *ever* say anything optimistic?'

He held her face between his hands. 'One day, maybe,' he said, 'but in the meantime, let's celebrate a new beginning. Give us a kiss.'

CONCLUSION

On a warm September evening, Kestrel Road, with its houses set back behind neat privet hedges, was a pleasure to look at. Harry Cartarett, his day's work finished, cycled towards home and, dismounting at the corner, stopped to survey the place he'd brought his wife Esther and their children to fifteen years'earlier. The last rays of the setting sun danced off the rooftops and glinted orange on the upstairs windows, the shadows of the evening falling softly on the quiet, empty road. It was a lovely place to live, and, despite the loss of a child, all the problems they had faced, and a war that had lasted for almost six years, they were still happy.

The war had ended over two years' ago, and his thoughts now were on their children. There was David, free at last of the demons in his head, married to Sally, and the father of two children, and Alex who had decided to give up the sea and had used his demob gratuity to buy the little corner shop from Mr and Mrs Sherlock when they retired. He was doing well with the help of his wife Jenny, whose longing for a child would have to wait until they were on their feet. Then there was Edwin, the brains of the family, now well on the way to becoming a Journalist, and who had started writing his first book. Harry smiled to himself when he thought of his two daughters. Catherine, in her first job behind the counter of the Co-op, already courting at sixteen, and with no ambition other than to get married, have children and be like her mother. And April, their sweet natured youngest, who sang like a nightingale, and wanted nothing more than to stay in the school choir, and have singing lessons. He was proud of them all and the way they had turned out.

His thoughts turned to Esther, his wife, who had changed so much over the past few years. She had developed a fixation in her head about the treatment of women by their menfolk. 'We're nothing more than servants,' she'd said. 'And unpaid ones at that.' Once, she had thought about joining the Married Women's Association, but he had put a stop to all that nonsense. He'd no intention of living with a "Suffragette" for a wife, and had told her so in no uncertain terms.

He pushed his bicycle round the back of the house and went indoors to find a fire burning brightly in the grate, and Esther, her salt and pepper hair tied back, reading a magazine. His nostrils detected the smell of roast beef, and he sniffed the air appreciatively. 'I'm home for me dinner,' he said. She looked up at him and smiled, then went back to the item she had been reading.

ABOUT THE AUTHOR

Eileen Frost was born in 1931 in Portsmouth. Her love of writing and the English language began at an early age, and on the rare occasions she had pocket money, it was always spent on pens, paper and ink. Just before he died, her father told her she should write for a living but at seventeen, she joined the WRAF where she met and married husband Bill. When their four children were young, Eileen wrote for them but never considered publishing. When she retired, she bought a PC, taught herself to use it and wrote a Family History book for her grandchildren, which she printed and bound herself. *When Tomorrow Comes* is her first novel, although a sequel is in the pipeline.

Printed in Great Britain
by Amazon

78858997R00192